HEALTHCARE RECORDS

A Practical Legal Guide

Jonathan P. Tomes, J.D.

HFMA® HEALTHCARE FINANCIAL MANAGEMENT ASSOCIATION

TWO WESTBROOK CORPORATE CENTER
SUITE 700
WESTCHESTER, ILLINOIS 60154
TELEPHONE 708/531/9600

KENDALL/HUNT PUBLISHING COMPANY
2460 Kerper Boulevard P.O. Box 539 Dubuque, Iowa 52004-0539

Copyright © 1990 by Healthcare Financial Management Association

All rights reserved. No part of this publication may be reproduced, stored in a retrieval system, or transmitted, in any form or by any means, electronic, mechanical, photocopying, recording, or otherwise, without the prior written permission of the copyright owner.

Printed in the United States of America
10 9 8 7 6 5 4 3

Library of Congress Cataloging-in-Publication Data

Tomes, Jonathan P.
    Healthcare records: a practical legal guide / by Jonathan P. Tomes.
      p. cm
    ISBN 0–8403–5832–6 (Kendall-Hunt): $60.65 ($48.50 to members)
      1. Medical records—Law and legislation—United States.
2 Medical records—Law and legislation—United States—States.
I. Title.
    [DNLM: 1. Confidentiality—United States—legislation. 2. Medical Records—United States—legislation.   WX 33 A1 T6h]
KF3827.R4T66   1990
344.73'041—dc20
[347.30441]
DNLM/DLC   90–4272
for Library of Congress   CIP

Contents

Acknowledgments   vii

Preface   ix

Part I
What Is a Record, Who Owns It, and What Do You Do with It?   1

1   What Is a Record?   3

Records Generally   3
Medical Records   3
State Laws   4

2   Who Owns Healthcare Records?   61

Ownership Generally   61
Federal Laws   62
State Laws   62

3   What Records Must You Keep and for How Long?   67

Why Must You Keep Records?   67
    To Comply with the Law   67
    To Provide Better Health Care   67
    To Minimize Litigation Losses   68
What Records Must You Keep and for How Long?   68
    Statutes of Limitations   69
    Federal Laws   70
    State Laws   74

Part II
How Do You Keep Your Records? 119

4 What Media Can You Use to Keep Your Records? 121

Media Generally 121
Federal Laws 122
State Laws 123

5 How to Store Records 137

Storage Generally 137
    Personnel Security 137
    Physical Security 138
    System Security 139
State Laws 139

6 Correcting Records 147

What Do You Do If a Record Is Inaccurate? 147
Federal Laws 148
State Laws 148

Part III
When Can You Disclose Information? 151

7 Reporting Child and Other Forms of Abuse 153

Reporting Generally 153
State Laws 153

8 Drug and Alcohol Abuse Records and Reports 171

Introduction 171
Federal Laws 171
State Laws 172

9 Reporting and Release of Communicable Disease Information 179

Introduction 179
State Laws 179

Contents   v

10 Assessing Patient Care, Inspections, and Credentialing   193

    Introduction   **193**
    Federal Laws   **193**
    State Laws   **193**

11 Disclosure When a Court Orders You To   203

    Introduction   **203**
    State Laws   **203**

12 Disclosure for Medical Research   215

    Introduction   **215**
    State Laws   **215**

13 Disclosure Upon Request   219

    Introduction   **219**
    Federal Laws   **219**
    State Laws   **219**

Part IV

When Should You Refuse to Release Records?   231

14 Patients' Rights to Privacy   233

    Definition of the Right to Privacy   **233**
    Federal Laws   **233**
    State Laws   **234**

15 The Physician-Patient Privilege   255

    Introduction   **255**
    Federal Laws   **255**
    State Laws   **255**
    Medical Ethics and Privacy   **268**

Part V

How Do You Dispose of Your Records? 269

16 How Do You Destroy Your Records? 271

Introduction 271
Federal Laws 272
State Laws 272

17 Disposing of Records During Acquisitions, Mergers, and Closings 279

Introduction 279
State Laws 280

Appendix A   Condition of Participation: Medical Record Services, Health Care Financing Administration, 42 CFR, Chapter 4, §482.24   285
          B   State Statutes of Limitations   287
          C   Administrative Rules of Montana 16, 32, 138–142, Annual Reports by Healthcare Facilities   291
          D   Recommended Retention Periods for Hospital Records   297
          E   American Medical Association's Confidentiality Statement   305

Glossary 307

Index 311

About the Author 321

Acknowledgments

This book would not have been possible without the indefatigable assistance of my main research tool, Mr. Thomas Dimitroff, B.C.L.

Special thanks also go to Ms. Alice McCart, Manager of Editorial Development at Healthcare Financial Management Association, who was going to see this book in print or else, and to Ira Berlin, who provided helpful guidance and assistance.

Besides the thanks due the faculty and students at Illinois Institute of Technology, Chicago-Kent College of Law, who so graciously put up with me while I wrote this book, special thanks are due Lou Ann Schraffenberger, RRA, of the American Medical Record Association, to Lois Kuehl at HFMA, and to Robert Shelton, FHFMA, Thomas J. Gryzbek, J. D., Carol Campbell, Fred Krizman, Ron Anspaugh, Bob Taylor, Rose Dunn, and Ellen Mount, who provided helpful reviews and comments, and to Carol Johnson, Yuri Shkeyrov, Martha Niles, and Kenda Hicks, who provided valuable assistance in the preparation of this manuscript.

Preface

Almost a decade has gone by since the Healthcare Financial Management Association published its last *Guide to the Retention and Preservation of Records with Destruction Schedules, Sixth Hospital Edition.* Time, however, has not lessened the need for a practical legal guide to healthcare records, especially medical records. With the increasing complexity of the law, with larger medical malpractice verdicts, and with advances in data-storage technology, the business of keeping proper medical and other records is more difficult now than a decade ago. And considering the pervasiveness of government regulation and the need to have proper records to avoid problems with the government as well as to limit malpractice or other liability, good record-keeping is more necessary now than a decade ago. Therefore, this book goes beyond the practical guide to retention HFMA used to publish. This book is a legal guide based on federal and state laws and regulations. The purpose of this new book is to help chief financial officers, hospital administrators, medical professionals, and records managers cope with the complex requirements of proper records management.

To assist you in developing or updating your records management, this book discusses the major topics in records management from the first question—what constitutes a record—through the last—how do you dispose of records. Each topic begins with an introduction to that area of records management and ends with a compilation of federal and state laws covering that particular aspect of record-keeping. The book focuses on medical records, but if a state or the federal government has a law or administrative regulation specifying requirements for other healthcare facility records, the federal or state law compilation summarizes those requirements. State laws vary widely. Some states have very comprehensive statutory and regulatory schemes for records management. Others have almost no requirements. Neither the federal government nor many states have specific requirements for certain aspects of records management. In such cases, you may want to follow the general guidance at the start of each chapter and look at some of the state provisions to adopt a rule for your facility that will serve its and its patients' and employees' needs. Of course, you should have an attorney review your plan even if your state has a law governing the particular aspect of records management you are interested in. Laws and regulations change frequently, and only a competent attorney can give you the assurance you need that your program is legally sufficient.

Use this book as a guide, not as a definitive statement of the law and certainly not as a substitute for a consultation with an attorney. Although the book contains citations to state and federal laws and regulations, in many instances the text paraphrases those laws and regulations to make them more understandable. Thus, you should seek legal counsel both to interpret existing laws and to provide guidance where the law is silent.

Part **I**

What Is a Record, Who Owns It, and What Do You Do with It?

In order to develop a good program for keeping healthcare records, you need to know what you are talking about. What's a record? What's a medical record? Chapter 1 will provide these definitions and start you on your way to developing a good records retention program. Chapter 2 answers the question of who owns hospital and medical records, and Chapter 3 specifies what records you must keep and for how long.

1

What Is a Record?

Records Generally

A record is nothing more than an account of an event preserved on some medium so that someone may read it at some later time. Rule 803 (5) of the Uniform Rules of Evidence, which more than half of the states have adopted, talks about business records, but its language applies to any record as being "a memorandum, report, record, or data compilation, in any form, of acts, events, conditions, opinions, or diagnoses, made at or near the time by, or from information transmitted by, a person with knowledge. . . ." § 1 (c) of the Uniform Preservation of Private Business Records Act defines business records as "books of account, vouchers, documents, cancelled checks, payrolls, correspondence, records of sales, personnel, equipment and production reports relating to any or all of such records, and other business papers."

Medical Records

Some states define the term medical record, and others merely specify what information such a record must contain. Colorado Code § 18-4-412, for example, defines a medical record as "the written or graphic documentation, sound recording, or computer record of services pertaining to medical and health care which are performed at the direction of a physician or other licensed health care provider on behalf of a patient by physicians, dentists, nurses, technicians, or other health care personnel. 'Medical record' includes such diagnostic documentation as X rays, electrocardiograms, electroencephalograms, and other test results." Other states define related terms, such as medical information (Arizona), health records (Indiana), hospital records (Louisiana), or healthcare records (Nevada). Some states, such as North Dakota, for example, do not define these terms as such, but state that medical records must contain sufficient information to justify the diagnosis and warrant the treatment and end results.

Perhaps a more important question than what medical records are is what they must include. Some states provide detailed guidelines on what a medical record must contain, either in a statute, in an administrative regulation, such as a regulation of the state department of health, or in a licensure rule or standard. Other states leave it up to the facility to define what a medical record comprises. In that event, "sufficient information to justify the diagnosis and warrant the treatment and end results" probably is not sufficient both to provide proper health care and to minimize litigation losses. Thus, to ensure that patients receive proper care and to avoid paying a malpractice claim because your facility cannot document that proper care, you must keep thorough medical records that document everything of significance (see Appendix A for Health Care Financing Administration guidelines). Each entry should be legible, accurate, complete, and objective. Illegible records don't help document that the care was proper. Accurate and complete records cover all required aspects of patient care without assigning blame or covering up an adverse event. You don't want to have to explain to a jury why you tried to hide something in a malpractice case. And, as far as the jury is concerned, if the record doesn't reflect that a treatment or medication was given, it wasn't. Use proper terminology, such as the Terminology of the International Classification of Diseases. Finally, document patient behavior and other items factually, not emotionally, so that you don't make the situation worse or allow a plaintiff's attorney to discredit you by showing that you were biased. For example, rather than charting that a patient was extremely upset, record what he said and what his actions were.

You should review what your state and other states require medical records to contain. You should also consult the Accreditation Manual for Hospitals of the Joint Commission on Accreditation of Healthcare Organizations. No jurisdiction prohibits healthcare providers from adding information that is not required by a statute or regulation to a medical record if the facility needs a record of that additional information.

State Laws

Alabama

Alabama does not define a medical record, but paragraph (3) of Rules of Alabama State Board of Health Division of Licensure and Certification 420-5-7.07 lists the following contents of medical records:

Admission Record:

- Name.
- Address.
- Age.
- Sex.
- Nationality.
- Marital status.
- Name and address of closest relative.

- Date of admission.
- Date of discharge or death.
- Any other personal and statistical particulars that the State Registrar of Vital Statistics requires in the certificates of birth, death, and stillbirths.

Medical and Surgical Record: As a minimum, the complete medical and surgical record shall include the following data, when applicable:

- Identification data (name, age, sex, referring and attending physician, and so forth).
- Complaint.
- Present illness.
- Past history.
- Family history.
- Review of systems.
- Physical examination.
- Provisional diagnosis.
- Clinical laboratory reports.
- X-ray reports.
- Consultations.
- Treatment (medical and surgical).
- Operative report.
- Tissue report.
- Progress notes.
- Final diagnosis.
- Discharge summary on cases longer than 48 hours.
- Autopsy findings, if performed.

Obstetrical Record: As a minimum, the complete obstetrical record shall include the following data:

- Prenatal record (medical and obstetric history).
- Labor record (observation and proceeding during labor).
- Postpartum record.

Newborn Record: As a minimum, the complete newborn record shall include the following data:

- Birth record and physical examination of the infant.
- Nurse's record (number and character of stools, bleeding from the umbilical cord, type and time of feeding and reaction of infant to feedings, or other such pertinent information).

6   Healthcare Records

Alaska

Alaska does not define a medical record, but regulations of the Department of Health and Social Services specify what information medical records must include. See 7 AAC 12.425 for medical records for birth centers, 7 AAC 12.530 for medical records for home health agencies, and 7 AAC 12.770 for all facilities except home health agencies, intermediate care facilities for the mentally retarded, and birth centers.

Inpatient Medical Records: 7 AAC 12.770 (c) specifies that inpatient medical records shall contain the following information as appropriate:

- Patient identification sheet:
    - Patient's name.
    - Medical record number.
    - Patient's address on admission.
    - Patient's date of birth.
    - Patient's sex.
    - Patient's marital status.
    - Patient's religious preference.
    - Date of admission.
    - Name, address, and telephone number of a contact person.
    - Name of patient's attending physician.
    - Initial diagnostic impression.
    - Date of discharge and final diagnosis.
    - Source of payment.
- Medical and psychiatric history and examination.
- Consultation reports, dental records, and reports of special studies.
- An order sheet that includes medication, treatment, and diet orders signed by a physician.
- Nurses' notes that must include these items:
    - Accurate record of care given.
    - Record of pertinent observations and response to treatment, including psychosocial and physical manifestations.
    - Assessment at time of admission.
    - Discharge plan.
    - Name, dosage, and time of administration of medication or treatment, route of administration and site of injection, if other than by oral administration, of medication, patient's response, and signature of person who administered the medication or treatment.
    - Record of any restraint used, showing duration of usage.
- Court orders relevant to involuntary treatment.
- Laboratory reports.
- X-ray reports.
- Consent forms.

- Operative report on inpatient and outpatient surgery, including preoperative and postoperative diagnosis, description of findings, techniques used, and tissue removed or altered, if appropriate.

Outpatient Clinic Records: The regulation adds that, in outpatient departments organized by clinics, the following information should be available:

- Patient's identification sheet.
- History and physical examination.
- Physician's orders.
- Any laboratory and other diagnostic tests, diagnosis, and treatment.
- Disposition.

Outpatient Services Record: If outpatient services are in other than an organized outpatient clinic, the following information should be available:

- Patient's identification.
- Information pertaining to the patient's chief complaint, including, but not limited to, physician's orders, treatment or service provided, and disposition.

Emergency Services Record:

- Patient identification.
- Record of any treatment patient received before arrival.
- History of disease or injury.
- Physical findings.
- Laboratory and X-ray reports, if applicable.
- Diagnosis.
- Record of treatment.
- Disposition.
- Name of physician who saw patient in the emergency room.

Arizona

Arizona Department of Health Services Regulation R9-1-311 defines medical information as including "all clinical records, medical reports, laboratory statements or reports, any file, film, record or report or oral statement relating to diagnostic findings and treatment of patients, as well as information relating to contacts, suspects and associates of communicable disease patients."

Arkansas

According to the Arkansas Register, Part 6, § 1, medical records must contain the following information:

Identification Data Record:

- Patient's full name and maiden name, if applicable.
- Patient's address, telephone number, and occupation.

- Date of birth.
- Age.
- Sex.
- Religion.
- Marital status.
- Dates and times of admission and of discharge.
- Full name of physician (and, if necessary, address and telephone number).
- Name and address of nearest relative or person or agency responsible for patient and occupation of responsible party.
- Name, address, and telephone number of person to notify in case of emergency.
- Hospital number or social security number.

Medical Data Record:

- Family history.
- Past history.
- Chief complaint(s).
- Present illness with dates.
- Physical examination.
- Orders and progress notes.
- Provisional or admitting diagnosis(es).
- Final diagnosis(es).
- A discharge summary that recapitulates the significant findings and events of the patient's hospitalization and condition on discharge.
- Date and time of death and signature of physician who pronounced patient dead.
- Cause of death. You may omit last two items in the event of a coroner's inquest and make a note to that effect in the medical record.

Special Treatment and Examination Records:

- Signed laboratory report(s).
- Signed X-ray report(s).
- Signed consultation reports.
- Pertinent surgical records, including the following data:
  - History and physical work up.
  - Preoperative and postoperative diagnosis.
  - Record of all medication, intravenous solutions, and blood transfusions given in the operating room.
  - Anesthetic report.
  - Postanesthetic follow-up note.
  - Operative report.
  - Recovery room record.
  - Signed pathological report of either macroscopic and/or microscopic examinations on all tissue surgically removed.

- Obstetrical records shall include the following data:
  - Pertinent prenatal record.
  - Labor record.
  - Nurse's postpartum record.
- Newborn records shall include the following data:
  - History of newborn delivery, including sex and date of birth, type of delivery, anesthetic given the mother during labor and delivery, and physical condition of the infant after birth.
  - Physician's record, including report of findings such as physical examination, weight, and date and time of birth.
  - Records of physical therapy treatment(s) and diagnostic treatment procedure(s).
  - Signed authorization for autopsy.
  - Autopsy findings.

Nurse's Notes:

- Mode of admission.
- Admission temperature, pulse, and respiration.
- Description of each patient on admission and discharge, indicating particularly any mark, bruise, discoloration, cut, abrasion, burn, rash, or irritation.
- Date and time of all treatments or dressings.
- Date, time, dosage, and manner of administration of all medications and initials of nurse administering medication.
- Diet.
- Objective signs and subjective symptoms.
- Complaints.
- Complete report of any injuries to the patient while hospitalized.
- Changes in appearance and mental conditions.
- The mode of discharge and to whom the facility discharged patient.
- Death notes, including the following information:
  - Time someone called physician and time physician pronounced patient dead.
  - Relatives present at time of death. (If relatives were not present, record their notification and disposition of the patient's belongings.)

Outpatient Record:

- Patient's history.
- Physical examination.
- Laboratory and other diagnostic tests.
- Diagnosis.
- Treatment.

Emergency Room Patient's Medical Record:
- Patient identification.
- Date.
- History of disease or injury.
- Physical findings.
- Laboratory and X-ray reports.
- Diagnosis.
- Record of treatment.
- Disposition.
- Signature of attending physician.

California

California's Title 22, Health Facilities and Referral Agencies, § 70748, specifies what an inpatient medical record must contain:

Medical Record:
- Identification Sheet:
    - Name.
    - Address on admission.
    - Identification number, if applicable.
      - Social Security.
      - Medicare.
      - Medi-Cal.
    - Age.
    - Sex.
    - Marital status.
    - Religion.
    - Date of admission.
    - Date of discharge.
    - Name, address, and telephone number of person or agency responsible for patient.
    - Name of patient's attending physician.
    - Initial diagnostic impression.
    - Discharge and final diagnosis.
- History and Physical Examination Record.
- Consultation Reports.
- Order Sheet:
    - Medication.
    - Treatment.
    - Diet.
- Progress Notes, including current or working diagnosis.

- Nurse's Notes:
  - Concise and accurate record of nursing care administered.
  - Record of pertinent observations, including psychosocial and physical manifestations, as well as incidents and unusual occurrences, and relevant nursing interpretation of such observations.
  - Name, dosage, and time of administration of medications and treatment. Record route of administration and site of injection if other than by oral administration.
  - Record of type of restraint and time of application and removal, except for soft tie restraints used for support and protection of the patient.
- Vital Sign Sheet.
- Laboratory Test Reports.
- X-ray Reports.
- Consent Forms.
- Anesthesia Record, including preoperative diagnosis, if applicable.
- Operative Report:
  - Preoperative and postoperative diagnosis.
  - Description of findings.
  - Technique used.
  - Tissue removed or altered, if applicable.
- Pathological Report, if applicable.
- Labor Record, if applicable.
- Delivery Record, if applicable.
- Discharge Summary:
  - Significant findings and events of the patient's hospitalization.
  - Condition on discharge.
  - Any recommendations and arrangements for future care.

Colorado

In its statute that makes theft of medical records or medical information a crime (Colorado Code § 18-4-412), Colorado defines a medical record as "the written or graphic documentation, sound recording, or computer record of services pertaining to medical and health care which are performed at the direction of a physician or other licensed health care provider on behalf of a patient by physicians, dentists, nurses, technicians, or other health care personnel. 'Medical record' includes such diagnostic documentation as X rays, electrocardiograms, electroencephalograms, and other test results." Colorado Code § 18-4-412.

Colorado Regulations 6 CCR 1011-1 for general hospitals states that a complete medical record shall include the following information:

Admission and Discharge Record:

- Date and time of admission and discharge.
- Adequate identification and sociological data.
- Admission diagnosis.
- Final diagnosis.
- Secondary diagnosis.
- Complications.
- Operative procedures.
- Condition on discharge.
- Signature of attending physician.

Medical-Surgical Data:

- Chief complaint and present illness.
- Past, family, and personal history.
- Physical examination reports.
- Provisional diagnosis.
- Reports of any special examinations.
- Reports of consultations.
- Treatment and progress notes.
- Complete surgical and dental reports.
- Condition on discharge.
- Final diagnosis.
- Autopsy protocol.
- Discharge summary.
- Signed permissions for procedures.

Nursing Records

Surgical Records:

- History.
- Physical and special examinations.
- Diagnosis recorded before the operation.
- Anesthesia record, including postanesthetic condition.
- Complete description of operative procedures and findings, including postoperative diagnosis.
- Pathologist's report on all tissues removed.

Obstetric Records:

- Record of previous obstetric history and prenatal care, including blood serology and Rh factor determination.
- Admission obstetrical examination report describing condition of mother and fetus.

- Complete description of progress of labor and delivery, including reason for induction and operative procedures.
- Records of anesthesia, analgesia, and medications given in the course of labor and delivery.
- Records of fetal heart rate and vital signs.
- Signed reports of consultants.
- Names of assistants present during delivery.
- Progress notes, including descriptions of involution of uterus, type of lochia, condition of breast and nipples.
- Report of condition of infant following delivery.

Newborn's Records:

- Date and time of birth.
- Weight and length.
- Period of gestation.
- Sex.
- Parents' names and addresses.
- Type of identification.
- Description of complications of pregnancy or delivery.
- Condition at birth.
- Record of prophylactic instillation into each eye.
- Results of PKU tests.
- Report of initial physical examination.
- Progress notes, including temperature, weight, and feeding charts.
- Condition of eyes and umbilical cord.
- Number, consistency, and color of stools.
- Condition and color of skin.
- Motor behavior.

Connecticut

Connecticut Public Health Code § 19–13–D3 (d) (3) specifies what medical records must contain:

All Medical Records: Proper identification data.

Clinical Records: Sufficient information, including progress notes, to justify the diagnosis and warrant the treatment.

Doctor's Orders, Nurse's Notes, and All the Entries: Signature of the person responsible.

Obstetrics Record:

- Such information as the commissioner of health services may require.
- All items necessary to fill out a death certificate for the mother.

- All items necessary to fill out a birth certificate or a death certificate for the baby.

Chronic and Convalescent Nursing Homes and Rest Homes with Nursing Supervision Medical Records:

- Patient identification data.
- Name of patient's personal physician.
- Signed and dated admission history and reports of physical examination.
- Signed and dated hospital discharge summary, if applicable.
- Signed and dated transfer form, if applicable.
- Complete medical diagnosis.
- All initial and subsequent orders by the physician.
- Patient assessment, completed within seven days of admission:
  - Health history.
  - Physical, mental, and social status.
  - Evaluation of problems.
  - Rehabilitation potential.
- Patient care plan.
- Record of visits and progress notes by the physician.
- Nurse's notes:
  - Current condition.
  - Changes in patient condition.
  - Treatments.
  - Responses to such treatments.
- Record of medications administered:
  - Name and strength of drug.
  - Date, route, and time of administration.
  - Dosage administered.
  - With respect to PRN medications, reasons for administration and patient response/result observed.
- Documentation of all care and ancillary services provided.
- Summaries of conferences and records of consultations.
- Record of any treatment, medication, or service refused by the patient, including the visit of a physician.
- Discharge plans.

District of Columbia

The District of Columbia in D.C. Code § 32–501 defines primary health record as "the record of continuing care kept by a physician, psychologist, hospital, or extended care facility regarding a patient which reflects the diagnostic and therapeutic services rendered by the practitioner."

Florida

According to Chapter 10D–28.59(3), Rules of the Department of Health and Rehabilitative Services, medical records must contain the original of the following information:

- Identification data.
- Chief complaint.
- Present illness.
- Past history.
- Family history.
- Physical examination.
- Provisional diagnosis.
- Clinical laboratory reports.
- X-ray reports.
- Consultation reports.
- Medical and surgical treatment notes and reports.
- Tissue reports.
- Physician and nurse progress notes.
- Final diagnosis.
- Discharge summary.
- Autopsy findings when performed.

Georgia

In Georgia, a record is "a patient's health record, including, but not limited to, evaluations, diagnoses, prognoses, laboratory reports, X-rays, prescriptions, and other technical information used in assessing the patient's condition, or the pertinent portion of the record relating to a specific condition or a summary of the record." Chapter 33, Georgia Code, 31–33–1. (3).

Hawaii

Hawaii Title 33, Evidence § 622.58 (d), does not define medical records but states that the basic information that a healthcare facility must retain even after destruction of medical records after the retention period or after microfilming from a physician or surgeon shall include the following items:

Medical Record:

- Patient's name and birthdate.
- List of dated diagnoses and intrusive treatments.
- Record of all drugs prescribed or given.

Healthcare Facility Record:

- Patient's name and birthday.
- Dates of admission and discharge.

- Names of attending physicians.
- Final diagnosis.
- Major procedures performed.
- Operative reports.
- Pathology reports.
- Discharge summaries.

Illinois

77 Illinois Administrative Code § 250.1510 b) 2) specifies the following minimum requirements:

Medical Record:
- Patient identification and admission information.
- History of patient as to chief complaints.
- Present illness and pertinent past history.
- Family history.
- Social history.
- Physical examination report.
- Provisional diagnosis.
- Diagnostic and therapeutic reports.
- Laboratory test results.
- X-ray findings.
- Any surgical procedure performed.
- Any pathological examination.
- Any consultation.
- Any other diagnostic or therapeutic procedure performed.
- Orders and progress notes made by the attending physician and when applicable by other members of the medical staff and allied health personnel.
- Observation notes and vital sign charting made by nursing personnel.
- Conclusions as to the primary and any associated diagnoses.
- Brief clinical resume.
- Disposition at discharge, including instructions and/or medications.
- Any autopsy findings on a hospital death.

Obstetric Record:
- Findings during the prenatal period, which should be available in the maternity department before the patient's admission.
- Medical and obstetric history.
- Observations and proceedings during labor, delivery, and postpartum period.
- Laboratory and X-ray findings.

Infant Record:
- History of maternal health and prenatal course.
- Description of labor:

- Drugs administered.
- Method of delivery.
- Complications of labor and delivery.
- Description of placenta and amniotic fluid.
- Birth data:
  - Time of birth and condition of infant at birth, including Apgar score at one and five minutes.
  - Age respiration became spontaneous and sustained.
  - Description of resuscitation if required.
  - Description of abnormalities and problems occurring from birth until transfer from the delivery room.
- Reports of a complete and detailed physical examination:
  - Within 24 hours following birth.
  - Within 24 hours of discharge.
  - At least every three days during hospital stay.
- Physical measurements:
  - Length, weight, and head circumference at birth.
  - Weight every day.
  - Temperature twice daily, charted.
- Documentation of infant feeding: intake, content, and amount if by formula.
- Clinical course during hospital stay, including treatment provided and patient response.
- Clinical note of status at discharge.

Indiana

Indiana Code § 16 4–8–1 defines health records as "written or printed information possessed by a provider concerning any diagnosis, treatment, or prognosis of the patient."

Indiana State Board of Health Hospital Licensure Rules 410 IAC15–1–9 requires the following information:

Inpatient Hospital Record:

- Identification data.
- Chief complaint.
- Present illness.
- Past history.
- Physical examination.
- Progress notes.
- Reports on consultations.
- Copy of transfer form.
- Reports on laboratory, X-ray, and operative procedures.

- Special reports.
- Doctors' orders (signed and dated).
- Notes and observations.
- Treatment records of nurses, dietitian, therapists, and other personnel.
- Reports on vital signs.
- Final discharge summary.
- Summary sheet giving final diagnosis, complications, operative procedures, and signature of attending physician.

Readmission Record (for readmissions within a reasonable time with the same diagnosis): Readmission note on the patient's condition and the reason for readmission.

Short Form Record (for patients hospitalized for less than 48 hours):

- Identification data.
- Description of patient's condition.
- Physical findings.
- Treatments given.
- Procedures carried out.
- Operative procedures and anesthesia.
- Medical orders.
- Other data to support the diagnosis and treatment.
- Disposition.
- Necessary signatures.
- Dismissal diagnosis.

Emergency and Outpatient Record:

- Identification data.
- Description of the illness or injury.
- Description of the treatment.
- Signature of the physician.
- Instructions given on release.
- Condition on discharge.
- Follow-up care.
- Name of person giving instructions.
- Copy of transfer form.
- Reasons the facility does not provide care for the patient or transfers the patient elsewhere, if applicable.

Iowa

Iowa's only reference to what constitutes a medical record is in Public Health Regulations, Chapter 51, Hospitals, 641–51.5(135B), which states that "Accurate and complete medical records shall be written for all patients and signed by the attending physician." The regulation that covers emergency services, 641–51.28(135B), provides that hospitals must have written policies and procedures that require a medical record on every patient given treatment in the emergency service and establish the medical record documentation. The documentation should include at least the following data:

- Appropriate information regarding the medical screening provided.
- Notation of patient refusal to provide information.
- Physician documentation of the presence or absence of an emergency medical condition or active labor.
- Physician documentation of transfer or discharge, stating the basis for transfer or discharge.
- Transfer:
  - Identity of the facility of the transfer.
  - Acceptance of the patient by the facility of transfer.
  - Means of transfer of the patient.

Kansas

Kansas Administrative Regulations § 28–34–9a (e)(1)–(3) specifies that medical records shall contain sufficient information to identify the patient clearly, to justify the diagnosis and treatment, and to document the results accurately. That regulation and § 28–34–16(f) explain that medical and emergency records should contain at least the following information:

Medical Record:

- Notes by authorized house staff members and individuals who have clinical privileges.
- Consultation reports.
- Nurse's notes.
- Entries by specified professional personnel.
- Findings and results of any pathological or clinical laboratory examinations.
- Radiology examinations.
- Medical and surgical treatment.
- Other diagnostic or therapeutic procedures.
- Provisional diagnosis.
- Primary and secondary final diagnosis.
- Clinical resume.
- Necropsy reports.

Emergency Record:

- Patient identification.
- History of disease or injury.
- Physical findings.
- Laboratory and radiological reports.
- Diagnosis.

20 Healthcare Records

- Record of treatment.
- Disposition of the case.
- Signature of physician providing the service.

Kentucky

902 Kentucky Administrative Regulations (KAR) 20:016 § 3 (11) (d) specifies that medical records shall include the following data:

- Identification data and signed consent forms, including name and address of next of kin and of person or agency responsible for patient.
- Date of admission and name of attending medical staff member.
- Chief complaint.
- Medical history, including present illness, past history, family history, and physical examination.
- Report of special examinations or procedures, such as consultations, clinical laboratory tests, X-ray interpretations, EKG interpretations, and so forth.
- Provisional diagnosis or reason for admission.
- Orders for diet, diagnostic tests, therapeutic procedures, and medications, including patient limitations, signed and dated by the medical staff member, and, if given verbally, undersigned by the medical staff member upon next visit to hospital.
- Medical, surgical, and dental treatment notes and reports, signed and dated by physician or dentist, when applicable, including records of all medication administered to the patient.
- Complete surgical record signed by attending surgeon or oral surgeon, including anesthesia record signed by anesthesiologist or anesthetist, preoperative physical examination and diagnosis, description of operative procedures and findings, postoperative diagnosis, and tissue diagnosis by qualified pathologist on tissue surgically removed.
- Physician's or dentist's progress notes, when applicable, and nurse's observations.
- Record of temperature, blood pressure, pulse, and respiration.
- Final diagnosis using terminology in the current version of the International Classification of Diseases or the American Psychiatric Association's Diagnostic and Statistical Manual, as applicable.
- Discharge summary, including condition of patient on discharge and date of discharge.
- In case of death, autopsy findings, if performed.
- In case of death, indication of patient evaluation for organ donation in accordance with hospital protocol.

Louisiana

Title 40, Louisiana Statutes § 2144 A. (5), defines hospital record as "a compilation of the reports of the various clinical departments within a hospital, as well as reports from health care providers, as are customarily catalogued and maintained by the hospital medical records department." Hospital records include reports of procedures, such as X rays and electrocardiograms, but they do not include the image or graphic matter produced by such procedures.

Maine

Medical records in Maine must contain sufficient information to justify the diagnosis and warrant the treatment and results. According to chapter XII G. of the Regulations Governing the Licensing and Functioning of General and Specialty Hospitals, the medical records should contain the following information:

- Identification data.
- Chief complaint.
- Present illness.
- Past history.
- Family history.
- Physical examination.
- Provisional diagnosis.
- Clinical laboratory reports.
- X-ray reports.
- Consultations.
- Treatment, medical and surgical.
- Tissue report.
- Progress notes.
- Final diagnosis.
- Discharge summary.
- Autopsy findings.

Maryland

Maryland Code § 4–302 defines medical record as "each record of medical care that a facility keeps on an individual and includes records kept in manual or automated form." The Code of Maryland Regulations 10.07.02.20 discusses maintenance of clinical records and specifies their contents:

- Identification and summary sheet or sheets:
  - Patient's name.
  - Social security number.
  - Armed forces status.
  - Citizenship.
  - Marital status.

22 Healthcare Records

- Age.
- Sex.
- Home address.
- Religion.
- Names, addresses, and telephone numbers of referral agencies, personal physician, dentist, parents' names or next of kin, or authorized representative.
- Documented evidence of assessment of the needs of the patient, of establishment of an appropriate plan of initial and ongoing treatment, and of the care and services provided.
- Authentication of hospital diagnoses (discharge summary, report from patient's attending physician, or transfer form).
- Consent forms when required.
- Medical and social history of patient.
- Report of physical examination.
- Diagnostic and therapeutic orders.
- Consultation reports.
- Observations and progress notes.
- Reports of medication administration, treatments, and clinical findings.
- Discharge summary, including final diagnosis and prognosis.
- Discipline assessment.
- Interdisciplinary care plan.

Massachusetts

The Department of Public Health, by Department of Health Regulation 130.112 and 105 CMR 130.690, has defined the contents of records:

Medical Records:

- Date of admission.
- Identification data.
- Chief complaint.
- History of present illness.
- Past history.
- Family history.
- Physical examination.
- Provisional diagnosis.
- Reports of special examinations or procedures, including consultation.
- Clinical, laboratory, and X-ray reports.
- Complete surgical and dental records.
- Medical, surgical, and dental treatment.
- Progress notes.
- Graphic bedside charts.
- Final diagnosis.

- Condition on discharge.
- Date of discharge.
- Autopsy report, if any.

Operative Reports:

- Record of preoperative physical examinations and diagnosis.
- Anesthesia record.
- Complete description of operative procedures and findings, including postoperative diagnosis.
- Report of pathological examinations on all tissues removed at operation.

Clinical Record of Newborn:

- Obstetrical history of mother's previous pregnancies.
- Description of complications of pregnancy or delivery.
- List of complicating maternal diseases.
- Drugs taken during pregnancy, labor, and delivery.
- Duration of ruptured membranes.
- Maternal antenatal blood serology, blood typing, Rh factor, and Coombs test for maternal antibodies where indicated.
- Complete description of progress of labor, including reasons for induction and operative procedures, if any, signed by attending physician.
- Anesthesia, analgesia, and medications given to mother and infant.
- Condition of infant at birth:
  - Apgar Score (or its equivalent) at one minute and repeat ratings in five minutes.
  - Resuscitation.
  - Time of sustained respiration.
  - Details of physical abnormalities.
  - Pathological states.
  - Treatments up to transfer to the nursery.
- Number of cord vessels and any abnormalities of the placenta.
- Date and hour of birth, birth weight and length, and period of gestation.
- Written verification of eye prophylaxis.
- Report of initial physical examination, including any abnormalities, signed by attending physician.
- Progress notes, written by a physician, at intervals appropriate to the infant's condition, but at least every four days, with notation of any abnormalities, complications, or unusual conditions.
- Discharge physical examination (including head circumference), recommendations, and signature of attending physician or delegate.
- Listing of all diagnoses since birth, including discharge diagnosis.
- Specific follow-up plans for infant's care.

Michigan

Department of Public Health Administrative Rules and Procedures R 325.1028 lists the following requirements:

Medical Record:

- Admission date.
- Admitting diagnosis.
- History and physical examination.
- Physician's progress notes.
- Operation and treatment notes and consultations.
- Physician's orders.
- Nurse's notes, including temperature, pulse, respiration, conditions observed, and medication given.
- Record of discharge or death.
- Final diagnosis.
- Reports of special examinations, such as laboratory, X ray, and pathology.

Surgical Record:

- Details of preoperative study and diagnosis.
- Preoperative medication.
- Name of surgeon and assistants.
- Method of anesthesia.
- Amount of anesthetic when measurable.
- Name of anesthetist.
- Postoperative diagnosis, including pathological findings.

Minnesota

Minnesota Hospital Licensing and Operation Regulations 4640.1000, subparagraph 3, requires keeping accurate and complete medical records on all patients from the time of admission to the time of discharge.

Medical Record:

- Adequate identification data.
- Admitting diagnosis completed within 24 to 48 hours.
- History and physical examination, including history of pregnancy in maternity cases, completed within 24 to 48 hours.
- Progress notes.
- Signed doctor's orders.
- Operative notes, where applicable, including course of delivery in maternity cases.
- Special reports and examinations, including clinical and laboratory findings, X-ray findings, records of consultations, and anesthesia reports.

- Nurse's notes.
- Discharge diagnosis.
- Autopsy report, where applicable.

Additional information on all maternity patients:

- Full and true names of patient and her husband.
- Place of residence of the patient before hospitalization.
- Place of residence following discharge.

Medical Record on Newborn Infant:

- Physical examination.
- Statement of physical condition of the infant at discharge.
- True name of the person or persons with whom the child leaves and the residence where the child will go, if the child leaves the hospital with any person other than a parent.

Mississippi

Mississippi's Statute § 41–9–61 (b) defines hospital records as "those medical histories, records, reports, summaries, diagnoses, and prognoses, records of treatment and medication ordered and given, notes, entries, X-rays, and other written or graphic data prepared, kept, made or maintained in hospitals that pertain to hospital confinements or hospital services rendered to patients admitted to hospitals or receiving emergency room or outpatient care. Such records shall also include abstracts of the foregoing data customarily made or provided. . . . Such records shall not, however, include ordinary business records pertaining to patient's accounts or the administration of the institution nor shall 'hospital records' include any records consisting of nursing audits, physician audits, departmental evaluations or other evaluations or reviews which are used only for inservice education programs, or which are required only for accreditation or for participation in federal health programs."

The statute in § 41–9–61 (f) also defines business records as "all those books, ledgers, records, papers and other documents prepared, kept, made or received in hospitals that pertain to the organization, administration or management of the business and affairs of hospitals, but which do not constitute hospital records as hereinabove defined."

Missouri

Title 13 Department of Social Services, Division 50—Division of Health, Chapter 20—Hospitals 13 CSR 50—20.021 (3) (D) 9 and Regulations Governing Skilled Nursing and Intermediate Care Facilities in the State of Missouri 13 CSR 15–14.042 (92)–(95) govern medical record contents in Missouri.

Patient Medical Record:

- Unique identifying record number.
- Pertinent identifying and personal data.

- History of present illness or complaint.
- Past history.
- Family history.
- Physical examination.
- Provisional admitting diagnosis.
- Medical staff orders.
- Progress notes.
- Nurse's notes.
- Discharge summary.
- Final diagnosis.
- Evidence of appropriate informed consent.
- Reports:
    - Clinical.
    - Laboratory.
    - X ray.
    - Consultation.
    - Electrocardiogram.
    - Surgical procedures.
    - Therapy.
    - Anesthesia.
    - Pathology.
    - Autopsy.
    - Any other reports pertinent to the patient's care.
- Date and time of death.
- Autopsy permit, if granted.
- Disposition of the body.

Nursing Home General Information Record:

- Resident name.
- Previous address.
- Age (birthdate).
- Sex.
- Marital status.
- Social security number.
- Date of admission.
- Name, address, and telephone number of responsible party.
- Name, address, and telephone number of attending physician.
- Height and weight on admission.
- Inventory of resident's personal possessions upon admission.
- Names of preferred dentist, pharmacist, and mortician.

Nursing Home Medical Record:

- Admission diagnosis.
- Admission physical and findings of subsequent examinations.
- Progress notes.
- Orders for all medications and treatments.
- Orders for extent of activity.
- Orders for restraints, including type and reason for such restraint.
- Orders for diet.
- Discharge diagnosis.
- Cause of death.

Nursing Home Nursing Progress Notes:

- Observations concerning the general condition of the resident.
- Any change in the resident's physical or mental condition.
- Any change in appetite.
- Any injury, incident, or accident.
- Observation of restraint of any resident.
- Any significant item of care provided to the resident.
- Monthly weights.
- Physician's visits.

Nursing Home Discharge Record:

- Date, condition, and reason for transfer or discharge.
- Name of person to whom facility discharges resident.
- Forwarding address.
- Date and time of death and disposition of the body.

Montana

Montana law does not define medical records or enumerate what records should contain. Chapter 23 of the Montana Hospital Association manual, however, suggests that patient records contain certain information. Administrative Rules of Montana, Health and Environmental Sciences, Chapter 32, Rules 16.32.323, 16.32.328, 16.32.328 (4), 16.32.340 (4), 16.32.355 (3), and 16.32.381 (1), however, list what must constitute certain specialized records.

Patient Record:

- Patient's name, address, age, sex, and marital status.
- Date of admission and date of discharge.
- Name, address, and telephone number of person or agency responsible for patient.
- Name, address, and telephone number of attending physician.
- Diagnosis on admission.

- Progress notes by physician.
- Nurse's notes.
- Medication and treatment orders.
- Temperature chart, including pulse and respiration.
- Condition and diagnosis of patient at time of discharge.
- Complete surgical record, including anesthesia record, preoperative diagnosis, operative procedure and findings, postoperative diagnosis, and tissue diagnosis on all specimens surgically removed.
- Complete obstetrical record, including prenatal record (if available), labor record, delivery record, and complete newborn record.

Delivery Record:

- Starting time of patient's labor.
- Time of birth of patient's newborn.
- Anesthesia used on patient.
- Whether physician performed an episiotomy on patient.
- Whether physician used forceps in delivery.
- Names of attending physicians.
- Names of attending nurses.
- Names of all other persons attending delivery.
- Sex of the newborn.
- Time of eye prophylactic treatment and name of drug used.

Obstetrical Record:

- Prenatal record.
- Labor notes.
- Obstetrical anesthesia notes.
- Delivery record.

Record for Newborn:

- Observations of newborn after birth.
- Delivery room care of newborn.
- Physical examinations performed on newborn.
- Temperature of newborn.
- Weight of newborn.
- Time of newborn's first urination.
- Number, character, and consistency of newborn's stool.
- Type of feeding administered to newborn.
- Phenylketonuria report for newborn.
- Name of person to whom facility releases newborn.

Hospice Medical Record:

- Patient identification, diagnosis, and prognosis.
- Patient's medical history.
- Patient/family plan of care.
- Record of all doctor's orders, verified at appropriate intervals.
- Progress notes, dated and signed.
- Evidence of timely action by the patient care team.

Core Record (abridgment following 10-year retention date):

- Patient identification data, including name, maiden name if relevant, address, date of birth, sex, and, if available, social security number.
- Medical history.
- Physical examination report.
- Consultation reports.
- Report of operation.
- Pathology report.
- Discharge summary (or final progress note for newborns and others for whom no discharge summary is available).
- Autopsy findings.
- For each maternity patient, the information listed above.
- For each newborn, the information listed above.

Infirmary and Outpatient Facility Medical Record:

- Identification data.
- Chief complaint.
- Present illness.
- Medical History.
- Physical examination.
- Laboratory and X-ray reports.
- Treatment administered.
- Tissue report.
- Progress reports.
- Discharge summary.

Personal Care Facility Resident Record:

- Admission record, including dates of admission and discharge.
- Name and address of resident.
- Birthdate.
- Marital status.
- Financial responsibility.
- Religious affiliation.
- Telephone number of physician and of person to notify in an emergency.

- Discharge information concerning disposition of a resident's personal belongings.
- Care record, including date and dosage of each medication.
- Date and time of visit to or by physician.

Nebraska

Medical records in Nebraska should contain sufficient information to justify the diagnosis and warrant the treatment and results:

Medical Record:

- Identification data.
- Chief complaint.
- Present illness.
- History and physical examination.
- Provisional diagnosis.
- Clinical pathology laboratory reports.
- Radiology reports.
- Consultations.
- Treatment.
- Tissue reports.
- Progress notes.
- Discharge summary.
- Autopsy findings.

For purposes of retention and inclusion, Nebraska does not include original X-ray film or laboratory samples, slides, or tissues in medical records, according to Title 175, Chapter 9, 003.04A.

Nevada

Nevada Statutes § 629.021 defines healthcare records as "any written reports, notes, orders, photographs, X-rays or other written record received or produced by a provider of health care, or any person employed by him, which contains information relating to the medical history, examination, diagnosis or treatment of the patient."

New Hampshire

The Department of Health and Human Services Regulations He–P 802.11, He–P 903.06, He–P 804.04, He–P 805.05, He–P 806.10, He–P 807.07, He–P 808.12, and He–P 809.07 list the contents of various records.

Complete Hospital Medical Records:

- Identification data.
- Complaint.

- Personal and family history.
- History of present illness.
- Physical examination.
- Special examinations, such as consultant, clinical laboratory, X-ray, and other examinations.
- Provisional or working diagnosis.
- Medical or surgical treatment.
- Gross and microscopical pathological findings.
- Progress notes.
- Final diagnosis.
- Condition on discharge.
- Follow-up.
- Autopsy findings.

Nursing Home Record:
- Admission data:
    - Date of admission.
    - Admitted from.
    - Name.
    - Address.
    - Date of birth.
    - Marital status.
    - Sex.
    - Name, address, and telephone number of nearest relative or other person responsible for the resident.
    - Name and telephone number of the resident's physician.
- Initial physician examination.
- Periodic medical evaluation findings.
- Medical history.
- Diagnoses.
- Orders for medications, treatments, diet, and activities.
- Physician's visits and progress notes.
- Nurse's notes:
    - Condition of resident on admission.
    - Pertinent observations.
    - Changes in the resident's physical or emotional condition.
    - Medications and treatments, including reactions (if any).
    - Vital signs.
    - Record of restraint monitoring.
- Reports of accidents, injuries, or unusual incidents.
- Consultation reports.
- Laboratory reports and other medical data.

- Discharge or transfer information, including date, time, health status, and future address.
- In the case of a deceased resident, the record must contain a licensed funeral director's receipt for removal of the body.

Sheltered Care Facilities Medical Record:

- Admission data.
- Name and telephone number of next of kin or person responsible for the resident.
- Telephone number of the resident's physician.
- Admission health assessment.
- Personal care and services needed by the resident.
- Accounting of the patient's funds if managed by the facility.
- Record of any accidents or injuries while in the facility.
- In the case of a deceased resident, a receipt from a licensed funeral director.

Sheltered Care Facilities with Nursing Units Medical Record:

- Date of admission.
- Name.
- Address.
- Date of birth.
- Sex.
- Telephone number of the resident's physician.
- Periodic medical evaluation findings.
- Diagnoses.
- Orders for medications, treatments, diet, and activities.
- Physician's visits and progress notes.
- Nurse's notes:
    - Condition of resident on admission.
    - Pertinent observations.
    - Changes in the resident's physical or emotional condition.
    - All medications and treatments, including reactions (if any).
    - Vital signs.
    - Record of restraint monitoring.
- Reports of accidents, injuries, or unusual incidents.
- Consultation reports, laboratory reports, and other medical data, when applicable.
- Discharge or transfer information, including time, date, health status, and future address of the resident.
- In the case of a deceased resident, a licensed funeral director's receipt for removal of the body.

Outpatient Clinic Medical Record:

- Patient/client identification data.
- Health assessment.
- Medical evaluation and physical examination or other appropriate evaluation and diagnosis.
- Physician orders for medications, treatments, diets, and laboratory tests.
- Progress notes by physician, health professional, and health worker.
- Documentation of all services provided.
- Laboratory, X-ray, and other diagnostic tests and consultation reports.
- Discharge summary.
- Instructions given to patient/client.

Residential Treatment and Rehabilitation Facilities Record:

- Identification data.
- Pertinent history, assessment, diagnosis, rehabilitation problems, goals, and prognosis.
- Physician orders for medications, special diets, treatments, and diagnostic services.
- Individual treatment plan.
- Progress notes.
- Reports from consultation, laboratory, and all other diagnostic services.
- Unusual events or occurrences and incident reports.
- Discharge summary.

Clinical Laboratories Accession Log:

- Laboratory number identifying the specimen.
- Identification of the person from whom the specimen came.
- Name or other identification of the licensed physician, other authorized person, clinical laboratory, or collecting depot that submitted the specimen.
- Date and time (if timing is critical) of collection of the specimen.
- Date and hour laboratory received the specimen if collected outside the laboratory doing the test.
- Condition of the specimen when received if unsatisfactory.
- Analysis performed.
- Results of the laboratory test.
- Date laboratory sent any required report to the division of public health services or to other agencies.

Home Healthcare Providers Care Record:

- Plan of care and goals.
- Client identification data, including at least name, address, age, pertinent history, and diagnosis.

Healthcare Records

- Documentation of service provided.
- Discharge summary.

New Jersey

New Jersey defines medical records as "all records in a licensed hospital which pertain to the patient including X-ray films." Standards for Hospital Facilities § 8:43B-7.4. (c) 3. i. According to 8:43B-7.2 (b), patients' individual medical records should contain enough information to justify the diagnosis and treatment and to document the results accurately. Subsection (c) notes what medical records should contain, and § 8:43B-8.17, § 8:43B-8.25, and § 8:43B-17.10 list what obstetrical, newborn, renal dialysis, and cardiac diagnostic and surgical services medical records should contain.

Medical Record:

- Identification data and consent forms.
- Admission and provisional diagnosis.
- History.
- Physical examination.
- Physician's progress notes.
- Operative record.
- Radiological diagnostic and treatment reports.
- Laboratory reports.
- Nursing notes.
- Physician's orders.
- Medication and treatment record.
- Consultations.
- Record of discharge or death.
- Autopsy findings.
- Final diagnosis.
- Discharge summary.

Obstetric Medical Records:

- Patient identification data.
- Names of patient's physicians.
- Physician's signed and dated admission note, medical and surgical history, and report of physical examination, completed within 24 hours of admission. Updating the prenatal record fulfills this standard.
- Completed prenatal record.
- Documentation of complete blood count and dipstick urinalysis, including protein and sugar upon admission.
- Reports of laboratory, radiological, and other tests done before admission.
- Documentation of course of labor, delivery, and immediate postpartum period.
- All orders for the patient, written, signed, and dated.

- Documentation of the patient's vital signs, condition of the uterus, blood loss, and any complications, before transfer to the postpartum unit.
- Nursing care plan.
- Signed informed consents.
- Operative report, if applicable, recorded by the physician who performed the surgery:
  - Description of the technique used.
  - Surgical procedures.
  - Tissue removed or altered.
  - Sponge count.
  - Condition of the patient upon leaving the operating or delivery room.
  - Estimated blood loss.
  - Postoperative diagnosis.
  - Names of the physician-in-charge and assistants.
- For patients receiving anesthesia:
  - Preanesthesia record, including at least drug history, anesthesia history, and potential anesthetic problems.
  - Anesthesia record, describing at least induction and maintenance of anesthesia, including volume, route of admission, patient's vital signs, duration of anesthesia, any complications of anesthesia or analgesia management, and drugs, intravenous fluids, blood, and/or blood components administered.
  - Postanesthesia note by the anesthetist describing presence or absence of anesthesia-related complications, recorded after the patient's recovery from anesthesia.
- Documentation of accidents and incidents, if any.
- Record of any treatment, medication, or service refused by the patient, including a physician's visit.
- Documentation of any medication released to the patient upon discharge.
- Progress notes by the physician.
- Clinical notes.
- Record of medications administered, including name and strength of drug, date and time of administration, dosage administered, method of administration, and signature and title of person administering the drug.
- Any referrals to outside resources.
- Discharge summary.
- Page 4 of the Prenatal Record, Form MCH-13, of the Maternal and Child Health Program of the Department, or other form that includes the same information, included at the time of discharge.

Newborn Record:
- Summary of the mother's obstetric history.
- Summary of labor and delivery:

- Anesthesia.
- Analgesia.
- Medications given to the mother.
- Reasons for induction of labor and operative procedures (if performed).
- Condition of the newborn at birth, including the one- and five-minute Apgar scores or the equivalent.
- Time of sustained respirations.
- Details of any physical abnormalities.
- Any pathological states observed and treatment given before transfer to the nursery.
- Any abnormalities of the placenta and cord vessels.
- Date and time of birth.
- Birth weight and length.
- Length of gestation.
- Procedures performed in the delivery room.
- Verification of eye prophylaxis.
* Newborn's identification.
* Record of newborn assessment performed by a physician or registered professional nurse upon the newborn's admission to the newborn nursery.
* Nursing care plan.
* Record of the initial physical examination.
* Physical examination on discharge or transfer to another facility, including head circumference and body length (unless previously measured), signed by a physician.

Renal Dialysis Records:

* Signed and dated admission and medical history.
* Report of physical examination.
* Medical, nursing, social service, and dietary portions of the patient care plan.
* Clinical notes.

Cardiac Diagnostic and Surgical Services Medical Record:

* Signed, and dated admission, medical, and surgical history and a report of physical examination, completed within 24 hours of admission, including results of all tests and procedures performed, diagnoses, prognosis, and rehabilitation potential.
* All orders for the patient, written, signed, and dated by the physician.
* Physician's care plan, initiated upon admission and kept current.
* Nursing care plan and a care plan for each of the services providing care to the patient, initiated upon admission and kept current.
* Signed informed consent before catheterization or surgery.

What Is a Record? 37

- Cardiac catheterization summary sheet, if applicable, including pre- and postcatheterization diagnoses and complications of the procedure, if any.
- Operative report, if applicable, recorded immediately after surgery by the cardiovascular surgeon who performed the surgery and including a description of findings, technique used, surgical procedures, tissue removed or altered, sponge count, estimated blood loss, postoperative diagnosis, and names of the surgeon and assistants.
- Preanesthesia record, including at least drug history, anesthesia history, and potential anesthetic problems.
- Anesthesia record describing at least induction and maintenance of anesthesia, including volume, route of administration, patient's vital signs, duration of anesthesia, any complications of anesthesia or analgesia management, and other drugs, intravenous fluids, blood, and blood components administered.
- Postanesthetic note by the anesthesiologist describing any postoperative abnormalities or complications and stating blood pressure, pulse, presence or absence of swallowing reflexes, cyanosis, and ability to move extremities.
- Clinical notes.
- Progress notes by physicians.
- Record of medications administered, including name and strength of the drug, date and time of administration, dosage administered, route of administration, and signature of the licensed nurse who administered the drug.
- Summaries of conferences and consultations.
- Any referrals to outside resources and documentation of follow-up.
- Clinical resume.
- Discharge plan for each of the services providing care to the patient.

New Mexico

According to chapter 5A.2 of the New Mexico Hospital Association Legal Handbook, regulations of the New Mexico Health and Social Services Department require that medical records include the following information:

- Identification data.
- Complaint.
- Personal and family history.
- History of present illness.
- Physical examination.
- Nursing notes.
- Temperature chart.
- Special examinations and consultations.
- Clinical laboratory examinations.
- X-ray examinations.
- Other examinations.

38 Healthcare Records

- Provisional and final diagnosis.
- Treatment.
- Pathological findings.
- Progress notes.
- Condition on discharge.
- Follow-up.
- Autopsy findings.

New York

New York's Department of Health Memorandum, Health Facilities Series H-40, requires an accurate, clear, and comprehensive medical record for every person evaluated or treated as an inpatient, ambulatory patient, emergency patient, or outpatient of the hospital. The record shall contain information to justify admission and continued hospitalization, support the diagnosis, and describe the patient's progress and response to medications and services. More detailed requirements appear in §§ 405.10 and 405.21.

All Records:

- Evidence of a physical examination, including a health history, performed no more than seven days before admission or within 24 hours after admission, and a statement of the conclusion or impressions drawn.
- Admitting diagnosis.
- Results of all consultative evaluations of the patient and findings by clinical and other staff involved in the care of the patient.
- Documentation of all complications, hospital acquired infections, and unfavorable reactions to drugs and anesthesia.
- Properly executed consent forms for procedures and treatments.
- All practitioners' diagnostic and therapeutic orders, nursing documentation and care plans, reports of treatment, medication records, radiology, and laboratory reports, vital signs, and other information necessary to monitor the patient's condition.
- Discharge summary with outcome of hospitalization, disposition of case, and provisions for follow-up care.
- Final diagnosis.
- Signed physician's attestation sheet:
    - Patient's age.
    - Sex.
    - Principal and other diagnoses.
    - Principal and other procedures performed.
    - Certification for licensed attending physician to sign: "I certify that the narrative descriptions of the principal and secondary diagnoses and the major procedures performed are accurate and complete to the best of my knowledge."

Maternity Patient Medical Record:

- Copy or abstract of the prenatal record, if available:
  - Maternal history.
  - Physical examination.
  - Results of maternal and fetal risk assessment.
  - Ongoing assessments of fetal growth and development and maternal health.
- Results of a current physical examination.
- Labor and birth information and postpartum assessment.

Newborn Record (cross-referenced with the mother's):

- Newborn physical assessment:
  - Apgar scores.
  - Presence or absence of three cord vessels.
  - Description of maternal-newborn interaction.
  - Ability to feed.
  - Eye prophylaxis.
  - Vital signs.
  - Accommodation to extrauterine life.
- Orders for newborn screening tests.
- Infant footprint and mother's fingerprint or other comparable positive newborn patient identification.

North Carolina

North Carolina's hospital licensing rules T10:03C.1404 prescribes the minimum requirements for medical records as sufficient recorded information to justify the diagnosis, verify the treatment, and warrant the end results. Further, Nursing Home Licensure Regulations § 10 North Carolina Administrative Code 3H.0609 sets forth requirements for nursing home records.

Medical Record:

- Identification data (name, address, age, sex, marital status).
- Date of admission.
- Date of discharge.
- Personal and family history.
- Chief complaint.
- History of present illness.
- Physical examination.
- Special examinations, if any, such as consultations, clinical laboratory, or X rays.
- Provisional or admitting diagnosis.
- Medical treatment.
- Surgical record:

40 Healthcare Records

- Anesthesia record.
- Preoperative diagnosis.
- Operative procedure and findings.
- Postoperative diagnosis.
- Tissue diagnosis (on all specimens examined).
• Progress and nurse's notes.
• Temperature chart, including pulse, respiration, and medications.
• Final diagnosis.
• Summary and condition on discharge.
• In case of death, autopsy findings, if performed.

Nursing Home Record:
- Identification data (name, address; age; sex; marital status; name, address, and telephone number of next of kin and/or legal guardian).
- Admission data, including medical history and physical examination, hospital discharge summary, admission diagnosis, and rehabilitation potential.
- Transfer form.
- Diagnostic reports.
- Consultation reports.
- Physician's orders.
- Physician's progress notes.
- Medical and treatment records, including laboratory, X-ray, dental examination, and physical therapy reports.
- Graphic sheet.
- Medication administration sheet.
- Diabetic sheets.
- Patient assessment and progress notes by various disciplines.
- Miscellaneous, such as consent and release forms, copy of transfer forms to the receiving institution, discharge order or release of liability for the facility if the patient or resident leaves against doctor's orders.
- Discharge summary, including admitting and final diagnosis and/or prognosis or cause of death.

North Dakota

North Dakota's Hospital Licensing Rules §33–07–01–16. 8. requires that hospital medical records contain sufficient information to justify the diagnosis and warrant the treatment and end results. They shall contain:

Hospital Medical Record:
- Identification data.
- Chief complaint (concise statement of the complaints that led the patient to consult the physician and the date of onset and duration of each).
- Present illness.

- Past history.
- Family history.
- Physical examination (all positive and negative findings resulting from an inventory of systems).
- Provisional diagnosis and diagnostic treatment procedures.
- Clinical laboratory reports.
- X-ray reports.
- Consultations.
- Treatment, medical and surgical.
- Tissue reports (report of microscopic findings if hospital regulations require such an examination; otherwise, a gross description).
- Progress notes.
- Final diagnosis.
- Discharge summary.
- Nurse's notes.
- Autopsy findings.

Long-term Care Facilities Clinical Record:
- Identification and summary sheet:
    - Resident's name.
    - Social security number.
    - Marital status.
    - Age.
    - Sex.
    - Home address.
    - Religion.
    - Names, addresses, and telephone numbers of referral agency, personal physician, dentist, and designated representative or other responsible person.
    - Admitting diagnosis.
    - Final diagnosis.
    - Conditions on discharge.
    - Disposition.
- Initial medical evaluation:
    - Medical history.
    - Physical examination.
    - Diagnosis.
    - Estimation of restoration potential.
- Authentication of hospital diagnosis, such as hospital summary discharge sheet, report from the physician who attended the resident in the hospital, or transfer form used under a transfer agreement.

- Physician's orders, including all medication, treatments, diet, and restorative and special medical procedures required for the safety and well-being of the resident.
- Physician's progress notes describing significant changes in the resident's condition, written at the time of each visit.
- Nurse's notes containing observations made by the nursing personnel.
- Medication and treatment records, including all medications, treatments, and special procedures performed for the safety and well-being of the resident.
- Laboratory and X-ray reports.
- Consultation reports.
- Dental reports.
- Social service notes.
- Resident care referral reports.

Ohio

According to Ohio Code § 3701.74, medical record means "any document or combination of documents that pertains to a patient's medical history, diagnosis, prognosis, or medical condition and that is generated and maintained in the process of the patient's health care treatment in a hospital." A final medical record is one that is complete according to the hospital's bylaws.

Specifically, medical records of maternity home residents must include prenatal history, physical examination, and physician's orders and observations, and the infant's record must contain history of gestation, delivery, and immediate postnatal period, physical examination, and physician's orders and observations.

Oklahoma

According to the Oklahoma Department of Health, Oklahoma has no statutory or regulatory definition of a medical record.

Oregon

Oregon Administrative Rules 333–70–055 lists what various records must contain, including those for chiropractic facilities.

Medical Record:
- Admitting identification data, including date of admission.
- Chief complaint.
- Pertinent family and personal history.
- Medical history, physical examination report, and provisional diagnosis.
- Clinical laboratory reports and reports on any special examinations.
- X-ray reports with identification (authentication) of the originator of the interpretation.
- Signed consultant's report.
- Orders of physician, dentist, podiatrist, or other authorized professional (dated and signed or authenticated by a signed stamp or computer key if the person has

a signed statement in the administrative offices that he or she is the only person who has possession of and will use the stamp or key).
- Dated progress notes.
- Graphic charts and appropriate personnel notes.
- Summary, including final diagnosis.
- Date of discharge and discharge note as applicable.
- Autopsy report if applicable.

Medical Record of Surgical Patient:
- Preoperative history, physical examination, and diagnosis charted before operation.
- Anesthesia record, including postanesthetic condition.
- A record of operation dictated or written following surgery and including a complete description of the operation procedures and findings, postoperative diagnostic impression, and description of the tissues removed and appliances, if any.
- Pathology report on tissues removed and appliances, if any (§ 333-70-055 (2)(d) lists six categories exempt from pathology exam).

Obstetrical Record:
- Date and hour of birth.
- Birth weight and length.
- Period of gestation.
- Sex.
- Condition of infant on delivery.
- Mother's name and hospital number.
- Record of ophthalmic prophylaxis.
- Physical examination at birth and discharge.
- Progress and nurse's notes:
    - Temperature.
    - Weight and feeding charts.
    - Number, consistency, and color of stools.
    - Condition of eyes and umbilical cord.
    - Condition and color of skin.
    - Motor behavior.
- PKU or metabolic disorders report (if the original PKU/metabolic disorders report is not in the medical record, the hospital shall keep a separate filing system for the maintenance and retrieval of such reports).
- Type of identification placed on infant in delivery room.

Emergency Room, Outpatient, and Clinic Records:
- Patient identification.
- Chief complaint and brief history of the disease or injury.
- Physical findings.

- Laboratory, X-ray, and special examination reports.
- Diagnosis.
- Record of treatment.
- Disposition of case with instructions to patient.
- Signature or authentication of attending physician.
- Copy of the prehospital report form (when patient arrives by ambulance) attached to the emergency room record.

Pennsylvania

An adequate medical record shall contain data from all episodes of care and treatment of the patient, whether inpatient, outpatient, or emergency, according to 28 Pennsylvania Statutes § 115.31. Further, § 115.32 specifies the contents of records: sufficient information to identify the patient clearly, to justify the diagnosis and treatment, and to document the results accurately. If a member of the hospital's medical staff has performed a physical examination within 30 days before the patient's admission, a copy of the examination record may substitute for an admission history and report of physical examination. Such a substitution, however, requires an interval admission note, including any additions to the history and changes in the physical findings. If another hospital has admitted the patient within 30 days before the current admission, the staff or attending physician shall determine whether to record for the hospital its own complete history and physical examination and, with the patient's written authorization, request records from the other hospital as soon as possible.

Medical Record:
- Notes by staff members and people who have clinical privileges.
- Consultation reports.
- Nurse's notes and entries by specified professional personnel.
- Findings and results of any pathological or clinical laboratory examinations, radiology examinations, medical and surgical treatment, and other diagnostic or therapeutic procedures.
- Provisional diagnosis.
- Primary and secondary final diagnoses.
- Clinical resume.
- Necropsy reports.

Rhode Island

Rhode Island does not specifically define medical records, but does define confidential healthcare information as "all information relating to a patient's health care history, diagnosis, condition, treatment or evaluation obtained from a health care provider who has treated the patient." § 5–37.3–3. The Rules and Regulations for Licensing of Hospitals, R23–17–HOSP §§ 25.6 and .7, state that medical records shall contain sufficient information to identify the patient and the problem and to describe the treatment and document the results. The content of all medical records, including inpatient, outpatient, ambulatory, and emergency, is to conform with the "Accreditation Manual for Hospitals," Joint Commission on Accreditation of Healthcare Organizations.

South Carolina

Extensive descriptions of what medical records should contain in South Carolina appear in the following state regulations: South Carolina Department of Health and Environmental Control Regulation No. 61–16, Minimum Standards for Licensing of Hospitals and Institutional General Infirmaries in South Carolina, § 601.5.A. and B.; Regulation No. 61–17, Minimum Standards for Licensing Nursing Care Facilities and Institutional Nursing Infirmaries in South Carolina, § 702.; § 502, Regulation 61–14, Minimum Standards for Licensing of Intermediate Care Facilities in South Carolina. § 504, Regulation 61–13, Minimum Standards for Licensing Intermediate Care Facilities—Mental Retardation—Providing Sleeping Accommodations for 15 Residents or Less.

Hospital or Institutional Medical Facility Medical Record:

- Admission record:
    - Name.
    - Address, including county.
    - Occupation.
    - Age.
    - Date of birth.
    - Sex.
    - Marital status.
    - Religion.
    - County of birth.
    - Father's name.
    - Mother's maiden name.
    - Husband's or wife's name.
    - Dates of military service.
    - Health insurance number.
    - Provisional diagnosis.
    - Case number.
    - Days of care.
    - Social security number.
    - Name of the person providing information.
    - Name, address, and telephone number of person or persons to notify in emergency.
    - Name and address of referring physician.
    - Name, address, and telephone number of attending physician.
    - Date and hour of admission.

- History and physical within 48 hours after admission.
- Provisional or working diagnosis.
- Preoperative diagnosis.
- Medical treatment.
- Complete surgical record, if any, including technique of operation and findings, statement of tissue and organs removed, and postoperative diagnosis.
- Report of anesthesia.
- Nurse's notes.
- Progress notes.
- Gross pathological and microscopic findings.
- Temperature chart, including pulse and respiration.
- Medication administration record or similar document for recording medications, treatments, and other pertinent data. Nurses must sign the record after each medication administered or treatment provided.
- Final diagnosis and discharge summary.
- Date and hour of discharge summary.
- In case of death, cause and any autopsy findings.
- Special examinations, if any, such as consultations, clinical laboratory, X-ray, and other examinations.

Newborn Record:

- History of hereditary conditions in mother's and/or father's family.
- First day of the last menstrual period and estimated day of confinement.
- Mother's blood group and Rh type—evidence of sensitization and/or immunization.
- Serological test for syphilis (including dates performed).
- Number, duration, and outcome of previous pregnancies, with dates.
- Maternal diseases, such as diabetes, hypertension, preeclampsia, and infections.
- Drugs taken during pregnancy, labor, and delivery.
- Results of measurement of fetal maturity and well-being, such as lung maturity and ultrasonography.
- Duration of ruptured membranes and labor, including length of second state.
- Method of delivery, including indications for operative or instrumental interference.
- Complications of labor and delivery, such as hemorrhage or evidence of fetal distress, including a representative strip of the fetal ECG if recorded.
- Description of placenta at delivery, including number of umbilical vessels.
- Estimated amount and description of amniotic fluid.
- Apgar scores at one and five minutes of age.
- Description of resuscitation, if required.
- Detailed descriptions of abnormalities and problems occurring from birth until transfer to the special nursery or the referral facility.

What Is a Record? 47

- Test results and date of specimen collection for PKU and hypothyroid newborn screening test (except only in cases in which the parents object because of religious reasons, and in such cases, file a copy of an executed "Statement of Religious Objection" form).

Nursing Home and Intermediate Care Facility Record:

- Identification data:
    - Name.
    - County.
    - Occupation.
    - Age.
    - Date of birth.
    - Sex.
    - Marital status.
    - Religion.
    - County of birth.
    - Father's name.
    - Mother's maiden name.
    - Husband's or wife's name.
    - Dates of military service.
    - Health insurance number.
    - Social security number.
    - Diagnosis.
    - Case number and dates of care.
    - Consent form for treatment signed by patient or patient's representative.
    - Name and telephone number of attending physician.
    - Date and hour of admission.
    - Date and hour of discharge.
    - Signature of physician authorizing discharge.
    - Condition on discharge.
    - Name of person providing information.
    - Name, address, and telephone number of person or persons to notify in emergency.
- Record of physical examination before admission or within 48 hours after admission:
    - Medical history.
    - Physical findings.
    - Diagnosis.
    - Physician's orders for medication, treatment, care, and diet, which physician must review and reorder at least once every 30 days.
- Record of all physician's visits after admission:

- Date of visit.
- Progress notes.
- Orders for medications, treatment, care, and diet, which the physician must review and reorder at least once every 30 days.
- Nursing record:
  - Date, time, dosage, and method of administration of all medications and signature of nurse administering.
  - Complete record of all safety precautions, including time, type, reason, and authority for applying.
  - Record of all pertinent factors pertaining to the patient's condition.
  - Date and time of all treatments and dressing.
  - Incidents occurring while the patient is in the institution, including drug reactions and medication errors.

Health Records of Residents of Intermediate Care Facilities—Mental Retardation—Providing Sleeping Accommodations for 15 Residents or Less:
- Identification date, including name, marital status, age, sex, social security number, and home address.
- Name, address, and telephone number of patient's physician.
- Name, address, and telephone number of referral source.
- Name and address of next of kin or other responsible person.
- Date and time of admission and discharge.
- Record of physician's or psychologist's findings and recommendation in the preadmission evaluation and in subsequent reevaluations.

South Dakota

Administrative Rules of South Dakota (ARSD), Title 44, Department of Health, specifies what hospital and nursing home records must contain.

Hospital and Nursing Home Medical Record:
- Identification data.
- Consent forms, except when unobtainable.
- History of the patient or resident.
- Current overall plan of care.
- Reports of initial and periodic physical examinations, evaluations, and all plans of care with subsequent changes.
- Diagnostic and therapeutic orders.
- Progress notes from all disciplines, including practitioners, physical therapy, occupational therapy, and speech pathology.
- Laboratory and radiology reports.
- Descriptions of treatments, diet, and services provided and medications administered.
- All indications of illness or injury, including date, time, and action taken.

- Final diagnosis.
- Discharge summary, including all discharge instructions for home care. ARSD 44:04:09:05.

Supervised Personal Care Facility Record:
- Admission and discharge data.
- Report of physician's admission physical evaluation for resident.
- Physician orders.
- Medication entries.
- Observations by personnel, resident's physician, or other persons authorized to care for the resident. ARSD 44:04:09:06.

Tennessee

" 'Hospital records' means those medical histories, records, reports, summaries, diagnoses, prognoses, records of treatment and medication ordered and given, entries, X-rays, radiology interpretations, and other written or graphic data prepared, kept, made, or maintained in hospitals that pertain to hospital confinements or hospital services rendered to patients admitted to hospitals or receiving emergency room or outpatient care. Such records shall also include reduction of the original records upon photographic film of convenient size. . . . Such records shall not, however, include ordinary business records pertaining to patients' accounts or the administration of the institution.'' Tennessee Code 68–11–302 (5). The Code also defines, in (2), business records as all "books, ledgers, records, papers, and other documents prepared, kept, made, or received at hospitals that pertain to the organization, administration, or management of the business and affairs of hospitals, but which do not constitute hospital records as defined in subdivision (5) of this section." Rules of the Tennessee Department of Health and Environment, Board for Licensing Health Care Facilities, 1200–8–4–.03, specify what medical records shall include.

Inpatient Medical Record:
- Identification data.
- Date and time of admission.
- Date and time of transfer.
- Date and time of discharge.
- Attending and consulting physicians' names.
- Written admission note within 24 hours of admission.
- Diagnostic and therapeutic orders.
- Policy on informed consent developed by a medical staff and governing body and consistent with legal requirements.
- Preanesthetic assessment documented by an anesthesiologist or attending physician before surgery. A postanesthetic assessment shall document the presence or absence of anesthesia-related complications.

- Progress notes sufficient to denote patient's status, frequency and detail of changes, and condition of the patient.
- Operative description, including preoperative diagnosis, findings at time of procedure, postoperative diagnosis, techniques used, and specimens removed.
- Reports of all procedures, tests performed, and results, authenticated by the appropriate personnel.
- Nursing notes, including nursing observations, vital signs, and other pertinent information regarding the patient.
- Discharge summary completed and authenticated:
  - Provisional diagnosis.
  - Primary and secondary final diagnoses.
  - Clinical resume.
  - Condition on discharge or transfer.
  - Instructions to the patient.
  - Necropsy results.
- Final diagnosis recorded in acceptable nomenclature at the time of discharge by the attending physician, dentist, or podiatrist.

Emergency Room Medical Record:
- Identification data.
- Information concerning time of arrival, means, and by whom transported.
- Pertinent history of injury or illness, including chief complaint and onset of injury or illness.
- Significant physical findings.
- Description of laboratory, X-ray, and EKG findings.
- Treatment provided.
- Condition of patient on discharge or transfer.
- Diagnosis on discharge.
- Instructions given to patient or patient's family.
- Control register listing chronologically the patient visits to the emergency room. The record shall contain at least the patient's name, date and time of arrival, and record number and the names of those dead on arrival.

Texas

Texas Department of Health Hospital Licensing Standards 1–22 list what medical records must contain that hospitals must preserve.

Medical Record:
- Identification data.
- Medical history of the patient.
- Reports of relevant physical examinations.
- Diagnostic and therapeutic orders.
- Evidence of appropriate informed consent.

- Clinical observations, including results of therapy.
- Reports of procedures, tests, and their results, including laboratory, pathology, and radiology reports.
- Conclusions at termination of hospitalization or evaluation/treatment.

Special Care Facility Medical Record:

- Identification data:
  - Full name.
  - Sex.
  - Date of birth.
  - Usual occupation.
  - Social security number.
  - Family/friend name, address, and telephone number.
  - Physician names and telephone numbers, including emergency numbers.
- Medical history and physical exam reports.
- Any physician orders and progress notes.
- Any documentation of the resident's change in health condition requiring emergency procedures and/or health services provided by facility personnel.
- If appropriate, documentation of assistance with medications as stated in pharmacy services.
- Other documents or reports related to the care of the resident as required by facility policy.
- If appropriate, documentation of nursing services provided and nursing staff observation as required by facility policy.
- Separation or discharge report completed at the time of the resident's discharge:
  - Date of departure.
  - Destination.
  - Reason for leaving.
  - Resident's health status.
  - Referral information, if any.
  - How to contact, if appropriate.

Utah

Utah Administration Code, Health Facility Licensure Rules R432–100–7.407, 7.408, 7.409, 7.410, and 7.411, prescribes the contents of medical records generally and specifically.

All Medical Records:

- Identification data.
- Medical history.
- Relevant physical examination.
- Diagnoses, including principal, provisional, final, and associate diagnoses.
- Laboratory reports.

- X-ray reports.
- Evidence of informed consent or the reason it is unattainable.
- Diagnostic and therapeutic orders by physicians and other authorized practitioners.
- Medical staff orders for medications and treatments.
- Anesthesia record.
- Pathology report.
- Clinical observations, including progress notes, consultation reports, and nursing notes.
- Discharge summary.
- Autopsy findings.
- Reports of procedures, tests, and results (requires identification of facility if report is from a facility outside the hospital).
- Physician identification.

Obstetrical Records:

- Admission history and physical examination.
- Labor notes.
- Obstetrical anesthesia record.
- Delivery records.
- Operative report, where indicated.
- Discharge summary for complicated deliveries. In the case of an uncomplicated delivery, a final progress note may substitute for the discharge summary.
- Record of administration of Rh immune globulin.

Newborn Infant Record:

- Copy of the maternal history from the mother's record, including relevant family history, serological test for syphilis, Rh status, analgesia, anesthesia, length of labor, and type of delivery.
- Date and hour of birth, period of gestation, sex, reactions after birth, delivery room care, temperature, weight, time of first urination, and number, character, and consistency of stools.
- PKU instruction and reports, including number of screening kit.
- Record of ophthalmic prophylaxis.
- If the hospital discharges the infant to any person other than the infant's parents, then the hospital shall record the name and address of such person and where the infant will go.

Emergency Room Records (Integrate into the patient's overall record or record identification system):

- Patient identification.
- Time and means of arrival.
- Emergency care given to patient before arrival.

- Short history.
- Physical findings.
- Lab and X-ray reports, if performed.
- Diagnosis.
- Record of treatment.
- Prognosis.
- Disposition of case.
- Discharge instructions.
- Signature of physician providing service.
- When a patient leaves against medical advice, a statement to that effect.
- Discharge instructions (for outpatient records).

Vermont

In Vermont, the State Hospital Licensure Regulations, § 3–946, lists what a medical record must contain. Further, Residential Care Home Licensing Regulations and State Nursing Home Regulations specify what kinds of records residential care and nursing homes must keep.

Medical Record:
- Identification data.
- Complaint.
- Personal and family history.
- History of present illness.
- Physical examination.
- Special examinations.
- Clinical laboratory reports.
- X-ray and other examinations.
- Provisional or working diagnosis.
- Medical or surgical treatments.
- Gross and microscopic pathology findings.
- Progress notes.
- Final diagnosis.
- Condition on discharge.
- Follow-up.
- Autopsy findings.

Records for Residential Care Homes Level III (homes serving persons requiring both personal and nursing care) and Level IV (homes serving persons needing only personal care:
- Resident register.
- Resident record:
    - Resident's name.
    - Emergency notification numbers.

- Name, address, and telephone number of responsible person, if any.
    - Physician's name, address, and telephone number.
    - Instructions in case of resident's death.
    - Accident reports.
    - Signed contract with a description of services and charges.
    - Medication documentation.
- Additional data for Level III homes:
    - Initial assessment.
    - Annual reassessment.
    - Physician's admission statement and current orders.
    - Staff progress notes, including changes in the resident's condition, illness, and action taken.
    - Reports of physician visits.
    - Signed telephone orders.
    - Treatment documentation.
- Written report when a fire occurs in the home, regardless of size or damage, submitted to the Licensing Agency and the Department of Labor and Industry within 24 hours.
- Written report of any accident or illness that involves physician follow-up, emergency room treatment, or admission to a hospital, placed in the resident's folder and, for Level IV, a copy sent within 48 hours to the Licensing Agency.
- Report of any unexplained absence of a resident from a home reported to the police and responsible person, if any, and provided to the Licensing Agency within 24 hours of disappearance.
- Written report of any breakdown to the home's physical plant (plumbing, heat, water supply, and so forth) or supplied service that disrupts the normal course of operation.

Nursing Homes Records:

- Resident register.
- Admission and discharge records.
- Record of medical history, examination, and diagnosis.
- Physician's order record.
- Physician's progress record.
- Nursing record (including records of medication, treatment, and nurse's observation).
- Narcotic and barbiturate records.

Virginia

The Rules and Regulations for the Licensure of Hospitals in Virginia, Department of Health § 208.5, states that the content of medical records shall conform to the standards of the "Accreditation Manual for Hospitals" of the Joint Commission on Accreditation of Healthcare Organizations.

The Rules and Regulations for the Licensure of Nursing Homes in Virginia, § 24.9, lists what medical records in nursing homes shall include.

Nursing Home Medical Record:
- Patient identification.
- Designation of physician having primary responsibility for the patient's care.
- Admitting information, including recent patient history, physical examination, and diagnosis.
- Physician orders, including all medications, treatments, diet, and restorative and special medical procedures required.
- Physician progress notes written at the time of each visit.
- Documented evidence of assessment of patient's needs, establishment of an appropriate treatment plan, and plans of care and services provided.
- Nurse's notes.
- Medication and treatment record, including all medications, treatments, and special procedures performed.
- Pertinent copies of radiology, laboratory, and other consultation reports.
- Discharge summary.

Washington

Washington Department of Social and Health Services Hospital Rules and Regulations, WAC 248–18–440 (6), requires hospitals to include the following information, when relevant, in a medical record for each inpatient or outpatient except referred outpatient diagnostic services and outpatient emergency care services:

Medical Record:
- Admission data:
    - Identifying and sociological data.
    - Full name, address, and telephone number of patient's next of kin or other legally responsible person.
    - Date of admission.
    - Name(s) of the patient's attending physician(s).
    - Admitting (provisional) diagnosis or medical problem.
- Report on any medical history obtained from the patient.
- Report(s) on the findings of physical examination(s) performed on the patient.
- Entry on any known allergies of the patient or known idiosyncratic reaction to a drug or other agent.
- Authenticated orders for any drug or other therapy administered to a patient and for any diet served to a patient, including any standing medical orders used in the care and treatment of the patient except standing medical emergency orders.
- Authenticated orders for any restraint of the patient.

- Reports on all roentgenologic examinations, clinical laboratory tests or examinations, macroscopic and microscopic examinations of tissue, and other diagnostic procedures or examinations performed upon the patient or specimens taken from the patient. (X-ray films, laboratory slides, tissue specimens, medical photographs, and other comparable materials obtained through procedures used in diagnosing a patient's condition or assessing clinical course are original clinical evidence and are not medical records).
- Entry on each administration of therapy (including drug therapy) to the patient.
- Entries on nursing services to the patient:
  - Report on all significant nursing observations and assessments of the patient's condition or response to care and treatment.
  - Nursing interventions and other significant direct nursing care.
  - All administration of drugs or other therapy.
  - Entry on time of and reason for each notification of a physician or patient's family regarding a significant change in the patient's condition.
  - Record of other significant nursing action on behalf of the patient.
- Entry on any significant health education, training, or instruction related to the patient's health care provided to the patient or the patient's family.
- Entry on any social services provided to the patient.
- Entry regarding any adverse drug reaction of the patient and any other untoward incident or accident involving the patient that occurred during hospitalization or on an occasion of the patient's visit to the hospital for outpatient services.
- Operative reports on all surgery.
- Entry or report on each anesthetic administered.
- Reports on consultations.
- For any woman who gave birth in the hospital, reports regarding her labor, delivery, and postpartum period.
- For any infant born in or en route to the hospital, date and time of birth, condition at birth or upon arrival, sex, and weight.
- Progress notes.
- In the event an inpatient leaves without medical approval, an entry on any known events leading to the patient's decision to leave, a record of notification of the physician, and time of departure.
- Discharge data, including final diagnosis, any associated or secondary diagnoses or complications, and titles of all operations performed.
- Discharge summary for any inpatient whose hospitalization exceeded 48 hours, except a normal newborn or normal obstetrical patient):
  - Significant clinical findings and events during the patient's hospitalization.
  - Description of the patient's condition upon discharge or transfer.
  - Summary and recommendations and arrangements for future care.

- Entry on any transmittal of medical and related data to a healthcare facility or agency or other community resource to which the facility referred or transferred the patient.
- In the event of the patient's death in the hospital, pronouncement of death, authorization for autopsy, report on the autopsy findings (if performed), and entry on release of the body.
- Written consents, authorizations, or releases given by the patient or by a person or agency who can legally exercise control over the patient.

West Virginia

West Virginia Statutes § 57-5-4a defines hospital records as "those medical histories, records, reports, summaries, diagnoses and prognoses, records of treatment and medication ordered and given, notes, entries, X-rays, and other written or graphic data prepared, kept, made or maintained in hospitals that pertain to hospital confinements or hospital services rendered to patients admitted to hospitals or receiving emergency room or outpatient care. Such records shall not, however, include ordinary business records pertaining to patients' accounts or the administration of the institution."

West Virginia Regulations for Hospital Licensure, 64 CSR 10.3b, specifies what a complete medical record must contain. Further, 10.3d provides for a short form record for patients staying in the hospital less than 48 hours other than maternity or newborn patients. The short form record may contain only information that is necessary for proper diagnosis and treatment.

Complete Medical Record:
- Patient identification.
- Date.
- Complaints.
- History of present illness.
- Personal and family history.
- Physical examination.
- Doctor's orders, including dietary orders, special examinations, and consultations.
- Clinical laboratory, X-ray, and other examinations.
- Provisional or working diagnosis.
- Treatment and medications given.
- Surgical reports, including operative and anesthesia records.
- Gross and microscopic pathological findings.
- Progress notes.
- Final diagnosis.
- Condition on discharge.
- Discharge summary.
- Autopsy findings, if performed.

Wisconsin

Statutes 146.81 defines patient healthcare records as all records related to the health of a patient prepared by or under the supervision of a healthcare provider except records subject to Statute 51:30, relating to treatment of individuals for mental illness, developmental disabilities, alcoholism, or drug dependence, records of chemical tests for intoxication administered under Statute 343.305, or fetal monitor tracings. Healthcare providers may destroy fetal monitor tracings only if the healthcare provider provides notice to the patient 35 days before deletion or destruction of such tracings. Also, 146.815 requires that inpatient records include the patient's and patient's parents' occupations and industries so that if health problems are related to occupation, the physician can ensure that the record contains information about these occupations and any potential health hazards related to these occupations.

Wisconsin's Health and Social Services Regulations, HSS 124.14n (3), mandates what the medical, maternal, and newborn records should contain.

Medical Record:

- Accurate patient identification data.
- Concise statement of complaints.
- Health history, containing a description of present illness, past history of illness, and pertinent family and social history.
- Statement about the results of the physical examination.
- Provisional diagnosis.
- All diagnostic and therapeutic orders.
- All clinical laboratory, X-ray reports, and other diagnostic reports.
- Consultation reports.
- Appropriate history and physical work-up before surgery, except in an emergency.
- Operative report.
- Tissue reports.
- Physician and nonphysician notes.
- Definitive final diagnosis.
- Discharge summary.
- Autopsy findings.

Maternal Medical Records:

- Prenatal history and findings.
- Labor and delivery record, including anesthesia.
- Physician's progress record.
- Physician's order sheet.
- Medicine and treatment sheet, including nurse's notes.
- Any laboratory and X-ray reports.

- Any medical consultant's notes.
- Estimate of blood loss.

Newborn Medical Records:

- Record of pertinent maternal data, type of labor and delivery, and condition of the infant at birth.
- Record of physical examinations.
- Progress sheet recording medicines and treatments, weights, feedings, and temperatures.
- Notes of any medical consultant.
- In the case of fetal death, weight and length of the fetus recorded on the delivery record.

Wyoming

According to the Wyoming Public Hospital Records Management Manual, permanent medical records include the following information:

- Admission and discharge records.
- Names of attending physician(s).
- Record of diagnosis and operations.
- Operative reports.
- Pathology reports.
- Discharge summaries.

2

Who Owns Healthcare Records?

Ownership Generally

What do you tell patients who demand their medical records, stating that the records are *their* records? It's easy to tell them that, no, the records are not theirs, but doing so is more effective if you know what the law is on the ownership of healthcare records and what rights, if any, patients have with regard to "their" records.

Hospitals own their own records, including medical records, but some states give patients the right to review or copy their medical records. One way to look at the question of ownership is to realize that while the healthcare facility owns the record and, consequently, has the right to physical possession and control, the patient has a right to the information contained therein. Many states have statutes that specify that the healthcare facility owns its medical records, with some states adding that the facility's ownership is subject to the patient's right of access to the medical information contained in the record. Even if the state statute or an administrative regulation does not specify who owns medical records, a facility may safely assume, in the absence of a statute or court decision to the contrary, that the facility, not the patient, owns the medical records. Similarly, physicians practicing in a private office rather than in a healthcare institution own their medical records subject, again, to rights of access by patients.

Because neither patients nor their authorized representatives have the right to physical possession of the records, the owners, whether hospitals or private physicians, should not permit anyone to remove the records from their control unless a court order so requires.

Although, generally speaking, no strict legal duty to do so exists, when patients change physicians, as when physicians leave practice, the physicians should transfer the records, or copies or summaries thereof, to the current physicians. When, however, hospitals transfer patients to other facilities or physicians send patients to specialists, they have a legal obligation to provide the receiving facilities or physicians all medical information from the records that is necessary to treat the patients.

Federal Laws

All medical records in federal healthcare facilities belong to the United States, subject to patients' rights to access.

State Laws

Alabama

Rules of Alabama State Board of Health Division of Licensure and Certification 420–5–7.07 (d) provides that medical records of patients are the physical property of the hospital and that control of them rests with the hospital administrator.

Arkansas

Arkansas's rules covering medical records, Part Six, Section I. E., provides that no one shall remove medical records from the hospital environment, except upon the issuance of a subpoena, strongly implying thereby that the hospital owns its medical records.

California

In California, the facility owns the medical record, including X-ray films. California law Title 22 § 70751 (b), however, considers that the facility maintains the information documented within the medical record for the benefit of the patient.

Colorado

Colorado Criminal Code § 18–4–412 makes it a class 5 felony for unauthorized people to knowingly obtain a medical record or medical information with the intent to appropriate it to their own use or another's, to steal or disclose to an unauthorized person medical information or a medical record, or to, without authority, copy such. This statute implies that the record belongs to the healthcare facility and that the patient has a right to confidentiality.

Georgia

Under Georgia Code § 31–33–3, the healthcare provider owns the records, subject to access thereto by the patient.

Idaho

Idaho Code 39–1392d's reference to patient access to the official hospital chart implies that medical records are the property of the hospital.

Indiana

The original health record of the patient is the property of the provider, and the provider may use it without written authorization for legitimate business purposes. Indiana Code § 16-4-8-8.

Kansas

Kansas Administrative Regulation 28-34-9a (6) provides that medical records are the property of the hospital and that only the hospital, Kansas law, or a court order may authorize removal of medical records from the hospital.

Kentucky

The medical record is the property of the health facility, 902 KAR 20:016 (11)(c), and may not leave the hospital except by court order or by order of physicians or dentists for consultation.

Louisiana

Louisiana statutes do not expressly state who owns medical records, but the language of 40 Statutes 2144 B., that hospital records are subject to reasonable access to the information contained therein by the patient or the patient's authorized representative, strongly implies that the hospital owns the record subject to the patient's right to access.

Mississippi

Mississippi statutes provide that hospital records are the property of the hospital subject to reasonable access upon good cause shown by the patient, the patient's personal representative or heirs, the patient's attending medical personnel, and the patient's duly authorized nominees and upon payment of any reasonable charges for such access. Statutes § 41-9-65.

Missouri

Medical records are the property of the hospital and may not leave the premises except by court order, by subpoena, for microfilming, or for off-site storage approved by the governing body. 13 CSR 50-20.021 (3) (D) 6.

Montana

Montana law does not specify who owns medical records, but Chapter 23-4 of the Montana Health Association Consent Manual states that the hospital has the obligation to retain possession of the record but may release X rays for not more than 30 days to physicians who require them for backup care. 23-4.1A.

64 Healthcare Records

New Jersey

New Jersey Standards for Hospital Facilities § 8:43B–7.1 (c) 5 states that medical records should not leave the hospital environment except upon subpoena, thereby implying that they are the property of the hospital.

New Mexico

The New Mexico Hospital Association Legal Handbook states that the pieces of paper that make up hospital medical records are the property of the hospital, but that patients or third parties may have the right of access to the information in the records. Chapter 5B.

North Carolina

North Carolina's Administrative Code states that records of patients are the property of the hospital. T10:03C.1403(d).

Oregon

All medical records are the property of the hospital or related institution. They may not leave the institution except where necessary for a judicial or administrative proceeding. Oregon Administrative Rules 333–70–055.

Pennsylvania

Medical records are the property of the hospital and may not leave its premises, except for court purposes. Copies may be available for authorized purposes, such as insurance claims and physician review, consistent with confidentiality requirements. 28 Pennsylvania Statutes § 115.28.

South Carolina

Regulation No. 61–16, Minimum Standards for Licensure of Hospitals and Institutional Care Facilities in South Carolina, Regulation No. 61–14, covering intermediate care facilities, Regulation No. 61–17, governing nursing care facilities, and Regulation No. 61–13, Minimum Standards for Licensing Intermediate Care Facilities—Mental Retardation—Providing Sleeping Accommodations for 15 Residents or Less, specify that the facility owns the medical records. Section 601.4 of No. 61–16, Section 504.4 of No. 61–14, and Section 704.4 of No. 61–17 add that records of patients must not leave the hospital property except by court order. Section 502 of No. 61–13 notes that only competent authorities may take records.

Tennessee

In Tennessee, hospital records are the hospital's property, subject, however, to court order to produce the same. The hospital also shall provide reasonable access, upon good cause shown, to the patient, to the patient's personal representative or heirs, or to the patient's attending medical personnel and upon payment of any reasonable charge for such service. Tennessee Code § 68–11–304.

Utah

Medical records are the property of the hospital and may not leave the hospital's control except by court order or subpoena. Health Facility Licensure Rule 7.404 D.

West Virginia

Written and other records of interviews, reports, statements, minutes, memoranda, charts, and physical property or materials of any kind used in connection with or relating to any such items or investigation or hearing or research discipline or medical study of a medical staff committee or medical society are the property of the hospital or medical society. § 39–1392d. Patients do, however, have the right to copy and inspect their records under § 16–29–1.

3

What Records Must You Keep and for How Long?

Why Must You Keep Records?

Healthcare providers must keep records for a number of reasons: to comply with the law, to provide better health care, and to minimize litigation losses.

To Comply with the Law

First, all levels of government have the undoubted authority to require you to keep records. A statute, an executive order, or an agency regulation may lawfully require record keeping. See appendix A for Health Care Financing Administration requirements, for example. The government's power to require records and reports in the area of health services is necessary to ensure the public welfare. Without records and reports, the government cannot properly fulfill this function. And if the government can require a report, the government can also inspect the report.

The government, whether acting through the courts or through an administrative agency, such as a health department, also has the power to enforce sanctions for failure to maintain required records. Such sanctions may include fines, contempt citations, default judgments, and the like.

To Provide Better Health Care

Second, even if the law did not require a hospital or other healthcare facility to keep medical records, such records would still be necessary to provide proper care for patients. Cases are legion in which information contained in a patient's medical record saved a patient's life. In addition, health records have important roles in research, evaluation, and education. Other records, such as administrative and financial, also are necessary to enable you to meet your goals and objectives efficiently.

To Minimize Litigation Losses

Third, attorneys who are involved in medical malpractice cases know that the most favorable situation a plaintiff who is alleging medical malpractice can be in is that in which the relevant medical records that the law requires the healthcare provider to keep are lost, incomplete, or otherwise defective (see appendix B for how long you may have to make good records available under various states' statutes of limitations). On the other hand, good medical records that show that the plaintiff received care that met the standard of care are the best defense against a malpractice suit to show, for example, that the plaintiff's injury is nothing more than an unfortunate result from proper care. Often, malpractice attorneys will either refuse to take a case or drop one when the records fail to show malpractice. Even in the worst-case scenario in which the record shows malpractice occurred, having a record is still valuable because, on the basis of such information, the defendant's attorney can attempt to settle the case to avoid costly litigation and the risk of an aberrant and excessive jury damage award.

Good records management must be a part of your risk management program for at least a couple of other reasons, too. For one thing, creating and maintaining proper records will document the health care at the time it occurs rather than forcing your medical personnel to rely upon their imperfect memories months or years after they provided the care. In addition, records can show that you have complied with the multitude of federal, state, and local regulatory requirements.

What Records Must You Keep and for How Long?

Now that you're convinced that you need to keep records, you need to figure out which records and for how long. It's not hard to determine what records you need to keep. Often a federal, state, or local law or regulation will tell you what records to keep, and your experience will undoubtedly add more. See appendix C for a sample of a list of records, including financial and administrative records, that one state requires hospitals to keep. The question of how long you must keep various records, however, has no easy answer. The answer is easier when a law, whether a state, federal, or local statute or regulation, provides for a specific retention period. But even when a law provides for such a period, other considerations may require you to keep the record even longer. And various laws may conflict. A state regulation may, for example, provide for a longer retention period for a particular record than a federal statute does. Other laws may require you to keep certain records, but contain no retention period. Sometimes you should keep records that no law or regulation mandates that you keep but other considerations do, such as sound management practices or litigation protection. Practical concerns, like the availability of resources such as space and funding, will also affect your decision as to how long to retain records.

Once you determine what records to keep and for how long, establish a records retention schedule, and have it approved by your lawyer and your hospital administration (see appendix D for a recommended retention schedule). Having a written retention schedule is powerful evidence that you destroyed records pursuant to your normal course of business instead of to gain an advantage in an investigation or litigation. Make certain that your schedule includes all records, even those that you want to retain permanently, and addresses retention and destruction of both original records and copies because copies usually have the same legal significance as originals (see chapter 4). Then make certain that you adhere to your destruction schedule and properly document the destruction of your records (see chapter 16). Of course, you should never destroy records that are involved in an investigation or in litigation, even if they are due for destruction on your retention schedule.

Statutes of Limitations

Regardless of whether a regulation specifies how long to retain a record, you must consider the effect of statutes of limitations. A statute of limitations specifics a period of time within which a plaintiff must begin a lawsuit. After the expiration of that period, the statute bars the plaintiff from bringing the suit. Statutes of limitations usually run from the date of the incident, such as the malpractice, or from the date the plaintiff learns of or reasonably should have learned of the incident, whichever is later. Thus, at a minimum, you should retain records for the period of the statute of limitations. See appendix B for state statutes of limitations for contracts, wrongful death, and medical malpractice suits. And because the statute may not begin to run until the prospective plaintiff learns of the causal relation between his injury and the treatment he received, you should keep the records for a longer period than the statute of limitations. Also, if the patient was a minor or under some other legal disability, such as insanity, you should keep the records until the patient reaches the age of majority or becomes competent plus the period of the statute of limitations. Even if a law or regulation specifies how long you must keep a record, good risk management may dictate keeping it for the period of the statute of limitations plus an additional period to cover the situation in which the statute does not begin to run until the plaintiff learns of the alleged malpractice. Another complicating factor, which stresses the need for an attorney's help in verifying what statute of limitations applies and how long it is, is that if the plaintiff's harm, such as an injury caused by malpractice, occurred before the effective date of the current statute of limitations, the old period of limitations may apply.

Most states have different statutes of limitations for different lawsuits. Different time periods may apply to suits based on contract and to negligence actions, for example. If a state does not have a separate statute of limitations for medical malpractice, the state's personal injury statute of limitations would cover medical malpractice. Many states have different statutes of limitations for cases in which the plaintiff is a minor or otherwise incompetent. Again, because statutes of limitations are so complex, *you must consult your attorney* to make certain which statute of limitations governs your situation.

The Federal Tort Claims Act, which covers medical malpractice and other negligent acts of federal government employees acting within the scope of their authority, has a two-year statute of limitations commencing on the date the harm happened or the plaintiff knew of or should have known of the harm.

State statutes of limitations vary widely. The following states commence the statute of limitations in medical malpractice cases on the date of the last treatment: Michigan, Minnesota, New York, and Virginia. The following states permit the plaintiff to use the date of discovery of the malpractice to start the statute of limitations: Alabama, California, Colorado, Connecticut, Delaware, the District of Columbia, Florida, Hawaii, Idaho, Illinois, Iowa, Kansas, Kentucky, Louisiana, Maryland, Michigan,[1] Mississippi, Missouri,[2] Montana, Nebraska, Nevada, New Hampshire, New Jersey, North Carolina, North Dakota, Oklahoma, Oregon, Puerto Rico, Rhode Island, South Carolina, South Dakota, Tennessee, Utah, Vermont, Washington, West Virginia, Wisconsin, and Wyoming. Many of these states that use the time of discovery to begin the statute of limitations have an overall limit. For example, Florida law provides "but in no event to exceed seven years from the date giving rise to the injury."

Some states have limited the rule permitting the plaintiff to use the date of discovery to cases involving foreign objects left in the body. States following the foreign-body exception include these: Arizona, Arkansas, California, Colorado, Connecticut, Georgia, Idaho, Iowa, Maryland, Missouri, New Hampshire, New Jersey, New York, North Carolina, Ohio, South Carolina, Tennessee, Utah, Vermont, Virgin Islands, West Virginia, and Wisconsin.

Federal Laws

The federal government has many specific record-keeping requirements. Many federal statutes and administrative regulations, however, only imply a responsibility to keep records. Thus, if the government requires a healthcare provider to comply with a regulation, that requirement probably implies that the provider must keep a record of such compliance. If you are not certain whether you should keep such a record, check with your attorney. Some specific federal record-keeping requirements follow.

Department of Labor

Fair Labor Standards Act: The Department of Labor requires employers to comply with several record-keeping acts and regulations. Employers subject to this act must keep employment records relating to wages, hours, sex, occupation, condition of employment, and so forth for three years for records containing employment information, payrolls, and certificates and for two years for basic employment and earnings

---

[1] Michigan draws a distinction between malpractice in a hospital, in which case the statute of limitations runs from the date of the injury, and other malpractice, in which the statute runs from the date of discovery.

[2] In Missouri, malpractice cases are an exception to the rule that the tort claim arises at the time of injury. In malpractice cases, the statute runs from the time of discovery.

records, wage rate tables, work time schedules, order shipping and billing records, job evaluations, merit or seniority systems, other matters that describe or explain the basis for any wage differentials to employees of the opposite sex in the same establishment, and records of deductions from or additions to pay. 29 C.F.R. §§ 516.2, 516.3, 516.5, 516.6, 516.11–.29.

Employment Retirement Security Act: Employers with an employee benefit or pension plan must file a summary of the plan with the Department of Labor under the Employee Retirement Security Act of 1974, 29 U.S.C. Chapter 18, and keep sufficient records to provide in sufficient detail the basic information and data for not less than six years after filing the required reports.

Welfare and Pension Plans Disclosure Act: Employers must keep records of reports under the Welfare and Pension Plans Disclosure Act, 29 U.S. Code § 308, on matters of which the act requires disclosure for five years. 29 C.F.R. Part 486.

Federal Employees' Compensation Act: Physicians and hospitals treating federal employees covered by the Federal Employees' Compensation Act must keep records of all injury cases they have treated sufficient to give the Office of Federal Employees' Compensation a history of the employee's accident, the exact description, nature, location, and extent of injury, the degree of disability arising therefrom, any X-ray findings, the nature of the treatment provided, and the degree of disability arising from the injury. 20 C.F.R. § 10.410. The department has not specified a retention period.

Federal Regulations: Hospitals and institutions employing patient workers must maintain records of disability, productivity, prevailing wage, production standards, evaluation and training records, work activities and group minimum wage records, and patient worker exceptions, 29 C.F.R. Part 519. The facility must keep the following information for at least three years: payroll records; certificates, agreements, plans, notices, and so forth of collective bargaining agreements, plans trusts, and employee contracts; and sales and purchase records concerning such employees. 29 C.F.R. § 516.5. The facility must keep supplementary basic records, including basic employment and earnings records and wage rate tables, for at least two years. § 516.6.

Equal Employment Opportunity Commission

The Equal Employment Opportunity Commission requires employers to keep various records, including records of their compliance with the law.

Civil Rights Act and Equal Pay Act: Employers subject to the Civil Rights Act (prohibiting discrimination against employees for reasons of race, color, national origin, or sex) must maintain personnel and employment records having to do with hiring, promotion, demotion, transfer, layoff or termination, rates of pay, and selection for training or apprenticeship for six months from the making of the record of personnel action involved, whichever is later. In the case of a discrimination complaint, retain the record until final disposition of the complaint. 29 C.F.R. § 1602.14. Similarly, employers should keep records to show compliance with the Equal Pay Act, which prevents wage discrimination between the sexes of those who perform the same work.

Federal Regulation: Employers must keep records to show they did not discriminate against workers because of age. 29 C.F.R. § 1627. Employers must keep records of each employee containing name, address, date of birth, occupation, rate of pay, and compensation earned each week for three years. They must also keep personnel records related to job applications, promotion or discharge, job orders submitted to employment agencies or labor organizations for recruitment of personnel, test papers of employer-administered aptitude tests, results of physical examinations, and advertisements for one year. They must also keep records of employee benefit plans for one year after termination of the plan and temporary position application forms for 90 days.

Food and Drug Administration

Investigators of new drugs must maintain records concerning delivery of the drugs and their disposition for two years after shipment and delivery and for three years after completion or discontinuance of the study. 21 C.F.R. §§ 201.150, 701.9, and 801.150. Persons petitioning for exemption from certification for antibiotic drugs intended for local or topical use must keep records of all laboratory tests and assays required as a condition for certification on each batch produced and of all shipments and deliveries thereof for three years after the date of shipment or delivery. Photostatic or other permanent reproductions may substitute for such records after two years.

Health Care Financing Administration

Skilled nursing and intermediate care facilities receiving medical assistance under a state plan for medical assistance must retain records for various periods. 42 C.F.R. 405, Subpart K.

Internal Revenue Service

Facilities should keep records of employment tax (social security) documents for four years after the due date of such tax. If a claimant files a claim, the facility should keep the record for four years after the date of filing. 26 C.F.R. § 31.6001.

Employers should keep withholding tax statements (W-2 Forms) and exemption certificates (W-4 Forms) for four years. 26 C.F.R. § 31.6001–1. Employers who are subject to income tax must keep records for as long as they are material in the administration of the tax laws. 26 U.S.C. § 6501 (a) states that, except as otherwise provided, the government must assess any tax within three years after you file a return unless you understate gross income, estate, gift, or excise tax by more than 25 percent, fail to declare constructive dividends, or operate a personal holding company. In such cases, the period of assessment is six years. If, however, you file a false return, willfully try to avoid tax, or fail to file a return, the government may extend the period of assessment indefinitely.

Occupational Safety and Health Administration

The Occupational Safety and Health Administration requires employers to keep records of both medical and other employees who are exposed to toxic substances and harmful physical agents. Employers must maintain such records for 30 years.

Health and Human Services Department

Hospitals participating in Medicare must keep medical records for each inpatient and outpatient, records of radiologic services, and records on nuclear medicine services, including copies of nuclear medicine reports and records of the receipt and disposition of radiopharmaceuticals for five years. 42 C.F.R. §§ 482.24, .26, and .53. Psychiatric hospitals participating in Medicare must maintain special medical records that include development of assessment/diagnostic data, treatment plan, recording progress and discharge planning, and discharge summary for five years.

Facilities certified as comprehensive outpatient rehabilitation facilities (CORFs) under the Medicare program must maintain clinical records that contain sufficient information to identify the patient clearly and to justify the diagnosis and treatment for five years after patient discharge. 42 C.F.R. § 485.60.

Rural health clinics qualifying for reimbursement under Medicare and Medicaid must retain patient records for at least six years from the date of last entry and longer if required by state statute.

42 Code of Federal Regulations contains many specific records retention requirements for various healthcare programs administered by the Public Health Service, including the following regulations governing specific situations:

- § 52.8. Individuals or institutions receiving grants for research projects.
- § 52.8. Public or nonprofit private hospitals or schools of medicine or other agencies receiving National Heart, Lung, and Blood Institute Grants for National Research and Demonstration Centers.
- § 526.6. Agencies receiving National Cancer Institute Grants.
- § 52d. Schools of medicine, osteopathy, dentistry, or public health affiliated teaching hospitals or specialized cancer institutes receiving grants under the National Cancer Institute Clinical Cancer Education Program.
- § 57.215. Institutions participating in the health professions and the nursing student loan programs.
- § 57.2913. Institutions receiving grants for training U.S. citizen foreign medical students.
- § 60.35–.61. Health Education Assistance Loan (HEAL) Program lenders.
- § 64.4. Institutions receiving federal grants for National Institutes of Health and National Library of Medicine training.
- §§ 74.2, 74.50, 74.52, and 74.53. Clinical laboratories.
- § 124.8. Applicants for project grants for public medical facility construction and modernization.

74 Healthcare Records

These regulations also have detailed requirements for various categories of health professions schools and for institutions receiving federal health insurance other than those mentioned above.

State Laws

Alabama

Rules of Alabama State Board of Health Division of Licensure and Certification, Chapter 420–5–7, Hospitals, set up the requirements for records retention in Alabama hospitals. Under these rules, the administrator is responsible for supervision, preparation, and filing of records. The administrator may delegate this responsibility to a medical records librarian or other employee. 420–5–7.07 (a).

420–5–7.07 (c), titled Preservation of Records, requires hospitals to keep patients' records current from the time of admission to the time of discharge or death and to store the records at least 22 years, either as original records, abstracts, microfilm, or otherwise. Hospitals may delete nurse's notes from the permanent record. 420–5–7.07 (f) requires hospitals to establish a medical record committee to be responsible for maintaining complete medical records, and (g) requires the attending physician to authenticate the records.

420–5–7.07 requires each hospital to maintain the following records:

Administrative Records and Documents:

- Articles of incorporation or certified copies thereof.
- Current copy of the approved constitution and/or bylaws of the governing authority, with a current roster of the membership of the governing authority.
- Copy of the minutes of the governing authority.
- Current copy of the approved constitution and/or bylaws and rules and regulations of the medical staff with a current roster of the membership of the medical staff.
- Minutes of the meetings of the medical staff and/or services, departments, or committees or other basis of the clinical experience of the staff.
- Narcotic permit.
- Narcotic records. 420–5–7.11 (i) requires hospitals to keep records of all stock supplies of all controlled substances, giving an accounting of all items received and dispensed.
- Current personnel records.
- License or registration number of all employees, such as nurses, therapists, technicians, and so forth, who have such credentials.
- Current record on each member of the medical staff, including application for membership on the staff, privileges granted by the governing authority, and so forth.

Reports. Hospitals must make the following reports:
- Vital Statistics Report.
- Destitute Children Report.
- Annual Report.

Medical Records: Other sections of this regulation require hospitals to keep complete reports of laboratory tests and tissue examinations with the patient's chart.

Chapter 420–5–10 covers nursing homes. 420–5–10.16 requires maintaining and filing medical records with at least three months of information in the records and maintaining documents such as histories and physicals, assessments, nursing histories, and so forth at all times. Nursing home medical records include identifying data, current medical evaluation, physician orders, observations and progress notes, reports of treatments and clinical findings, a medication administration record and treatment record, evidence of a treatment plan, discharge summary, copies of transfer sheets received upon admission and discharge, laboratory and X-ray reports, evaluations of services and consultations from other health professionals, medications given to the patient upon discharge, and copies of official death certificates. The nursing home business office must keep copies of vital statistics reports, employees' health certificates and reports of physical examination, annual report, and other records relating to licensure. Nursing homes must maintain medical records for five years from date of discharge or, in the case of a minor, three years after the minor becomes of age.

Alaska

Alaska Statutes § 18.20.085 provides that, unless otherwise specified by the Department of Health and Social Services, "a hospital shall retain and preserve records that related directly to the care and treatment of a patient for a period of seven years following the discharge of the patient. However, the records of a patient under 19 years of age shall be kept until at least two years after the patient has reached the age of 19 years or until seven years following the discharge of the patient, whichever is longer. Records consisting of X-ray film are required to be retained for five years."

The Department of Health and Social Services has defined by regulation the types of records and the information required in medical records and may specify records and information hospitals must retain for longer periods than those set out above. 7 AAC 12.770 (h). Section (f)(2) notes that hospitals must maintain the following records in a form and manner acceptable to the Department of Health and Social Services and make such reports from them as requested:

- Record of admission and discharges, total patient days, average length of stay, and number of autopsies performed. Hospitals must maintain separate data for adults and children, excluding newborns, and for newborn infants, excluding stillbirths.
- Register of births.
- Register of deaths.

- Official original records of birth, death, and stillbirth, required by law for each of these events, are the prime responsibility of the attending physician. The hospital shall be responsible for the completeness and accuracy of the data furnished from its records and for the prompt filing of the original with the proper U.S. Commissioner when so requested by the attending physician in accordance with instructions by the Bureau of Vital Statistics.
- Register of operations.
- Register of outpatients.
- Hospitals shall handle narcotics in complete conformance with the Federal Narcotic Law and the Uniform Narcotic Act as adopted by the State of Alaska, AS 17.10 and AS 17.12. Hospitals shall keep a daily record of the kind and quantity of narcotics dispensed or administered and the name of the physician upon whose authority and the purpose for which they were dispensed or administered.

7 AAC 12.110 (c)(5) requires medical staffs to maintain complete records on investigational drugs, including protocol and side effects.

7 AAC 12.210 specifies that the medical staff shall adopt bylaws and rules that provide for the appointment of committees, including executive, credentials, medical records, tissue and transfusion, infection control, pharmacy and therapeutics, and utilization review committees, which must keep for at least five years written minutes and records of attendance of their meetings, including committee activities and recommendations and election of officers.

7 AAC 43.005 requires providers of health care to Medicaid recipients to retain all fiscal, patient care, and related records for three years following the year in which they provide services unless the Department of Health and Social Services requests retention for a longer period.

Pharmacists must maintain a bound record book for dispensing controlled substances containing name and address of purchaser, name and quantity of controlled substance purchased, date of each purchase, and name or initials of pharmacist or pharmacy intern who dispensed the substance.

Arizona

Arizona Revised Statute R9–10–213 (6) and (8) discuss what records a hospital must maintain:

Records and Reports:
- Bylaws of the governing body.
- Bylaws and rules and regulations of the medical staff.
- Policies and procedures for all established hospital services.
- Reports of all inspections and reviews related to licensure for the preceding five years together with corrective actions taken.
- Binding contracts and agreements related to licensure.
- Appropriate documents evidencing control and ownership.

- Current copy of the following Title 9 Health Care Regulations available from the Office of the Secretary of State:
  - Chapter 1, Article 4, Codes and Standards referenced.
  - Chapter 8, Article 1, Food and Drink.
  - Chapter 9, Articles 1, 2, 3, Health Care Institutions: Establishment and Modification.
  - Chapter 10, Article 1, Health Care Institutions: Licensure.
  - Chapter 11, Articles 1, 2, Health Care Institutions: Rates and Charges.

Personnel Records: A hospital must maintain a record of each employee that includes the following information:

- Employee's identification, including name, address, and next of kin.
- Resume of education and work experience.
- Verification of valid license, if required, education, and training.
- Payroll and attendance records for the preceding twelve-month period shall be available for review by Arizona Department of Health Services personnel.
- Every position shall have a written description that explains the duties of the position.

R9–10–216, Surgical Services, requires a hospital to maintain in the surgical suite a chronological register of surgical operations.

Under R9–10–217, concerning pertinent observations and information related to special diets, the hospital shall record patients' food habits and dietetic treatment in the patient's medical record. The dietetic services office shall keep on file a written order for modified diet prescriptions as recorded in the patient's medical record throughout the duration of the order.

R9–10–219, concerning disaster preparedness, requires hospitals to write a disaster plan that includes the establishment of an emergency treatment record for external disasters, such as mine explosions, bus accidents, floods, earthquakes, and so forth. The section also has specifications for internal disasters.

R9–10–220 requires hospitals to maintain records to assure that qualified personnel periodically accomplish appropriate inspections and maintenance of hospital physical plant equipment.

R9–10–221, concerning medical records services, requires a medical records department under the direction of a qualified person and with adequate staff and facilities to perform all required functions. The department must maintain a medical record for every person receiving treatment as an inpatient, as an outpatient, or on an emergency basis in any unit of the hospital. The records shall be available to other units engaged in care and treatment of the patient. Only authorized personnel shall have access to the records.

For licensing purposes, hospital medical records shall be readily retrievable for a period of not less than three years, except that A.R.S. § 36–343 requires retention of vital records, such as records concerning births and deaths, and statistics for ten years. By letter dated July 28, 1989, the Arizona Department of Health Services recommends that if a healthcare facility anticipates use of its records in a criminal case, it should retain the records for the seven-year criminal statute of limitations. The Arizona Department of Library, Archives and Public Records noted that it found no case of retrieving medical records after seven years and recommended a ten-year retention period.

Arizona R9–10–222, concerning laboratory services, requires hospitals to report results of laboratory tests to the physician and to enter the results in the patient's chart. People performing examinations must record their observations concurrently with the performance of each step in the examination of specimens and record the actual results of all control procedures. Records shall identify the individual performing the examination. The laboratory shall retain such records, as well as duplicate copies of laboratory reports, in the laboratory area for at least one year after reporting the results. No clinical interpretation, diagnosis, prognosis, or suggested treatment may appear on the laboratory report form except that a report made by a physician may include such information. When another laboratory performs the analysis, the report must include name, address, and name of the director of the laboratory actually performing the analysis. Each laboratory must participate in a proficiency testing program provided by the American Association of Bioanalysts or the College of American Pathologists for each authorized specialty and subspecialty. Laboratories shall keep records of such testing for two years and make them available for examination by representatives of the Department.

The Arizona Legislature recently repealed A.R.S. § 25–103.06, which had required maintaining copies of premarital serology results for five years.

R9–10–222 G requires hospitals to keep records of the donor and recipient of all blood handled and report all transfusion reactions occurring in the hospital.

R9–10–225 A, concerning quality assurance, requires hospitals to maintain a record of quality assurance activities.

R9–10–225 B requires hospitals to establish a discharge planning program to provide for transfer of information between hospitals and other healthcare facilities or agencies to facilitate continuity of care.

R9–10–227, Respiratory Care Services, requires that reports of respiratory care services become part of the patient's medical record.

R9–10–231 requires hospitals with an organized social service department to record social services information and to establish policies and procedures to specify the type and extent of this information that should appear in the medical record.

R9–14–110, concerning records, maintenance, availability, and retention, states:

Laboratories shall make records of observations, where appropriate, concurrently with the performance of each step in the examination of specimens and record the actual results of all control procedures. The individual performing the examination shall initial or sign the record. The laboratory shall retain records as well as duplicate copies of laboratory reports for a period of at least one year after the date the results are reported except as otherwise prescribed by law and make them available for inspection by representatives of the Department.

R9-14-111 covers personnel records. Hospitals must maintain on a current basis personnel records that include a complete resume of each employee's training, experience, duties, and date or dates of employment. Hospitals must also maintain attendance records for each employee for one year.

R9-14-112, concerning records of specimens examined, requires hospitals to maintain records containing the following information for each specimen examined:

- Laboratory number or other identification.
- Name and other identification of the person from whom the specimen came, if available.
- Name of the licensed physician or other person or laboratory that submitted the specimen.
- Date the physician or other authorized person collected the specimen.
- Date the laboratory received the specimen.
- Condition of unsatisfactory specimens and packages when received, such as broken, leaked, hemolyzed, or turbid.
- Examination requested and result in units of measurement where applicable.
- Where requested or indicated, the normal values for the method used.
- Initials or signature of the individual conducting examination.

Arizona appears to have no specific requirements for nursing homes.

Arkansas

Hospitals must maintain all records either in original form or on microfilm for ten years after the most recent admission. Hospitals must also retain complete medical records of minors for seven years after the age of minority.

Hospitals must have written policies and procedures covering all functions of the medical record department and review and update them annually.

California

Generally, Title 22 California Administrative Code § 70751 requires hospitals to keep records on all patients admitted or accepted for treatment. The hospital should have a medical records service, under the supervision of a registered records administrator or accredited records technician, and maintain the records, either as originals or accurate reproductions, in such form as to be legible and readily available.

Register of Operations: Hospitals should keep a register of operations, including the following information, for each surgical procedure performed:

- Name, age, sex, and hospital admitting number of the patient.
- Date and time of the operation and the operating room number.
- Preoperative and postoperative diagnosis.

- Name of surgeon, assistants, anesthetists, and scrub and circulating assistants.
- Surgical procedure performed and anesthetic agent used.
- Complications, if any, during the operation.

Records of Unusual Occurrences: § 70333 (a) (8) of Title 22 of the California Administrative Code requires that each hospital maintain reports of unusual occurrences for the preceding two years.

Medical Records: Hospitals must maintain medical records for a minimum of seven years following discharge except for minors. Hospitals must maintain records for minors for at least one year after they have reached the age of 18, but in no event for less than seven years. Title 22 § 70751(c). The California Hospital Association, however, recommends retaining medical records, including fetal heart rate monitoring, for at least ten years following discharge of the patient for adults and at least one year after a minor reaches age 18, but in no event for less than ten years following discharge.

Medi-Cal Patient Records: Each California healthcare provider must, under Title 32 § 51476, keep readily retrievable records necessary to fully disclose the type and extent of services provided to a Medi-Cal beneficiary, including the following information:

- Billings.
- Treatment authorization requests.
- All medical records, service reports, and orders prescribing treatment plans.
- Records of medications, drugs, assistive devices, or appliances prescribed, ordered for, or furnished to beneficiaries.
- Copies of original purchase invoices for medication, appliances, assistive devices, written requests for laboratory testing and all reports of test results, and drugs ordered for or supplied to beneficiaries.
- Copies of all remittance advices that accompany reimbursement to providers for services or supplies provided to beneficiaries.
- Identification of the person providing services. Records of each service provided by nonphysician medical practitioners shall include the signature of the nonphysician medical practitioner and the countersignature of the supervising physician.

Records of Institutional Medi-Cal Providers:

- Records of receipts and disbursements of personal funds of beneficiaries held in trust by the provider.
- Employment records, including shifts, schedules, and payroll records of employees.
- Book records of receipts and disbursements by the providers.

What Records Must You Keep and for How Long? 81

- Individual ledger accounts reflecting credit and debit balances for each beneficiary provided services.

Medi-Cal Providers' Records of Meeting Code I Restrictions for Medical Supplies and Drugs:

- Practitioner who issues a prescription for a Code I supply or drug shall document in the patient's chart the patient's diagnostic or clinical condition that fulfills the Code I restriction.
- Dispenser shall maintain readily retrievable documentation of the patient's diagnostic or clinical condition information that fulfills the Code I restriction. If transmission of this Code I diagnostic or clinical condition information to the dispenser occurs other than by personal handwritten order from the prescriber, the dispenser shall document the transmittal date and the name of the prescriber or the employee or agent legally authorized to transmit such information. The dispenser shall sign the documentation.

Medi-Cal Prescription Records: Every practitioner who issues prescriptions for Medi-Cal beneficiaries shall maintain, as part of the patient's chart, records that contain the following data for each prescription:

- Name of the patient.
- Date prescribed.
- Name, strength, and quantity of the item prescribed.
- Directions for use.

Medical Transportation Records: Records of medical transportation providers shall include, in addition to the information all providers must keep, the following data:

- Time and date of service for each beneficiary.
- Odometer readings at each pickup and delivery location.
- Provider-assigned vehicle identification code and name of the operator providing the service.
- Names of beneficiaries transported in total or partial group runs.

Records of Medi-Cal Psychiatric and Psychological Services: Providers of Medi-Cal psychiatric and psychological services shall include, in addition to the information all providers must keep, the following data: patient logs, appointment books, or similar documents showing the date and time allotted for appointment of each patient or group of patients and the time actually spent with such patients.

Medi-Cal Financial Records: A provider shall make available, during regular business hours, all pertinent financial books, all records concerning the provision of healthcare services to a Medi-Cal beneficiary, and all records this section requires a provider to make and retain to any duly authorized representative of the Department acting in the scope and course of employment, including, but not limited to, employees of the Attorney General, Medi-Cal Fraud Unit, duly authorized and acting within the scope and course of their employment. Failure to produce records may result in sanctions, audit adjustments, or recovery of overpayments.

Pharmacy Records: Under § 51476.1, providers must keep readily retrievable pharmacy records, including written prescription orders and records of oral orders reduced to writing. Such records describing the provision of a pharmaceutical service to a Medi-Cal beneficiary must include the following information:

- Full beneficiary name.
- Name, category of professional licensure, and license number of the prescriber.
- Name, strength, and quantity of the drug or medical supply dispensed, as applicable.
- Direction for use of the drug or medical supply.
- Name of the principal labeler of any multisource drug or medical supply dispensed when not specifically identified by the brand name of the drug dispensed.
- Date of service.
- Name or initials of the pharmacist that provided the service.
- Unique number to identify each pharmaceutical service billed to the program. This number shall be the "prescription number" required on the form.
- Documentation of compliance with Code I restrictions for medical supplies and drugs.

Clinical Laboratory Records: Clinical laboratories must maintain for at least two years the following information:

- Records of specimens received and tested, including identification of the patient, name of the submitter, dates of receipt and report, type of test performed, and test results.
- Records of inspection, validation, calibration, repair, and replacement to ensure proper maintenance and operation of equipment and proper reactivity of test materials.
- Manuals, card files, or flow charts for each procedure performed in the laboratory, including the following information:
  - Name of procedure.
  - Source of reference for the test method.
  - Date director or supervisor last reviewed or modified the procedure.
  - Current specific instructions for test performance.
  - Standards and controls required.
  - Instructions for collecting and handling specimens to ensure test reliability.
  - Records of quality control procedures in use in the various technical areas of the laboratory, including results on standards and reference materials and action limits when appropriate. Title 17 § 1050 (f) (1).

- Additional requirements for cytology: The laboratory shall retain all cytology slides and cell blocks for at least five years and all cytology reports for at least ten years. Title 17 § 78.1 (f) (1).
- Records indicating the daily accession of numbered specimens and an appropriate cross-filing system according to patient's name. Title 17 § 1050 (f) (2).

Hospital Records: As to other than medical records, Title 22 § 70733 requires each hospital to maintain the following records subject to inspection by the Department:

- Articles of incorporation or partnership agreement.
- Bylaws or rules and regulations of the governing body.
- Bylaws and rules and regulations of the medical staff.
- Minutes of the meetings of the governing body and the medical staff.
- Reports of inspections by local, state, and federal agents.
- All contracts, leases, and other agreements required by these regulations.
- Patient admission roster.
- Reports of unusual occurrences for the preceding two years.
- Personnel records.
- Policy manuals.
- Procedure manuals.
- Minutes and reports of the hospital Infection Control Committee.
- Any other records deemed necessary for the direct enforcement of these regulations by the Department.

Personnel Records: Title 22 § 70725 requires hospitals to maintain personnel records containing the following information for all employees for at least three years following termination of employment:

- Employee's full name.
- Social security number.
- License or registration number, if any.
- Brief resume of experience.
- Employment classification.
- Date of beginning employment.
- Date of termination of employment.
- The facility shall also keep records of hours and dates worked by all employees during at least the most recent six-month period.
- Title 22 § 70732 (c) requires hospitals to keep employee health records, including records of all required health examinations, for at least three years following termination of employment.

Colorado

Colorado's regulation, 6 CCR 1011-1 § 4.9, requires hospitals to keep the following records:

- Daily census.
- Hospital services statistics.
- Admissions and discharges analysis record.
- Register of all deliveries, including live and still births.
- Register of all surgeries performed (entered daily).
- Diagnostic index.
- Operative index.
- Physician index.
- Number index.
- Death register.
- Patient master card file.
- Register of outpatient and emergency room admissions and visits.

§ 4.3 requires a registered record administrator or other trained medical record practitioner to be responsible for the medical record department.

Colorado also requires that hospitals preserve medical records, as originals or on microfilm, for not less than ten years after the most recent patient care use except that hospitals must preserve records of minors for the period of minority plus ten years.

§ 5.3 requires the facility to keep personnel records on each person of the hospital staff, including employment application and verification of credentials.

Connecticut

Hospitals having 100 beds or more must have a medical record department with adequate space, equipment, and personnel, including at least one registered record librarian or person with equivalent training and experience. Short-term hospitals or hospices may have a person with training, expertise, and consultation from a medical record librarian in charge. State Department of Health Regulations §§ 19–13–D3 (d), 19–13–D4 (d). Hospitals must also have a medical record audit committee. The facility must keep records of attendance and minutes of all medical staff and departmental meetings. § 19–13–D4b.

Hospitals must keep medical records, other than nurse's notes, for at least 25 years after the patient's discharge, except that hospitals that microfilm the records by a process approved by the Department of Health may destroy the original records sooner.

Homes for the aged and rest homes must maintain records on each resident on forms approved by the State Department of Health, including the following data: name, residence, age, sex, nearest relative, religion, and other necessary information. § 19–13D6 (e). Homes for the aged, rest homes, and children's nursing homes must keep records, originals or copies, for at least ten years following the death or discharge of the patient. §§ 19–13D6 (5), 19–13D10 (6).

Licensed maternity hospitals must keep complete records that include information required by the State Department of Health. They must include all items necessary to fill out a death certificate for the mother and all items necessary to fill out a birth certificate or death certificate for the baby, together with steps for handling the case. § 19–13–D14 (e).

Industrial health facilities must also keep records for each individual who receives health services, including all medical and health related reports and letters received from laboratories, physicians, and others. The records must include an entry for every visit of such person to the facility. Industrial health facilities must keep noncurrent medical records and medical records of former employees for at least three years. § 19–13–D44 (e).

Dialysis units must keep records for a minimum of five years following the discharge of a patient. § 19–13–D55 (e).

Facilities must keep records, separate from the medical records, for controlled drugs, including narcotics, for three years following the transaction recorded. § 19–13–D44 (g) (5).

Delaware

Delaware is currently revising its healthcare retention schedules. Previously, it had followed the Guidelines of the American Hospital Association and the Joint Commission on Accreditation of Healthcare Organizations and the Medicare and Medicaid requirements.

Florida

Hospitals must have a medical records department with administrative responsibility for medical records and maintain a current and complete record for every patient admitted with a system of identification and filing to ensure the prompt location of the record. The department should index records according to disease, operation, and physician. Rules of the Department of Health and Rehabilitative Services, Hospital Licensure 10D–28.59.

Florida's General Records Schedule E–T1 applies to county, municipal, and special tax district hospitals and specifies that such a hospital must maintain its patient medical case files for 25 years following the last discharge. If the hospital microfilms the records, the hospital may destroy the paper records, provided the Division of Archives, History and Records Management, Department of State, has received and approved a notice of intent to destroy scheduled records. Such approval is also necessary for disposal at the end of 25 years. Outpatient and/or emergency room records follow the same rule, but hospitals need retain them for only 15 years. The schedule does not recommend microfilming X-ray films because the hospital need retain them for only five years. The hospital must retain its master index card file, for both inpatients and outpatients, permanently, but may microfilm upon approval as above.

Georgia

Hospitals must preserve medical records as originals, microfilms, or other usable forms in such a manner as to afford a basis for complete audit of professional information until the sixth anniversary of the patient's discharge or longer. The hospital must keep a minor's records until the patient's 27th birthday. The regulation requires hospitals to keep patient statistics and hospital operational records current and in such a way as to ensure rapid location with easy access to the following information (Rules of the Department of Human Resources, Public Health, Chapter 290–5–6, Hospitals 290–5–6–.11 (h)):

- Daily admission and disposition record.
- Monthly and yearly totals of admissions and discharges, excluding newborns.
- Number of patient days per month and year.
- Monthly and annual occupancy rate.
- Number of beds and bassinets.
- Number of births and fetal deaths.
- Number of deaths.
- Average census, daily, monthly, and annually.
- Number of autopsies.

290–5–6–.10 requires hospitals to maintain a separate personnel folder for each employee, containing all personal information concerning the employee, including application and qualification for employment, physical examination (including laboratory and X-ray reports), and job description.

Georgia hospitals must also maintain accurate records of their costs of care for providing health services for nonresident indigent patients and report the total cost to the commissioner.

Health maintenance organizations must maintain records of written complaints about their healthcare services for five years after filing and submit summary reports concerning the complaints to the Insurance Commissioner. Georgia Code § 33–21–9. They must also provide annual reports under § 33–21–15 to the Insurance Commissioner. Their accounts, financial records, and other records are subject to inspection by the Insurance Commissioner and the Commissioner of Human Resources. § 33–21–17.

Hawaii

In Hawaii, healthcare providers must retain medical records in the original or reproduced form for at least seven years after the last data entry except in the case of minors. The facility must keep a minor's records during the period of minority plus seven years after the minor reaches the age of majority. Title 33 § 622–58 (a). Section (b) exempts from the retention requirement the following records: public health mass screening records, pupils' health records, and related school health room records; preschool screening program records; communicable disease reports; mass testing epidemiological projects and studies records, including consents; topical fluoride application consents; psychological test booklets; laboratory copies of reports; pharmacy copies of prescriptions; patient medication profiles, hospital nutritionists' special diet orders, and similar records retained separately from the medical record but duplicated within it; social workers' case records; and diagnostic or evaluative studies for the department of education or other state agencies.

Subsection (c) notes that healthcare providers must retain X-ray films, electroencephalogram tracing, and similar imaging records for at least seven years, after which they may present the records to the patient or destroy the records, provided that the interpretations or separate reports of X-ray films, electroencephalogram tracing, and similar imaging records are basic information. Healthcare providers must retain basic information (defined in Chapter 1) for 25 years from the date of last entry, except for minors whose records must remain for the period of minority plus 25 years. § 622–58 (d).

Idaho

Idaho Code § 39–1394 specifies retention periods for patient care records: clinical laboratory test records and reports, three years after the date of the test; X-ray films, five years after the date of exposure or five years after the patient reaches the age of majority, whichever is later, if the hospital has written findings of a physician who has read such films.

Otherwise, Standard MR.4.6 of the Manual of the Joint Commission for the Accreditation of Healthcare Organizations states that the length of time you should retain medical records depends on the need for their use in continuing patient care and for legal, research, or educational purposes.

Skilled nursing and intermediate care facilities must keep records in a safe location protected from fire, theft, and water damage for not less than seven years. If the patient is a minor, the facility must preserve the record for not less than seven years following the patient's 18th birthday. 02.2203.04.b.

Proprietary home health agencies shall maintain clinical records for six years from the date of discharge or, in the case of minors, three years after the patient becomes of age. 2–5030.03.

For records other than medical records, Idaho Code § 72–1337 requires each employer to keep true and accurate records for such periods of time and containing such information as the Director of Employment Security shall prescribe.

Illinois

The Illinois Administrative Code § 250.1510 recommends that hospitals employ registered medical record administrators or accredited medical record technicians as directors of medical records departments with professional consultation services available to them. These directors must participate in educational programs relative to medical record activities, in on-the-job training and orientation of other medical record personnel, and in in-service medical record educational programs. A committee of the medical staff should be responsible for reviewing medical records to ensure adequate documentation, completeness, promptness, and clinical pertinence. The Illinois Hospital Association Record Retention Guide for Illinois Hospitals recommends retention of medical records for 10 to 22 years and notes that microfilming could take place at any time. The hospital shall preserve the records or photographs of such records in accordance with hospital policy based on American Hospital Association recommendations and legal opinion.

Hospitals must submit reports containing such pertinent data as the Department of Public Health requires, including birth, stillbirth, and death reports. § 250.1520.

Hospitals must keep personnel records during the term of employment of hospital personnel and for the years thereafter required by state agency or federal requirements. According to 77 Illinois Administrative Code § 250.420, minimum contents include the following information:

- Application form and/or resume with current and background information sufficient to justify the initial and continuing employment of the individual.
- Verification of license.
- Record of the employee's specialized education, training, and experience.
- Verification of identity.
- Employment health examination and subsequent health services provided to the employees to ensure that all are physically able to perform their duties.
- Record of orientation to the job.
- Continuing education.
- Current information or periodic work performance evaluations.

116 Illinois Statutes § 60 states that unless a law requires a longer retention period, any business records may be destroyed after three years.

Indiana

Indiana State Board of Health Hospital Licensure Rules 410 IAC15–1–9 requires that the hospital store all original films or microfilms thereof in the hospital for seven years. The hospital may substitute microfilms for the original records after three years. The Indiana Hospital Licensing Council may approve reduction of the three-year retention period upon request.

Healthcare providers must retain X-ray films for five years (in microfilm form). Providers must notify the patients of the retention for five years and that they may have copies of the X rays upon payment of the actual cost. Patients may pick up mammograms within 30 days of the end of the five-year period at no charge. Before that period, the patient may have a copy of a mammogram at the actual cost. § 16–4–8–13 (b) through (d).

The facility must have a responsible employee, preferably a registered record administrator or a qualified accredited record technician, in charge of medical records. If not, a consultant with one of those qualifications must assist the person in charge. The person in charge must perform the following duties: check records for completeness; maintain indices by patient, by disease, by procedure, by physician, and other as requested by the medical staff; provide assistance to physicians in their reviews and studies that involve medical records and in completing records as required by medical staff rules and regulations.

410 IAC 15-1-14 (7) requires original laboratory reports, including the pathologist's findings on specimen examinations, to be in the patient's chart. Such reports and records in the laboratory must include information on the daily accession of specimens, test methods used, and quality control procedures. The facility must keep such records for two years.

410 IAC 15-1-8, Recordkeeping Requirements, mandates, in (2), that each hospital keep a record of all admissions, deaths, surgical records, outpatient records, deliveries, births, and stillbirths with patient identification data, attending physician, results, and other pertinent data.

Other than medical records, the hospital must keep documents and records that show ownership and compliance with local, state, and federal laws and regulations and adherence to bylaws and regulations of the facility. Such records must be available to representatives of the Hospital Licensing Council and the Board of Health. 410–IAC 15-1-8 (1) requires the facility to maintain the following data:

- Certified copy of articles of incorporation (unless a governmental hospital or in cases of individual ownership).
- Constitutions, bylaws, and regulations of the governing body and medical staff (signed and dated).
- Minutes of meetings of both the governing body and medical staffs and their committees. Such minutes are confidential.
- Current roster of members of the medical staff and their designated privileges.
- Completed application for each member of the medical staff, including the following information:
  - Date of application.
  - Professional education and training.
  - Date of licensure and number thereof.
  - Drug Enforcement Administration number.
  - Experience.
  - Type of appointment and delineation of privileges.
  - Medicaid provider number.
  - Pledge to abide by rules and regulations of the hospital.
  - Other items specified by the hospital or its medical staff.
- Current Indiana licensure or certification and serial number issued by the applicable agency for physicians, dentists, pharmacists, nurses, physical therapists, and others.
- Personnel records for each employee, including the following data:
  - Personal data.
  - Education and experience.
  - Evidence of participation in job-related educational activities.
  - Records of employees that relate to preemployment and subsequent physical examinations, immunizations, chest X rays, and tuberculin tests.

- Pharmacy permit when required.
- Transfer agreements with nursing homes and other hospitals.

Iowa

Iowa Administrative Code requires hospitals to keep admission records, death records, birth records, and narcotic records. Hospitals must file and store medical records in an accessible manner in the hospital in accordance with the statute of limitations. Hospitals must also submit the Hospital Price Information Survey to the Commissioner of Public Health annually. § 641–51.5 (135B).

The pharmacy must keep records of transactions for the control and accountability of drugs, including a system of controls and records for requisitioning and dispensing supplies to nursing care units and to other departments or services of the hospital. It must also keep records of all medications and prescriptions dispensed. § 641–51.25 (2) b. (135B).

The dietetic service must keep copies of menus as served for at least 30 days and include pertinent dietary records in the patient's transfer discharge record. § 641–51.19 (135B).

According § 441–81.9 (249A), intermediate care facilities must keep the following information for three years:

- All records required by the Department of Public Health and the Department of Inspections and Appeals.
- Records of all treatments, drugs, and services for which the medical assistance program has paid or will pay, including the authority for and the date of administration of the treatment, drugs, or services.
- Documentation in each resident's records that will enable the department to verify that each charge is due and proper before payment.
- Financial records maintained in the standard specified form, including the facility's most recent audited cost report.
- All other records the department needs in determining compliance with any federal or state law or rule or regulation.
- Census records, including the date, number of residents at the beginning of each day, names of residents admitted, and names of residents discharged for residents in skilled, intermediate, and residential care. Monthly totals of census figures for each type of care shall indicate the number admitted, the number discharged, and the number of patient days. Failure to maintain acceptable census records shall result in computing the per diem rate on the basis of 100 percent occupancy and a request for funds covering indicated recipients of nursing care not properly accounted for.
- Resident accounts.
- Inservice education program records.
- Inspection reports pertaining to conformity with federal, state, and local laws.
- Resident's personal records.

- Resident's medical records.
- Disaster preparedness reports.

Healthcare providers shall maintain clinical and fiscal records in support of services medical assistance programs pay for and shall make such records available to authorized representatives of the department on request. The fiscal records shall support each item of service charged to the program, and the clinical records shall specify the procedure or procedures performed, the dates of service, the medications or other supplies or services prescribed or provided to the recipient, and information concerning progress of treatment. The provider must retain these records for five years.

Kansas

Each hospital shall have a medical records service adequately directed, staffed, and equipped to enable accurate processing, indexing, and filing of all medical records. The service shall be under the direction of a registered records administrator or an accredited records technician or one who meets the educational or training requirements for such certification. If not, the hospital shall employ such a qualified person as a consultant.

The medical staff shall hold regular meetings and keep records of attendance and minutes. 28–34–6 (c). Also, each hospital shall comply with vital statistics statutes and regulations regarding the completion and filing of birth, death, and fetal death certificates within a specified period. 28–34–3a (d). The hospital must also keep records indicating receipt, disposition, and other pertinent information of all blood and blood derivatives provided to patients. 28–34–11 (q). And the hospital must keep records of personnel radiation exposure monitoring. 28–34–12 (n).

Hospitals must keep each medical record for ten years after the date of last discharge of the patient or one year after the date that minor patients reach their majority, whichever is longer. Regulations 28–34–9a (d) (1).

Kentucky

902 KAR 20:016 § 3 (3) requires hospitals to establish, maintain, and use administrative reports as necessary to guide the operation, measure productivity, and reflect the programs of the facility, including minutes of the governing authority and staff meetings, financial records and reports, personnel records, inspection reports, incident investigation reports, and other pertinent reports made in the regular course of business. Licensure inspection reports and plans of correction shall be available to the public on request. The hospital must also have written policies and procedures governing all aspects of its operations and services. Also, the hospital must have medical staff bylaws that provide for, among other things, appointment of committees, the minutes and reports of which are to be part of the permanent records of the hospital.

According to 902 KAR 20:016 § 3 (b) (d), personnel records on each employee must contain the following data:

- Name, address, social security number.
- Health records (skin tests and chest X rays must be a permanent part of the personnel record).
- Evidence of current registration, certification, or licensure of personnel.
- Records of training and experience.
- Records of performance evaluation.

Hospitals must maintain medical records, under the control of a medical records service with administrative responsibility for all medical records, for every patient admitted or receiving outpatient services for at least five years from date of discharge or, in the case of a minor, three years after the patient reaches the age of majority under state law, whichever is longer. 902 KAR 20:016 § 3 (11) (a). A registered records administrator on either a full-time, part-time, or consultative basis or an accredited record technician on a full- or part-time basis must direct the medical records service.

The dietary service must keep its menus on file for 30 days. The hospital must also keep records of the pharmacy or drug room to maintain adequate control over requisitioning and dispensing of all drugs and drug supplies and charging patients for drugs and pharmaceutical supplies, including a record of the stock on hand and of dispensing of all controlled substances. Hospitals shall also keep records indicating the receipt and disposition of all blood provided to patients. Reports of all laboratory services and tissue examinations will be in the patient's medical record with duplicates kept in the department.

Louisiana

Hospitals must retain hospital records in their original, microfilmed, or similarly reproduced form for at least ten years after the patient's discharge. Hospitals must retain graphic matter, images, X-ray films, and like matter that are necessary to produce a diagnostic or therapeutic report in their original, microfilmed, or similarly reproduced form for three years from the date of the patient's discharge. When, however, an attending or consulting physician of the patient, the patient or someone acting legally in the patient's behalf, or legal counsel for a party having an interest affected by the patient's medical records so requests in writing, the hospital must retain such graphic matter and so forth for a longer period. 40 Louisiana Statutes § 2144 F.

Maine

Chapter XII C 1–2 of the Regulations for the Licensure of General and Specialty Hospitals in the State of Maine requires hospitals to have medical records departments that maintain medical records, in accordance with accepted professional principles, for every patient admitted for care. A registered medical record librarian should run the department. If not, the hospital should use a qualified consultant or a trained part-time medical record librarian to organize the department, train the personnel, and make periodic visits to evaluate the records and the operation of the department.

Hospitals must preserve medical records, either in the original or by microfilm, for a period not less than the statute of limitations. The regulation also requires keeping records of pharmacy transactions, activities of various departments, such as outpatient, emergency, dentistry, physical therapy, and so forth, and activities of the utilization review committee. A recent revision of the regulations requires documentation of discharge planning activity, XII B.

Maryland

Healthcare facilities must maintain medical records for not less than five years from the date of discharge or, in the case of a minor, three years after the patient becomes of age or five years, whichever is longer. Code § 4–305; Code of Maryland Regulations 10.07.02.20 F. Maryland Code 15 (b) § 2 specifies that, unless a law requires a longer retention period, any business records may be destroyed after three years.

Massachusetts

Hospitals or clinics subject to licensure by the department of public health or supported in whole or in part by the Commonwealth, shall keep records, including the medical history and nurse's notes. They may destroy any such record or part thereof 30 years after the discharge or final treatment of the patient to whom it relates. 111 Statutes § 70.

Department of Public Health Regulations 130.120 requires hospitals to maintain the following records (under the responsibility of a trained medical record librarian or other responsible hospital employee):

- Daily census.
- Register of admissions and discharges.
- Register of outpatients.
- Register of births.
- Register of deaths.
- Register of operations.
- Narcotic register.
- Emergency room admissions.

111 Statutes § 54 requires the Department of Public Health to audit medical records as necessary, but not more than once a year.

Michigan

According to the Chief Medical Consultant of the Bureau of Health Facilities, Department of Public Health, Michigan does "not have any definitive information about Michigan policy on hospital record retention and destruction. . . . [T]his is a topic under current discussion in both the regulatory and legislative arenas." Department of Public Health Rule 325.1028 (s) states that hospitals shall preserve medical records as original records, abstracts, microfilms, or otherwise and that the records shall be such as to afford a basis for a complete audit of professional information. The administrative records of the hospital shall include, as a minimum, the following data: records of admissions and discharges, patient's records, daily census records, narcotic register, statistics regarding number of deaths, and statistics regarding number of autopsies.

Tuberculosis hospitals and other communicable disease units must maintain complete records of employee health programs. R 325.1060 (6) (b).

Minnesota

Minnesota Hospital Licensing and Operation Rules, § 4640.1100, requires hospitals to maintain the following records in a form and manner acceptable to the commissioner of health:

- Record of admissions and discharges, total patient days, average length of stay, and number of autopsies performed. Hospitals shall maintain separate data for adults and children, excluding newborns, and newborn infants, excluding stillbirths.
- Register of births.
- Register of deaths.
- Register of operations.
- Register of outpatients.

Hospitals must keep individual permanent medical records, as defined by the commissioner of health (see chapter 1), permanently. Hospitals may destroy other portions of the record, including any miscellaneous documents, papers, and correspondence, after seven years without transfer to photographic film. Hospitals must, however, keep all portions of records relating to minors for seven years following the age of majority. § 145.32.

Under § 4640.1200, hospitals must maintain a record for all narcotics administered, containing date, hour, name of patient, name of physician, kind of narcotic, and name of person by whom administered.

On or before January 31 of each year, hospitals must file the annual hospital statistical report covering patient service data with the commissioner of health. On or before the tenth of each month, hospital administrators must file with the commissioner a report of all births and deaths or stillbirths occurring in the institution during the previous month. Also the attending physician and the hospital must report by mail within three days after the death to the Minnesota Department of Health, Section of Maternal and Child Health, any death associated with pregnancy, including abortion and extrauterine pregnancy, or the puerperium for a period of three months postpartum, whether or not the complication from pregnancy is the actual cause of death. § 4640.1300.

Every illegitimate birth must also be reported to the commissioner of human services within 24 hours after the birth. § 4640.1400, Subpart 1.

Mississippi

Mississippi Code § 41-9-63 specifies the basic requirement that all hospitals and their personnel make and maintain accurate records.

§ 41–9–69 establishes the retention period. Hospitals must retain, preserve, and properly store records for such periods of reasonable duration as prescribed by the rules and regulations of the licensing authority. Such rules may provide for different retention periods for the various parts of hospital records and for different medical conditions and may require that the hospital make an abstract of data from records. Under the statute, however, hospitals must retain complete records for at least seven years for patients discharged at death, for ten years for adult patients of sound mind at the time of discharge, and for the period of minority or other disability, such as insanity, plus seven years, but not to exceed 28 years. In cases in which the hospital discharged the patient because of death or the patient died within 30 days, and the survivors are under a disability, and if the hospital knows or has reason to know that the patient left one or more survivors under disability who are or claim to be entitled to damages for wrongful death of the patient, the hospital must maintain the records for the period of the disability of the survivors plus seven years, not to exceed 28 years.

The facility may retire X-ray film four years after the date of exposure if the radiologist has made written and signed findings and if the facility keeps those findings for the same period as other hospital records as above.

As to business records, § 41–9–81 provides that the commissioners or board of trustees of hospitals owned and operated by counties, cities, towns, supervisors districts, or election districts have the authority, in their discretion, to retire and destroy any of the following business records at any time three years after preparation of the records: intrahospital requisitions; inventory records of expendable supplies; temporary records pertaining to patients' charges; department reports; paid invoices; purchase orders; and similar documents of temporary use and value.

In addition, whenever such hospitals have retained business records that the law requires the hospitals to retain for indefinite periods or that are necessary on the basis of sound business practices and that hospitals have so retained and preserved for a period of six years, the commissioners or board of trustees shall have the authority, in their discretion, to retire the same. This statute, however, does not authorize retirement, destruction, or disposal of any of the following business records:

- Minutes or minute books.
- Bylaws or rules and regulations.
- General ledgers.
- Disbursement registers or journals.
- Cash receipts registers.
- Maintenance and investment accounts.
- Inventory records.
- Ledger cards.
- Sheets or other records of unpaid accounts receivable.
- Other evidence of unpaid indebtedness.
- Budgets.
- Audit reports.

- Licenses or permits.
- Abstracts or certificates of title.
- Geological reports.
- Engineering or architectural plans, specifications, or drawings.
- Any other business records that laws, court orders, rules and regulations, or sound business practices require hospitals to retain permanently or for longer than six years.

Privately owned hospitals may retire any business records at such times as dictated by sound business practices and the reasonable accommodation of other interested parties except as otherwise provided by law, court order, or regulations.

Any hospital may, at any time, microfilm or otherwise reproduce its business records. Microfilming or other means of reproducing records do not, however, permit destruction or retirement of any record that this statute requires hospitals to retain.

Willful violation of these statutes pertaining to medical records is a misdemeanor.

Missouri

The chief executive officer or chief operating officer of a hospital must appoint a director of the medical record services who is a qualified registered record administrator, an accredited record technician, or an individual with demonstrated competence and knowledge of medical record services supervised by a consultant who is a registered record administrator or accredited record technician. 13 CSR 50–20.021 (D) 1. The hospital must also have a mechanism for review and evaluation of medical records services on a regular basis. 13 CSR 50–20.021 (D) (17).

Hospitals must maintain medical records as required by the statute of limitations, but may preserve them longer to meet their needs for clinical, educational, statistical, or administrative purposes. 13 CSR 50–20.021 (D) 16. Chapter 515 Missouri Statutes § 516.105 establishes the statute of limitations for medical malpractice cases. Plaintiffs must bring such suits within two years of the date of the occurrence of the act of neglect complained of with two exceptions. Minors under the age of ten will have until their twelfth birthday to bring action. In cases in which the negligence was permitting any foreign object to remain in a living person's body, the plaintiff must bring the action within two years of the discovery of such negligence or from the date on which the patient in the exercise of ordinary care should have discovered such negligence, whichever occurs first. In no event, however, shall any action for damages for malpractice be commenced after ten years from the date of the act of neglect complained of.

Nursing homes must maintain records of medication destruction in the facility, including the resident's name, the date, the name, strength, and quantity of the medication, the prescription number, and the signatures of the participating parties. 12 CSR 15–14.042 (57). Nursing homes must also maintain records of medication released to the family or resident on discharge or to the pharmacy, and the records shall include the same information as records of medication destruction (58). These intermediate care and skilled nursing care facilities must also keep separate records of Schedule II medication for one year, including name of the resident, name of the physician, prescription number, medication, and signature of the person administering the drug (59). These facilities shall keep complete and accurate records of each resident in the facility from admission to discharge or death and for five years after the resident leaves the facility or reaches age 21, whichever is longer (91). When the home purges records, it must maintain a minimum of three months' documentation as well as the most recent report of physical examination and administrative information, with access to past records readily available in the medical records department of the facility (99). The facility must keep all financial records relating to facility operation for seven years (101).

Montana

The Administrative Rules of Montana, Chapter 32, Rule 16.32.328 (1), requires hospitals to maintain a patient's entire medical record, in either original or microfilmed form, for not less than ten years following the date of a patient's discharge or death, or, in the case of minors, for not less than ten years following the attainment of the age of majority. Hospitals must keep diagnostic imaging film and electrodiagnostic tracings for five years and their interpretations for the same period as medical records, above.

Healthcare facilities other than hospitals must maintain patients' or residents' health records for not less than five years following the date of their discharge or death. Rule 16.32.308.

Whenever a hospital or an independent clinical laboratory provides medical services to a patient with a reportable tumor (including the following kinds: malignant neoplasm, with the exception of a basal or squamous carcinoma of the skin; skin cancer of the labia, vulva, penis, or scrotum; benign tumor of the brain, including a meninioma [cerebral meninges], pinealoma [pineal gland], adenoma [pituitary gland]; carcinoid tumor), whether malignant, benign, or not otherwise specified, it must collect, record, and make available to the Tumor Registry, Department of Health and Environmental Services, information listed in Rules 16.32.501 through .504. Those of you who need very detailed information on this topic will find these administrative rules particularly helpful and worth looking up.

Rule 16.32.138 specifies the requirement for and contents of hospital annual reports, and .139 does the same for annual financial reports. Rule 16.32.140 specifies annual reports by long-term care and personal care facilities, and Rule 16.32.142 specifies annual reports by alcohol and drug treatment facilities. These facilities must collect and maintain the information required to fulfill these reporting requirements (see appendix C).

Nebraska

Hospitals must keep medical records in original, microfilm, or other approved copy for at least ten years following discharge. In the case of minors, the hospital must keep the record until three years after the minor has reached the age of majority. Title 175, Chapter 9, 003.04A6.

Nevada

Under Statutes § 629.051, healthcare providers will retain the healthcare records of their patients as part of their regularly maintained records for five years after receipt or production of the records.

All superintendents, managers, or others in charge of hospitals or other institutions to which persons go for treatment of diseases or to which the process of law commits persons shall make a record of all the personal and statistical particulars relative to the inmates of their institutions at the time of their admission. If a healthcare facility admits a person for medical treatment of disease, the physician in charge shall specify in the record the nature of the disease and where, in the physician's opinion, the patient contracted it. § 439.230.

Facilities that treat patients, including hospitals, convalescent care facilities, nursing care facilities, detoxification centers, and specialized medical healthcare facilities, must file with the Department of Human Resources the following financial statements and reports: a balance sheet detailing assets, liabilities, and net worth of the institution for its fiscal year and a statement of income and expenses for the fiscal year. Such reports are public records. § 449.490.

New Hampshire

Health facilities must keep current, written files on each resident on active file in the facility until the resident is discharged. Both hospitals and health facilities must maintain medical records for seven years (from date of the resident's discharge in the case of health facilities). Hospitals must retain children's records to the age of majority plus seven years. Each hospital must have a written policy in regard to the disposition of records. He–P 802.11 and 803.06. He–P 802.08 (B) (5) states that hospitals must store X-ray film for at least seven years and then may destroy it.

Sheltered care facilities must retain resident records in the facility until seven years from the date of the resident's discharge. He–P 804.04 (b). Outpatient clinics must store clinical records for seven years after discharge. Healthcare facilities must keep a minor's records until one year after the minor reaches age 18 but in no case less than seven years after discharge. He–P 806.10 (e). Residential treatment and rehabilitation facilities have the same retention period, except that they must keep a minor's records no less than three years. He–P 807 (d). Home healthcare providers must retain records for seven years after discharge. In the case of minors, home healthcare providers must keep their records until one year after the minor reaches age 18, but in no case less than seven years. He–P 809.07. Home healthcare provider business records must contain the following information:

- Documentation of services provided.
- Annual report.

- Current financial report.
- Current service contracts or agreements, including the following data:
  - Description of service provided.
  - Delineation of responsibility of each agency.
  - Fiscal arrangements.

He–P 808.12 requires clinical laboratories to keep all test records and reports for not less than two years. Such facilities must also keep current personnel records, including the employees' training, qualifications, and experience with verified dates of previous and current employment.

Unless a law designates a specific period, healthcare facilities my destroy business records three years after preparation of the records. Statutes § 337–A: 2.

New Jersey

New Jersey's Standards for Hospital Facilities requires hospitals to include in their bylaws requirements regarding the maintenance of complete medical records and the establishment of an acceptable format for retaining all necessary data. § 8:43B–6.2 (a) 9.

Hospitals must also have medical records departments that are under the supervision of a medical record librarian or other person qualified by education, training, and experience and employ such additional personnel as necessary for the efficient conduct of the department. If a professionally qualified person is not available on a full-time basis, the facility must employ a registered medical record librarian on a part-time or consultant basis to make regular visits to evaluate maintenance of records and to advise on the operation of the service.

Facilities must preserve medical records, either in the original or by microfilm, for a period of not less than ten years following the most recent discharge of the patient or until the discharged patient reaches the age of 23, whichever is longer. Hospitals must keep X-ray films for five years. § 8:43B–7.1 (b) (3).

Hospitals must maintain such additional records as required to fully document its operations and to provide statistical data required by the Department of Health, including the following information:

- Record of admissions and discharge.
- Case and clinical reports.
- Daily census.
- Register of births.
- Register of operative procedures.
- Narcotic register.
- Death records.
- Autopsy records.
- Consultations.
- Record of emergency and clinic services.

Hospitals must forward a summary report of their activities to the Department of Health within three months of the end of each calendar year. 8:43B–7.3.

Hospitals must also keep personnel records, including employment and health records, on all employees. The facility must ensure that each employee's record contains documentation of required tests, such as Mantoux tuberculin skin tests, chest X-rays, and rubella screening. § 8:43B–5.1(f) and (g).

Finally, § 8:43B–6.3 (d) requires hospitals to keep records of attendance and adequate minutes of all staff meetings.

New Mexico

New Mexico Statute 14–6–2 provides that unless otherwise provided in the statute, hospitals shall retain all records directly relating to the care and treatment of a patient for ten years following the patient's last discharge. Hospitals may destroy laboratory test records and reports one year after the date of the test if a copy is in the patient's record. If not, hospitals must retain them for four years. Hospitals may destroy X-ray films four years after exposure if the hospital records contain written findings of radiologists who read the X rays. After three years from exposure, patients may recover their X rays.

New York

Hospitals must have a department that has administrative responsibility for medical records and maintain a comprehensive medical record for every patient, whether an inpatient, ambulatory patient, emergency patient, or outpatient. Medical records must be legibly and accurately written, complete, properly filed and retained, and accessible. The hospital shall use a system of author identification and record maintenance that ensures the integrity of the authentication and protects the security of all record entries. § 405.10.

The facility must retain the records in their original or legally reproduced form for at least six years from the date of discharge or three years after the patient's age of majority (18 years), whichever is longer, or at least six years after death. § 405.10 (a)(3) Department of Health Memorandum, Health Facilities Series H–40.

The chief executive officer must develop and implement personnel policies that cover, among other items, the maintenance of an accurate, current, and complete personnel record for each hospital employee and the recorded medical history for all personnel along with their medical records. § 405.3 (b).

§ 405.3 (d) requires that the hospital maintain and, upon request, immediately furnish to the Department of Health copies of all documents, including, but not limited to, the following data:

- All records related to patient care and services.
- Certificate of incorporation or partnership agreement and certificate of conducting business under an assumed name as required by General Business Law, § 130.

What Records Must You Keep and for How Long? 101

- Reports of hospital inspections and surveys of outside agencies with statements attached specifying the steps taken to correct any hazards or deficiencies or to carry out the recommendations contained therein.
- All contracts, leases, and other agreements entered into by the governing authority pertaining to the ownership of the land, building, fixtures, and equipment used in connection with the operation of the hospital.
- All licenses, permits, and certificates required by law for the operation of the hospital and also for those departments and staff members, where required.
- Operating procedure manuals for all services or units of the hospital organization. Hospitals shall review these manuals at least biennially or more frequently as determined appropriate by each service or unit and make them available to all services and units of the hospital.
- All bylaws, rules, and regulations of the hospital and all amendments thereto; a listing of the names and addresses and titles of offices held for all members of the governing authority and revisions thereof; a copy of the bylaws, rules, and regulations of the medical staff and all amendments and revisions thereof; a copy of the current annual report and financial statements of the hospital.
- Copies of all complaints received regarding patient care and documentation of the follow-up actions taken as a result of the investigation of these complaints.
- Copies of all incident reports completed pursuant to § 405.8.
- Listing of names and titles of the members of each committee of the hospital.
- Written minutes of each committee's proceedings, including at least the following data:
  - Attendance.
  - Date and duration of the meeting.
  - Synopsis of issues discussed and actions or recommendations made.
- Any record required by this part. § 405.3 (d).

The hospital shall report in writing to the Office of Professional Medical Conduct with a copy to the appropriate Area Administrator of the Department's Office of Health Systems Management within thirty days of the occurrence of denial, suspension, restriction, termination, or curtailment of training, employment, association, or professional privileges or the denial of certification of the completion of training of any physician, registered physician's assistant, or registered specialist's assistant licensed/registered by the New York State Department of Education for reasons related in any way to any of the following occurrences:

- Alleged mental or physical impairment, incompetence, malpractice, misconduct, or endangerment of patient safety or welfare.
- Voluntary or involuntary resignation or withdrawal of association or of privileges with the hospital to avoid the imposition of disciplinary measures.
- Receipt of information concerning a conviction of a misdemeanor or a felony.

These reports must contain the name and address of the individual, the profession and license number, the date of the hospital's action, a description of the action taken, and the reason for the action or the nature of the action or conduct that led to the resignation or withdrawal and the date thereof. § 405.3 (e) (1). § (e) (2) establishes a similar requirement for health profession students serving in a clinical clerkship, an unlicensed health professional serving in a clinical fellowship or residency, or an unlicensed health professional practicing under a limited permit or a state license.

The infection control officer of the hospital must maintain a log of occurrences of infections and communicable diseases. § 405.11 (b) (4).

Hospitals shall file records of radiological services, including interpretations, consultations, and therapy, with the patient's record and keep duplicate copies in the radiology department. § 405.15 (a) (5).

The hospital will assure that all tests, examinations, and procedures of its laboratory services are properly recorded and reported, including filing reports with the patient's medical record and keeping duplicate copies in a manner that permits ready identification and accessibility. § 405.16 (c) (2) (ii). In addition, the facility must keep records on file indicating the receipt and disposition of all blood and blood products acquired by the hospital. § 405.16 (e) (5).

The director of the pharmacy will ensure that pharmacy personnel keep current and accurate records of the transactions of the pharmacy, including the following information:

- System of record and bookkeeping in accordance with the policies of the hospital for the following activities:
  - Maintaining adequate control over the requisitioning and dispensing of all drugs and pharmaceutical supplies.
  - Charging patients for drugs and pharmaceutical supplies.
- Record of inventory and dispensing of all controlled substances maintained.
- Labeling of all inpatient and outpatient medications.

Pharmacy personnel must report all abuses and losses of controlled substances to the director and the medical staff, as appropriate. §§ 405.17 (a) (7) and (c) (3).

The admission and discharge register of the emergency service must include the following information for every individual seeking care:

- Date, name, age, gender, zip code.
- Expected source of payment.
- Time and means of arrival, including name of ambulance service for patients arriving by ambulance.
- Complaint and disposition of the case.
- Time and means of departure, including name of ambulance service for patients transferred by ambulance.

The emergency service must develop a medical record for every patient seen in the service and integrate or cross-reference these records with the inpatient and outpatient medical records system to assure the timely availability of previous patient care information and shall contain the prehospital care report or equivalent report for patients who arrive by ambulance. §§ 405.19 (c) (6) and (7).

The hospital must also maintain in the maternity and newborn service a register of births containing the following data: name of each patient admitted; date of admission; date and time of birth; type of delivery; names of physicians, nurse midwives, assistants, and anesthetists; sex, weight, and gestational age of infant; location of delivery; and fetal outcome of delivery. This register shall list any delivery for which the institution is responsible for filing a birth certificate. §§ 405.21 (c) (2) through (4).

§ 405.8 requires hospitals to report immediately to the Department of Health's Office of Health Systems Management any of the following incidents, followed up by written notification within seven days:

- Patients' deaths in circumstances other than those related to the natural course of illness, disease, or proper treatment in accordance with generally accepted medical standards. Injuries and impairments of bodily functions in circumstances other than those related to the natural course of illness, disease, or proper treatment in accordance with generally accepted medical standards and that necessitate additional or more complicated treatment regimens or that result in a significant change in patient status are also reportable.
- Fires or internal disasters in the facility that disrupt the provision of patient care services or cause harm to patients or personnel.
- Equipment malfunction or equipment user error during treatment or diagnosis of a patient that adversely affected or could have adversely affected a patient or personnel.
- Poisoning occurring within the facility.
- Reportable infection outbreaks (as defined in § 405.11).
- Patient elopements and kidnapping.
- Strikes by personnel.
- Disasters and other emergency situations external to the hospital environment that adversely affect facility operations.
- Unscheduled termination of any services vital to the continued safe operations of the facility or to the health and safety of its patients and personnel, including but not limited to, the termination of telephone, electric, gas, fuel, water, heat, air conditioning, rodent or pest control, laundry services, food, or contract services.

The hospital will provide a copy of its investigative report to the Area Administrator within 24 hours of its completion, documenting all hospital efforts to identify and analyze the circumstances surrounding the incident and to develop and implement appropriate measures to improve the overall quality of patient care. The report shall include the following data:

- Explanation of the circumstances surrounding the incident.
- Updated assessment of the effect of the incident on the patient(s).
- Summary of current patient status, including follow-up care provided and post-incident diagnosis.
- Chronology of steps taken to investigate the incident that identifies the date(s) and person(s) or committee(s) involved in each review activity.
- Identification of all findings and conclusions associated with review of the incident.
- Summaries of any committee findings and recommendations associated with review of the incident.
- Summary of all actions taken to correct identified problems, to prevent recurrence of the incident, to improve overall patient care, and to comply with other requirements of this regulation. § 405.11 (d).

§ 400.18 of Part 400 of Article 1 of Subchapter A of Chapter V of Title 10 establishes policies for the Department of Health's collection, use, and disclosure of data from medical facilities. The New York State Statewide Planning and Research Cooperative System (SPARCS) is a statewide centralized healthcare system that incorporates data from the uniform bill and uniform discharge abstract. This law requires hospitals to submit to the Department the Patient Review Instrument Data required of residential healthcare facilities, and ambulatory surgery data submitted by hospitals and freestanding centers. Among other requirements, this law requires hospitals to maintain their accounts and records in accordance with the American Hospital Association's Chart of Accounts for Hospitals on an accrual basis except in cases in which the law requires an alternate system. Hospitals must submit a certified uniform financial report and a uniform statistical report of hospitals within 120 days after the close of the fiscal year.

North Carolina

North Carolina Administrative Code T10:03C.1405 provides that hospitals shall preserve or retain all original medical records or photographs of such records for at least the period outlined in the North Carolina Statute of Limitations and in accordance with the hospital policy based on American Hospital Association recommendations and guidance of the hospital's legal advisers.

North Carolina's Vital Statistics Statute, § 130A–117, however, requires all persons in charge of hospitals to maintain records for not less than three years of personal data concerning each person admitted or confined to the institution and to make such available for inspection by the State Registrar upon request. These records shall include information required for certificates of birth and death and spontaneous fetal death.

Nursing homes must have a full-time employee designated to be responsible for medical record services. If that employee is not qualified by education or experience, a registered record administrator or accredited record technician shall consult to assure compliance with the regulations. Nursing homes must maintain records in accordance with the statute of limitations for both adults and minors. § 10 NCAC 3H .0606.

North Dakota

North Dakota's Hospital Licensing Rules 33–07–01–16 requires the governing board of a hospital to establish and implement procedures to ensure that the hospital has a medical record department with administrative responsibility for medical records. The department shall maintain a record in accordance with accepted medical record principles for every patient admitted for care in the hospital.

The hospital must preserve records, either in original or any other method of preservation, for 25 years from the date of discharge except for the records of deceased patients, which hospitals need to retain for only seven years after the date of death. Hospitals may retain records longer if the governing body determines that they have a research, legal, or medical value.

If a registered record administrator or accredited record technician does not head the department, a consultant who is so qualified must organize the department, train the personnel, and make periodic visits to evaluate the records and the department's operation.

The hospital shall centralize all clinical information pertaining to a patient's stay in the patient's records with the original of all reports filed therein.

Long-term care facilities must retain their clinical records, either in the original or by any other method of preservation, such as microfilm, for ten years after discharge or seven years after the death of deceased residents. Such facilities must retain records of minors for the period of minority and ten years after discharge. Such facilities should receive consultation at least annually from an accredited record technician or registered record administrator if such a qualified person is not in charge of the records.

Ohio

Ohio's Minimum Standards for Hospitals Receiving Federal Aid requires in § 3701–11–04 that such hospitals keep accurate and complete medical records for all patients admitted to the hospital containing sufficient data to warrant the treatment administered. Hospitals shall file all reports as required by state law, by the Ohio Sanitary Code, or by the municipality or other political subdivision with the proper agency within the prescribed period. § 3701–11–03 adds that the governing board of such a hospital is responsible for keeping accurate records of its finances and activities.

§ 3727.11 (B) requires every hospital to disclose to the department of health the following data for nongovernmental patients, that is, those that do not have charges paid by various government programs:

- Total number of patients discharged.
- Mean, median, and range of total hospital charges.
- Mean, median, and range of length of stay.

- Number of admissions to the emergency room by transfer from another hospital and other sources.
- Number of nongovernmental patients falling within diagnosis related group numbers 468, 469, and 470 as defined in 42 C.F.R. Part 412.

§ 3701-7-35 requires maternity homes to keep medical records for not less than two years. Hospitals shall make this information available for inspection and copying by the public. But under no circumstances shall a hospital include name or social security number of patient or physician in this information.

Nursing homes must keep the following records:
- Individual medical records on each patient.
- All records required by federal and state laws and regulations as to purchase, dispensing, administering, and disposition of all narcotic and barbiturate drugs, including unused portions.
- Annual report submitted to the Director of Health.
- Records of all patients admitted to or discharged from the home, including any additional information necessary to complete the annual report.

Rest homes must keep a record on each resident, including name, residence, age, sex, race, religion, nearest relative, and guardian. Such homes must also keep records of medications, treatments, and unusual events or accidents involving residents, and name, address, and hours of duty of all persons who work in the home. All these records and reports must be available for inspection at all times by the director or representative.

Maternity hospitals must keep medical records of each maternity patient and each infant for not less than two years and a log of all deliveries in chronological order, including information pertinent to the delivery, the patient's condition, course, and disposition of newborn infant. Hospitals will identify newborn infants with special problems in a special log as prescribed by the Director of Health. § 3701-7-24.

Oklahoma

According to the Oklahoma Department of Health and Department of Libraries, public healthcare facilities must retain records as specified in the Records Management Act, 67 Oklahoma Statutes § 201 and following. Private facilities should maintain their records in accordance with the Uniform Preservation of Private Records Act, 67 Oklahoma Statutes § 251 and following. § 252 states that, unless another law specifies a different retention period, facilities may destroy business records three years after making such records. This section does not apply to minute books of corporations or to records of sales or other transactions involving weapons, poisons, or other dangerous articles or substances capable of use in the commission of crimes.

Oregon

Oregon Administrative Rules 333-70-055 (7) states that hospitals will maintain and keep permanently in written or computerized form the following records:

- Patient's register, containing admission and discharges.
- Patient's master index.
- Register of all deliveries, including live births and stillbirths.
- Register of all deaths.
- Register of operations.
- Register of outpatients (7 years).
- Emergency room register (7 years).

Oregon also requires visits, at least annually, by a qualified medical records consultant (a Registered Record Administrator, RRA, or an accredited Record Technician, ART) unless an individual qualified as an RRA or an ART is the Director of the Medical Records Department, to ensure the quality of record retention.

Oregon Administrative Rules 333-73-215 requires Termination of Pregnancy Hospitals to keep written records, including, but not limited to, the following information: admission and discharge notes; histories, including special problems of the patient; results of tests, including pregnancy diagnostic test; gross pathologic examination of the tissue removed, noting amount of tissue, presence of villi, presence or absence of molar degeneration, fetal parts, and microscopic examination of tissue removed; nurse's work sheets, counseling or social service notes, laboratory reports, operative procedure reports; progress notes, and so forth. Such records are to be available to the State Health Division, and the hospital must submit a "Report of Induced Termination of Pregnancy" report to the Vital Statistics Division of the Oregon State Health Division.

Pennsylvania

Pennsylvania has a comprehensive statutory scheme for medical record retention in Title 28, Pennsylvania Statutes. Its principle, as stated in § 115.1, is that the hospital maintain facilities and services adequate to provide medical records that are accurately documented and readily accessible to authorized persons requiring such access and that can be readily used for retrieving and compiling information. Its medical record service must be directed, staffed, and equipped to ensure the accurate processing, indexing, and filing of all medical records. § 115.2. The service shall be under the direction of a certified medical records practitioner. If none is available on a full-time basis, the facility must employ a certified person on a part-time or consulting basis. At least one full-time or part-time employee must provide regular medical record service. § 115.3. The hospital must also have education programs for such personnel, § 115.5, and written job descriptions for them, § 115.6.

The hospital must keep medical records, whether originals, reproductions, or microfilm, for seven years following discharge of the patient. The facility must keep minors' records until their majority and then for seven years or as long as the facility keeps the records of adult patients. § 115.23.

The hospital must have a medical records committee to periodically review such records. § 115.34.

Rhode Island

The Rules and Regulations for the Licensing of Hospitals require medical records to be under the direction of a registered medical record administrator who is certified by the American Medical Record Association or who possesses equivalent training and experience. The director may be full- or part-time or a consultant as required by the scope of service. The hospital must staff and equip the department to facilitate accurate processing, checking, indexing, filing, and retrieval of all medical records. §§ 25.1 and .2.

The regulations also require that the facility maintain records for every person treated on an inpatient, outpatient, or emergency basis and establish written policies and procedures regarding content and completion of medical records. § 25.3 and .4.

The retention period for medical records, in either original or accurately reproduced form, is five years following discharge of the patient, except that facilities must maintain a minor's records for at least five years after the minor reaches the age of 18 years. § 25.9.

Rhode Island also has a uniform reporting system that requires hospitals to establish and maintain records and data in such a manner as to make uniform the system of periodic reporting. Hospitals must report on a quarterly basis to the Department of Health, Office of Health Statistics, information pertaining to financial and statistical data of hospital inpatient services, including data on all discharges during the three-month periods ending on March 31, June 30, September 30, and December 31. Hospitals shall retain copies of such data for not less than one year from the end of the three-month period covered. See R23–17–HOSP for guidance as to what to report and authorized media.

South Carolina

The South Carolina Department of Health and Environmental Control's Regulation No. 61–16, Minimum Standards for Licensing of Hospitals and Institutional General Infirmaries in South Carolina, specifies that hospitals shall assign the responsibility for supervision, filing, and indexing of medical records to a responsible employee of the hospital who has had training in the field. Section 601.2. Hospitals must retain records for ten years and may destroy the records thereafter, provided that they retain records of minors until after the expiration of the one-year period of election following achievement of majority as prescribed by statute and that the hospitals retain an index, a register, or summary cards providing certain basic information (see chapter 16). Regulation No. 61–14 prescribes the same retention period for medical records in Section 504.1.

Nursing homes must store medical records in an inactive file after discharge or death of the patient and maintain them for ten years after discharge or death.

Intermediate care facilities for mental retardation must keep health records for five years after discharge. On discharge, the facility must complete the resident's record and file it in an inactive file. Regulation No. 61–13, Section 503.

South Dakota

The Administrative Rules of South Dakota require hospitals and nursing homes to have a medical record department staffed with trained personnel and equipped to facilitate accurate processing, checking, indexing, filing, and retrieval of all medical records. The individual in charge must be trained and knowledgeable in the field of medical records, and the facility must have written policies and procedures to govern the activities of the medical record department, including confidentiality, safeguarding, content, continuity, completeness, and entries of medical records. 44:04:09:04, Administrative Rules of South Dakota. 44:04:09:06 has a similar provision for record service for supervised personal care facilities.

Tennessee

Tennessee has one of the most comprehensive statutory schemes for records management. § 68–11–303 of its Code establishes hospitals' duty to keep "true and accurate hospital records, including records pertaining to abortions . . . complying with such methods, minimum standards, and contents thereof as may be prescribed by rules and regulations adopted by the board [the hospital licensing board]. The responsibility for supervision, filing, and indexing of medical records shall be delegated to a responsible employee of the hospital." Tennessee's Department of Health and Environment, Board for Licensing Health Care Facilities § 1200–8–4–.03 (1) (a), adds that the facility shall delegate the supervision of medical records services to a qualified medical record practitioner, either a Registered Record Administrator (RRA) or an Accredited Record Technician (ART) or other person qualified by work experience.

§ 68–11–305 requires hospitals to keep records relating to patient care for ten years following discharge or death of the patient. In cases involving patients under mental disability or minority, however, the hospital must keep their records for the period of disability or minority plus one year or ten years following the discharge of the patient, whichever is longer.

The facility may retire X-ray film four years after the date of exposure, provided that the facility retains the written findings or interpretations of a radiologist who read the film for the period required for medical records immediately above. § 68–11–305 (b).

§ 68–11–307 authorizes hospitals to retain records, either as originals or reproductions, for a longer period than the period of retention or as required by a court.

The hospital may, unless otherwise required by law, court order, or applicable rules or regulations, retire any business records at such time as in its judgment may conform to sound business practices and the reasonable accommodation of other interested parties. § 68–11–309.

Under § 68–11–311, willful violation of these records management statutes is a misdemeanor, but no hospital or employee may be civilly liable for such a violation except for actual damages in a civil action for willful or reckless or wanton acts or omissions.

Texas

A hospital may authorize the disposal of any medical record on or after the tenth anniversary of the date on which the hospital last treated the patient who is the subject of the record. If the patient was under 18 years old when last treated, the hospital may dispose of the patient's records on or after the date of the patient's 20th birthday or on or after the tenth anniversary of the date on which the hospital last treated the patient, whichever is later. Texas Hospital Licensing Law Title 71, Art. 4437 f. § 5A; Hospital Licensing Standard 1–22.

Special care facilities retention requirements are the same as those for hospitals. Standard 12–8.7.4.1 and .2. In addition, the standards require that the director of such facilities be responsible for the organization and management of medical records. 12–8.7.2. Personnel records must contain sufficient information to support placement in the assigned position (including a resume of training and experience). Where applicable, a current copy of the person's license or permit shall be in the file. 12–3.1.3.7.

Title 71 Texas Statutes Art. 4438e, § 3, requires each hospital to submit to the Department of Health financial and utilization data, based on its latest audited financial records, including the following information:

- Total gross revenue:
    - Medicare gross revenue.
    - Medicaid gross revenue.
    - Other revenue from state programs.
    - Revenue from local government programs.
    - Local tax support.
    - Charitable contributions.
    - Other third party payments.
    - Gross inpatient revenue.
    - Gross outpatient revenue.
- Total deductions from gross revenue:
    - Charity care.
    - Bad debt.
    - Contractual allowance.
    - Any other deductions.
- Total admissions:
    - Medicare admissions.
    - Medicaid admissions.
    - Admissions under a local government program.
    - Charity care admissions.
    - Any other type of admission.
- Total discharges.
- Total patient days.
- Average length of stay.

- Total outpatient visits.
- Total assets.
- Total liabilities.
- Total cost of reimbursed and unreimbursed care for indigent patients.
- Total cost of reimbursed and unreimbursed medical education.

Any portion of this information that relates to a specific patient or any financial information that refers to a provider or facility is confidential. Disclosure of such information is a misdemeanor.

Utah

Utah's Health Facility Licensure Rules requires every health facility to have a medical records service or department, under the direction of a person whose qualifications, authority, responsibilities, and duties the administrator has defined or approved. The health facility shall employ a Registered Records Administrator (RRA) or an Accredited Records Technician (ART) at least on a part time basis. If such employment is impossible, the hospital shall have an RRA or ART consultant who visits at least quarterly and provides written reports to the chief executive officer. 7.401. Each records department employee must have a written job description and participate in a continuing education program. 7.403. According to 7.414, the hospital must have written policies, approved by the medical staff and administration, providing for the following activities:

- Duties of the director and ART or RRA.
- Educational requirements for medical record personnel.
- Release of information, including child abuse records, psychiatric records, and drug and alcohol abuse records.
- Preparation of medical records.
- Filing and record storage.
- Transportation of medical records.
- Indexing.
- Coding.
- Statistical reporting.
- Security and confidentiality of records.
- Destruction of records.
- Authorization of individuals for access or nonaccess to the medical record.
- Retention of medical records.
- Prohibition against delegation of rubber stamp usage.
- Duration or revocation of consent and releases.

The facility must maintain a medical record on every patient admitted into the hospital or accepted for treatment. All records shall be readily available to the following people or organizations: attending physicians; the hospital, its medical staff, or authorized employees; authorized representatives of the Department of Health for determining compliance with licensure rules; and other persons authorized by consent forms. 7.404 A.

The retention period for medical records is ten years after the last date of patient care. 7.406. A.

Hospitals must maintain, in addition to medical records, the following information:

- Record of admissions, discharges, and number of autopsies performed.
- Vital statistics, including registers of births, deaths, operations, and narcotics. 7.412. In addition, 7.413 requires reports of vital statistics, including birth certificates, death certificates, and fetal death certificates.

Vermont

According to the Vermont State Hospital Licensing Regulations, § 3–496, hospitals must maintain medical records for ten years following the patient's discharge.

Hospitals must keep accounting records of all operating procedures on a monthly basis and compile complete operating and financial statements at least annually and keep them on file for 20 years. § 3–941. The licensee must file an annual report with the State Board of Health containing the following data:

- Total number of admissions during the year.
- Total number of discharges during the year.
- Total number of deaths during the year.
- Bed capacity.
- Average length of stay.
- Number of major operations.
- Number of minor operations.
- Number of outpatient visits.
- Number of autopsies.
- Maternity statistics.
- Report of any changes in structure and/or services within the past year.
- Report of any changes in the next year.

The hospital must also provide the agency a copy of its published annual report. § 3–492.

Level III and Level IV Residential Care Homes must keep resident records on file for at least seven years after the date of discharge or death of the resident, whichever occurs first. Licensing Regulations Section VI. 1. C. Such homes must also report fires to the Licensing Agency and the Department of Labor and Industry within 24 hours, and Level IV facilities must report to the licensing agency accidents or illnesses that require physician follow-up and emergency room treatment or admission to a hospital. All homes must file these reports in the resident's folder. Homes must also report unexplained absences of residents to the police and responsible persons and follow up with a report to the Licensing Agency within 24 hours. Finally, these homes must report breakdowns to their physical plants that disrupt normal operations. 9. b. Level III and Level IV Residential Care Home Licensing Regulations.

Nursing homes must keep resident's records for at least six years following discharge or death. Nursing Homes Regulations 3–29. Licensed nursing personnel must be responsible for the maintenance of medical records, and the facility must submit a semi-annual statistical report to the licensing agency as of December 31 and June 30 each year, due before February 1 and August 1, respectively. Nursing homes must also report all fires and provide Health Examination Certificates for all employees. Regulations 3–28.

Hospitals and physicians must report all fetal deaths of 20 or more weeks of gestation or, if gestational age is unknown, of 400 or more grams or 15 or more ounces and all therapeutic or induced abortions to the commissioner within seven days after delivery. Chapter 107 Vermont Statutes § 5222.

Virginia

In Virginia, hospitals must staff and equip their medical record departments to facilitate accurate processing, checking, indexing, filing, and retrieval of all medical records and establish written policies and procedures regarding content and completion of medical records. The regulations mandate that hospitals preserve either originals or accurate reproductions for at least five years following the patient's discharge, except for minor patients. Hospitals must keep their records for at least five years after the patient reaches the age of 18. Hospitals must keep birth and death information for ten years. Rules and Regulations for the Licensure of Hospitals in Virginia 208.

The same retention period applies to nursing homes. Rules and Regulations for the Licensure of Nursing Homes Section 24.5. Nursing homes must assign overall responsibility for maintenance, completion, and preservation of medical records to a full-time employee with work experience or training that is consistent with the nature and complexity of the record system. Rules 24.10.

Washington

Regulations require hospitals to have a well-defined medical record system and the facilities, staff, equipment, and supplies necessary for the development, maintenance, control, analysis, use, and preservation of patient care data and medical records in accordance with recognized principles of medical record management and applicable state laws and regulations. Hospitals must have the medical record service directed, staffed, and equipped to ensure timely, complete, and accurate checking, processing, indexing, filing, and preservation of medical records, and the compilation, maintenance, and distribution of patient care statistics. Title 70 Revised Code of Washington § 70.41.190. The hospital must have written policies and procedures concerning the medical record system, including format, access to and release of data, and retention, preservation, and destruction.

That regulation requires hospitals to retain all medical records that relate directly to the care and treatment of a patient for not less than ten years following the patient's most recent discharge. Hospitals must keep minors' records not less than three years following the minors' attainment of age 18 or ten years following their discharge, whichever is longer. Washington's Administrative Code § 248–18–440 adds that hospitals must keep the following information for as long as indicated:

- Reports on referred outpatient diagnostic services for at least two years.
- Master patient index card (or equivalents) for at least the same period as the medical record or records to which it pertains.
- Data in inpatient and outpatient registers for at least three years.
- Data in emergency services registers for at least the same period as the medical record.
- Data in the operation register, the disease and operation indexes, the physicians' index, and annual reports on analyses of hospital services for at least three years.
- Hospitals may elect to preserve an emergency service register for only three years after the last entry if they include all outpatient emergency care patients in the master patient index.

Hospitals must maintain current registers, including inpatient registers, one or more outpatient registers, an emergency service register, and an operations register. Further, hospitals must prepare daily inpatient census reports on admissions to inpatient services, births, and discharges, including deaths and transfers to another healthcare facility, and regular monthly or more frequent reports on admissions to outpatient services and the number of emergency care patients. For patients to whom the hospital provides only referred outpatient diagnostic services, the hospital may maintain a simple record system providing for identification, filing, and retrieval of authenticated reports on all tests or examinations provided to patients who received referred outpatient diagnostic services. § 248–18–440.

Personnel records must include a record of tuberculin skin tests, reports of X-ray findings, or exemptions. § 248–18–070. Other hospital records required by this regulation include equipment maintenance and inspection records, § 248–18–150, laundry inspections, § 248–18–170, and records of planned menus (kept for one month), § 248–18–180.

West Virginia

West Virginia Regulations for Hospital Licensure, 64 CSR 12 Section 10.3.1 e., states that hospitals must preserve records in the original form or by microfilm or electronic data process without specifying a retention period, thus implying that retention must be permanent.

Legislative Rule 16–5c Section 7.5, governing nursing homes, requires nursing homes to keep on file an admission contract governing the relationship of the patient to the facility for five years from the date the relationship terminated. Nursing homes must also keep records listed in sections 7.9 and 7.10 in their administrative offices (such records may be photocopies):

Administrative Records (Class III): The facility shall maintain on file in its administrative office the following records:

- Documentation of the facility's professional and administrative staff meetings.
- Documentation of visits by professional consultants employed by the facility in accordance with the requirements of these regulations.
- Current copy of these regulations.
- Copy of the facility's current policy and procedure manual containing copies of all policies and procedures required by the provisions of these regulations.
- Reports of all inspections by government agencies together with summaries of corrective action taken in response to each report during the previous five years.
- Reports of any other inspections required by these regulations.
- Copies of contracts and agreements, including agreement for the provision of professional services by outside agencies or contractors, to which the facility is a party.
- Documents demonstrating control and ownership of the facility.
- Bylaws of the governing body, if applicable.
- Reports of accidents or incidents involving patients as required by Section 9.6.1 and Section 11.8 of these regulations.
- Records of all transactions conducted by the facility involving personal funds of patients in the facility during the previous five years (see Section 9.9 of these regulations).
- All menus prepared by the facility in accordance with the requirements of section 12.3 of these regulations.
- Records of food purchases made in compliance with section 12.3 of these regulations.
- Copy of the facility's emergency evacuation plan as required by Section 8.2 of these regulations.
- Chronological record of all patients admitted to the facility with an identifying number, date of admission, and, where appropriate, date of discharge.
- All other records required by state or federal laws and regulations, except those for which maintenance elsewhere is required.

Personnel Records (Class III): The facility shall maintain a confidential personnel record for each employee containing sufficient information to support the employee's assignment. The record shall contain at least the following information:

- Dated application for employment that includes a resume of the applicant's training and experience and verification by references.

- Employee health record containing the results of pre-employment and annual physical examination, including tuberculosis screening if indicated by exposure or prevalence.
- Evaluations of work performance signed by employee and supervisor.
- Subsequent change of status forms, including change of address, salary adjustments, merit increases, and promotions.

Wisconsin

Health and Social Services Regulations in the Wisconsin Administrative Code, HSS 124.14 (1), requires that hospitals have a medical record service with administrative responsibility for all medical records maintained by the hospital with either a registered medical records administrator or an accredited records technician in charge, except that, if such a person is not in charge, a consultant who is so qualified must organize the service, train the personnel, and make periodic visits to evaluate the records and the operation of the service. HSS 124.14 (2) (d) 2. a.

The regulations provide that hospitals shall have a written policy for the preservation of medical records, either in the original or on microfilm. Hospitals may determine the retention periods based on historical research, legal, teaching, and patient care needs, but hospitals must keep medical records for at least five years. HSS 124.14 (c).

§ 69.186 requires each hospital, clinic, or other facility that performs an induced abortion to report to the Department of Health information concerning patients.

Wyoming

Wyoming Statutes § 35–2–803 empowers the State Health Care Data Authority to require healthcare facilities to assist in the collection and submission of facility-specific information, such as the following information:

- Financial information, including costs of operation, revenues, assets, liabilities, fund balances, other income, rates, charges, units of service, and wage and salary data.
- Scope and volume of service information, including, but not limited to, inpatient services, outpatient services, and ancillary services by type of service provided.
- Utilization information.
- New services and programs proposed for the coming fiscal year.
- Patient abstract and charge data.
- Cost of malpractice insurance, malpractice claims, and associated legal and litigation costs.
- Any other information the authority may require.

§ 35–6–107 requires the reporting of abortions without disclosing the identity of the patient. The physician must send such reports to the administrator of the division of health and medical services within 20 days after performing the abortion.

According to the Wyoming Public Health Records Management Manual, hospitals are to maintain patient medical records for 30 years and then destroy them. Hospitals, however, are to permanently keep administrative and discharge records, diagnoses of operations, operative reports, pathology reports, and discharge summaries. Hospitals are to keep nursing histories and care plans for three years. Hospitals must keep nuclear medicine records and blood bank laboratory reports for five years. Facilities must keep emergency care records, donor records, and outpatient records for ten years. Incident reports have an eight-year retention schedule.

Part **II**

How Do You Keep Your Records?

Now that you know what records you must keep and for how long, you must make sure that you use the right media and store the records properly. You must also be careful that you don't harm their effectiveness by making improper corrections. Chapters 4, 5, and 6 will discuss these issues.

4

What Media Can You Use to Keep Your Records?

Media Generally

Some states, by statute or by administrative regulation, specify what media are permissible for healthcare or other records. Others do not. See appendix A for Health Care Financing Administration guidelines. Regardless of whether your state specifically authorizes the use of particular media, you must carefully consider whether a particular medium is permissible and whether that medium is admissible in evidence. Records that are not admissible in evidence do not help you very much. If a record shows that the care one of your staff physicians provided a patient who is suing for malpractice was proper, but the record is inadmissible, the record won't help you avoid liability.

The dynamic nature of today's information technology provides both an opportunity and a challenge with regard to healthcare record retention. New diagnostic equipment, new information storage equipment, and the need for better documentation of patient care to avoid malpractice losses together have revolutionized medical and other healthcare record retention. How do you retain this critical information considering the possibility of litigation that might require you to produce the record and the practical and financial aspects of maintaining the records?

In most states, when you record information, such as patient examination data, on a computer or other electronic device, its output, such as a hard-copy printout, becomes the original physical record of that examination and thereby becomes a part of the patient's medical records, subject to the same retention requirements.

If the output, such as the printout, is visually intelligible, you may retain it in that form in the regular course of your business. The situation is more complicated when the output is not visually intelligible, such as a magnetic tape. In such cases, any future use of the data, as in a court case, would require turning the data into a written or visually understandable form. Should you retain the unintelligible "original" or reproduce the output in an intelligible form and store it? The answer depends, in part, on your state law. Under federal and many state laws, you can reproduce data from an unintelligible form and use it as evidence. The law calls such evidence "duplicate originals." Federal Rules of Evidence § 1001(4). Again, you must create and store the data in conformance with your established procedures in the normal course of your business. Your personnel must, of course, properly operate the recording devices for such information to be admissible in court.

Microfilming is permissible in almost all states and with the U.S. Government. 28 United States Code § 1732. You must, however, be certain that your staff conducts microfilming during the regular course of business and "in good faith," that is, not only to records that are involved in an investigation or litigation. You should also ensure that you can produce a readable copy of the microfilmed records. Microfilm is most appropriate for bulky records of the same size that do not require frequent access.

Computer stored data is likewise generally admissible into evidence if the record was made at or within a reasonable period of time after the event or transaction it memorialized and in the regular course of business and if the procedure, including the printout, was reliable. Optical storage media have aspects of both microfilm and computer stored data. Optically stored data are hard to alter, as is microfilm, but like magnetic computer data, optically stored data cannot be read without being translated into visually readable form. Consequently, the evidentiary advantage microfilm has over computer generated data, its unalterability, should result in unalterable optical storage data's admissibility. State statutes or evidence codes that talk about "any other information storage device" or similar language should encompass optical storage systems. Federal Rule of Evidence Rule § 1001(4)'s definition of "duplicate" as including "other equivalent techniques which accurately reproduce the original" would seem to authorize the use of optical storage systems. Check with your attorney before adopting new record storage media.

Federal Laws

28 United States Code § 1732 governs business and public records. The statute provides that, if any business, institution, member of a profession or calling, or any department or agency of government, in the regular course of business keeps any memorandum, writing, entry, print, or representation of any act, transaction, occurrence, or event, and in the regular course of business records, copies, or reproduces the original by any photographic, photostatic, microfilm, Microcard, miniature photographic, or other process that accurately reproduces the original, the entity may destroy the original unless the law requires its preservation. Such reproduction is admissible in evidence to the same extent as the original was.

42 U.S.C. § 2112(a) provides that when a statute requires indefinite retention of a record, the retention of a photographic, microphotographic, or other reproduction suffices.

44 U.S.C. § 3312 provides that photographs or microphotographs made in compliance with regulations promulgated pursuant to § 3303 have the same effect as the originals and are originals for the purposes of admissibility in evidence.

The Public Health Service permits microfilming or other adequate copies of records required of grantees. See 45 C.F.R. § 74.20.

The Internal Revenue Service also permits the use of microfilm. Revenue Procedure 81–46 and Revenue Ruling 75–265.

The Food and Drug Administration, Compliance Policy Guide 7132a.05, the Occupational Safety and Health Administration, 29 C.F.R. § 1910.20, and the Veterans Administration also permit microfilming of records.

Federal law also provides that you may not reproduce, by microfilm or otherwise, certain documents, such as naturalization records (that is, certificates of citizenship), military identification cards, obligations or securities of the United States, currency, stamps, social security cards, copyrighted material without permission of the copyright holder, and licenses.

State Laws

Alabama

Alabama's rules of the State Board of Health Division of Licensure and Certification permit storage of patient records either as original records, abstracts, microfilm, or otherwise. 420–5.7.07 (c).

Alabama Code § 12–21–44(a) covers business records generally and permits photographing or microphotographing them on plate or film. Such copies are admissible in evidence.

Alaska

The medical record retention requirements of the Alaska Administrative Code mandate that "originals or accurate reproductions of the originals of records, including x-rays, must be retained in a form which is legible and readily available . . . ." 7 AAC 12.425 and 530.

Hospitals may copy business records by photostatic, microfilm, Microcard, miniature photographic, or other reproduction in the regular course of business. Alaska Rules of Civil Procedure, Rule 44(c).

Arizona

Arizona permits microfilming of records that may be used in court regardless of the existence of hard copy. Hospitals may copy business records by photostatic, microfilm, Microcard, miniature photographic, or other reproduction in the regular course of business. Arizona Statutes § 12–2262.

Arkansas

Hospitals must retain records in either original form or microfilm. They may keep required indexes on punch cards or printout sheets kept in books in hospitals using automatic data processing. Rule 1003 of the Arkansas Rules of Evidence states that a copy is admissible to the same extent as an original unless a genuine question exists as to the authenticity of the original. Rule 1001 (4) defines "duplicates" as counterparts of the original made by photography, including enlargements or miniatures, or by other equivalent techniques that accurately reproduce the original. Hospitals may reproduce business records by photograph, microfilm, or photostat. Arkansas Statute § 16–501–03.

California

California Evidence Code § 1550 permits use of microfilm. Title 22 § 70751 requires hospitals to keep medical records either as originals "or accurate reproductions," which would seem to authorize any media that reproduce records accurately and legibly.

Colorado

Hospitals may preserve records either as originals or on microfilm. 6 CCR 1011 § 4.2. Colorado Statutes §§ 13–26–101–104 permits photographic copies of business records.

Connecticut

Connecticut permits microfilming of medical records. § 19–13–D4b (6). Connecticut Statutes § 52–180 permits copying of business and public records by any photographic, photostatic, microfilm, Microcard, miniature photographic, or other process that accurately reproduces or forms a durable medium for reproducing the original.

Delaware

Under Delaware's Uniform Rules of Evidence, a "duplicate" is a counterpart produced by the same impression as the original, or from the same matrix, or by means of photography, including enlargements and miniatures, or by mechanical or electronic re-recording, or by chemical reproduction or by other equivalent techniques that accurately reproduce the original. Duplicates are admissible to the same extent as the original unless a genuine question arises as to the authenticity of the original or unless it would be unfair to admit the duplicate instead of the original. Rules 1101(4)–1003.

District of Columbia

The District of Columbia follows the federal rules above.

Florida

Florida permits microfilming of records. General Records Schedule E–T–1. The Florida Evidence Code specifies that duplicates are admissible to the same extent as the original unless the document is a negotiable instrument, unless a genuine question arises as to the authenticity of the original, or unless it would be unfair to admit the duplicate instead of the original. A "duplicate" is a counterpart produced by the same impression as the original, or from the same matrix, or by means of photography, including enlargements and miniatures, or by mechanical or electronic re-recording, or by chemical reproduction or by other equivalent techniques that accurately reproduce the original or an executed carbon copy not intended by the parties to be an original. Florida Statutes §§ 90.951 and .953.

Georgia

Georgia permits preservation of medical records as originals, microfilms, or other usable forms. Chapter 290–5–6, Rules of the Department of Human Resources, Public Health, 290–5–6–.11 (h).

As to business records generally, Georgia Code § 38–710 provides that a microfilm of a record made in the regular course of business is admissible in evidence.

Hawaii

Hawaii's evidence code, Title 33, § 622–58 (a), permits computerizing or minifying records by the use of microfilm or other similar photographic process, provided that the method used creates an unalterable record. Rule 1001 of Hawaii's Uniform Rules of Evidence adds that a "duplicate" is a counterpart produced by the same impression as the original, or from the same matrix, or by means of photography, including enlargements and miniatures, or by mechanical or electronic re-recording, or by chemical reproduction, or by other equivalent techniques that accurately reproduce the original.

Idaho

Hospitals may preserve records relating to the care and treatment of a patient in microfilm or other photographically reproduced form. Iowa Code § 39–1394 (a). The statute considers such copies as originals for evidentiary purposes. Idaho Code § 9–417 provides that, if any business, institution, member of a profession or calling, or any department or agency of government in the regular course of business keeps any memorandum, writing, entry, print, or representation of any act, transaction, occurrence, or event and in the regular course of business records, copies, or reproduces the original by any photographic, photostatic, microfilm, Microcard, miniature photographic, or other process that accurately reproduces the original, the entity may destroy the original unless the law requires its preservation. Such reproduction is admissible in evidence to the same extent as the original was.

Illinois

116 Illinois Statutes § 59 defines "reproduction" as a "reproduction or durable medium for making a reproduction obtained by any photographic, photostatic, microfilm, microcard, miniature photographic or other process that accurately reproduces or forms a durable medium for reproducing the original." If made in the

regular course of business, such reproductions are admissible in evidence. 110 A Statutes § 236.

Indiana

Indiana's Hospital Licensure Rules permit the use of microfilm or computerized records that maintain confidentiality. 410 IAC 15-1-8 (2), 410 IAC 15-1-9 (1) and (2) (b) (1). Indiana Code § 34-3-15-1 authorizes a business to reproduce its records by any "photographic, photostatic or miniature photographic process which correctly, accurately, and permanently copies . . . the original."

Iowa

Iowa Code § 622.30. 2. provides that, if any business, institution, member of a profession or calling, or any department or agency of government in the regular course of business keeps any memorandum, writing, entry, print, or representation of any act, transaction, occurrence, or event and in the regular course of business records, copies, or reproduces the original by any photographic, photostatic, microfilm, Microcard, miniature photographic, or other process that accurately reproduces the original, the entity may destroy the original unless the law requires its preservation. Such reproduction is admissible in evidence to the same extent as the original was.

Kansas

Hospitals may microfilm medical records after completion. Regulations 28-34-9a (d) (5). Kansas Statutes § 17-6514 states that a corporation may, in the regular course of business, microfilm or reproduce by any other information storage device if the reports can be converted into clearly legible form within a reasonable period. § 60-469 makes photographic copies made in the regular course of business admissible in evidence.

Kentucky

Hospitals may microfilm or otherwise photographically reproduce medical records in Kentucky. Kentucky Revised Statutes 422.105 provides that, if any business, institution, member of a profession or calling, or any department or agency of government in the regular course of business keeps any memorandum, writing, entry, print, or representation of any act, transaction, occurrence, or event and in the regular course of business records, copies, or reproduces the original by any photographic, photostatic, microfilm, Microcard, miniature photographic, or other process that accurately reproduces the original, the entity may destroy the original unless the law requires its preservation. Such reproduction is admissible in evidence to the same extent as the original was.

Louisiana

Hospitals may, in their discretion, microfilm or similarly reproduce any hospital record or part thereof in order to efficiently store and preserve it. Louisiana Statutes §§ 40.2151(E)–(G).

Louisiana Statutes § 13:3733 allows any business to microfilm records if it does so in the regular course of business.

Maine

Hospitals may preserve either in the original or by microfilm, Chapter XII, B. Regulations for the Licensure of General and Specialty Hospitals in the State of Maine. Title 16 Maine Statutes § 357 authorizes hospitals to make photographic or microphotographic copies. 16 Maine Statutes § 456 governs business records and provides that, if in the regular course of business a hospital keeps any memorandum, writing, entry, print, or representation of any act, transaction, occurrence, or event and in the regular course of business records, copies, or reproduces the original by any photographic, photostatic, microfilm, Microcard, miniature photographic, or other process that accurately reproduces the original, such reproduction is admissible in evidence to the same extent as the original was.

Maryland

The Maryland Code, in Article 15B, defines "reproduction" as a "reproduction or durable medium for making a reproduction obtained by any photographic, photostatic, microfilm, microcard, miniature photographic or other process which accurately reproduces or forms a durable medium for so reproducing the original." Such reproductions are admissible in evidence if made in the regular course of business. § 10–102.

Massachusetts

Massachusetts provides for photographic or microphotographic copies of medical records, 111 Massachusetts General Laws § 70. 233 Massachusetts General Laws § 79e specifies that, if any business, institution, member of a profession or calling, or any department or agency of government in the regular course of business keeps any memorandum, writing, entry, print, or representation of any act, transaction, occurrence, or event and in the regular course of business records, copies, or reproduces the original by any photographic, photostatic, microfilm, Microcard, miniature photographic, or other process that accurately reproduces the original, the entity may destroy the original unless the law requires its preservation. Such reproduction is admissible in evidence to the same extent as the original was.

Michigan

Hospitals may preserve medical records as originals, abstracts, microfilms, or otherwise. Department of Public Health Rule 325.1028 (5). Photographic or photostatic copies of business records made in the usual course of business are admissible under Michigan Laws §§ 600.2146–48.

Minnesota

Minnesota Statute 145.30 permits the transfer and recording of any or all of the original files and records of the hospital dealing with the case history, physical examination, and daily hospital records of individual patients, including any miscellaneous documents, upon photographic film of convenient size. § 145.31 permits use of photostatic copies of hospital files and records as evidence. Statute 600.135 provides similar authority for business records. Evidence Rule 1003 makes duplicates admissible to the same extent as originals.

Mississippi

§ 41-9-77, Mississippi Code, permits reproduction of any hospital record or part thereof on film or other material by microfilming, photographing, photostating, or other appropriate process. The law deems them originals for all purposes, including admission into evidence. Code § 13-1-151 permits businesses to reproduce their records by any photographic, photostatic, or miniature photographic process that correctly, accurately, and permanently reproduces the original on a film or other durable material.

Missouri

Missouri Statutes § 109.130 deems such photostatic copy, photograph, microphotograph, or photographic film of the original records to be an original for all purposes and to be admissible in evidence in all courts or administrative agencies.

Montana

Administrative Rules of Montana, Chapter 32, Rule 16.32.308 (3), permits microfilming if the healthcare facility has the equipment to reproduce records on the premises.

Montana Rules of Evidence provide that a duplicate—a counterpart of the original produced by means of photography, by mechanical or electric re-recording, or by other equivalent techniques that accurately reproduce the original—is admissible to the same extent as the original unless someone raises a genuine question as to the original's authenticity. Rule 1003.

Nebraska

Nebraska law provides that hospitals may preserve medical records in original, microfilm, or other approved copy. Statute § 27-1003 provides that a duplicate is admissible to the same extent as an original unless a genuine question exists as to the authenticity of the original or it would be unfair to admit the duplicate.

Nevada

Nevada healthcare providers may retain healthcare records on microfilm or any other recognized form of size reduction that does not adversely affect their use for inspections by the patients or the State Board of Medical Examiners. Statutes § 629.061.

Nevada defines a "duplicate" as a counterpart produced by a number of methods, including by photography, including enlargements and miniatures, or by mechanical or electronic re-recording, Statutes Ch. 52. § 195 makes a duplicate admissible to the same extent as an original unless a genuine question exists as to the authenticity of the original or it would be unfair to admit the duplicate. A duplicate is also admissible if the custodian was authorized to destroy the original after duplicating it and did so.

New Hampshire

He-P 802.11 (b) requires storage of all original hospital records or "photographs" of such records, presumably authorizing microfilm or other similar means of reproduction.

As to business records in general, Statutes §§ 337-A:1 to A:6 define "reproduction" as a "reproduction or durable medium for making a reproduction obtained by any photographic, photostatic, microfilm, microcard, miniature photographic or other process which accurately reproduces or forms a durable medium for so reproducing the original" and notes that keeping such reproductions complies with all state laws requiring preservation of business records. §§ 520:1 to :3 make records made in the regular course of business, including reproductions, admissible in evidence.

New Jersey

Hospitals shall preserve medical records either in the original or by microfilm. § 8.43B-7.1 (b) 3. Standards for Hospital Facilities. Statutes 2A:82-38 provide that, if any business, institution, member of a profession or calling, or any department or agency of government in the regular course of business keeps any memorandum, writing, entry, print, or representation of any act, transaction, occurrence, or event and in the regular course of business records, copies, or reproduces the original by any photographic, photostatic, microfilm, Microcard, miniature photographic, or other process that accurately reproduces the original, the entity may destroy the original unless the law requires its preservation. Such reproduction is admissible in evidence to the same extent as the original was.

New Mexico

Hospitals may microfilm or otherwise photographically reproduce medical records under New Mexico Statute 14-6-2. A. The New Mexico rules of evidence deem such reproductions originals for evidentiary purposes.

Rule 1001 of the New Mexico Rules of Evidence defines a duplicate as "a counterpart produced by the same impression as the original, or from the same matrix, or by means of photography, including enlargements or miniatures, or by mechanical or electronic re-recording, or by chemical reproduction, or by other equivalent technique which accurately reproduces the original." Rule 1003 makes a duplicate admissible to the same extent as an original unless a genuine question arises as to the authenticity of the original or it would be unfair to admit the duplicate into evidence.

New York

Hospitals are to maintain medical records in their original or "legally reproduced form." § 405.10 (3), Department of Health, Health Facilities Series H–40. If any business or professional records, copies, or reproduces a writing, entry, print, or representation by any process that accurately reproduces or forms a durable medium for reproducing the original, such reproduction is admissible in evidence. Civil Practice Rule 4518.

North Carolina

Hospitals shall preserve medical records or "photographs" of such records. T10: 03C .1405. For nursing homes, the regulations speak in terms of originals or "copies." § 10 NCAC 3H. 0607. North Carolina statutes allow corporations, § 55-37.1, and nonprofit organizations, § 55A–27.1, to reproduce records or keep them on any information storage device, provided that they can be converted to legible form within a reasonable time. Such duplicates are admissible in evidence. § 8–45.1 states that, if any business, member of a profession, and so forth, in the regular course of business kept or recorded a memorandum, writing, entry, print, or representation and recorded, copied, or reproduced it by any photographic, photostatic, microfilm, Microcard, miniature photographic, or other process that accurately reproduces or forms a durable medium for reproducing the original, the entity may destroy the original in the regular course of business unless it holds the record in a custodial or fiduciary capacity or unless the law requires its preservation. Such reproductions are admissible in evidence.

North Dakota

North Dakota specifies that hospitals may preserve their records either in originals or any other method of preservation, such as microfilm. Regulations 33–07–01–16. 3. As to business records, North Dakota provides that, if any business, member of a profession, and so forth, in the regular course of business kept or recorded a memorandum, writing, entry, print, or representation and recorded, copied, or reproduced it by any photographic, photostatic, microfilm, Microcard, miniature photographic, or other process that accurately reproduces or forms a durable medium for reproducing the original, the entity may destroy the original in the regular course of business unless the law requires its preservation. Such reproductions are admissible in evidence. Rules of Evidence Rule 1003.

Ohio

Ohio Code § 2317.41 specifies that a "photograph" includes a microphotograph, a roll or strip of film, a strip of microfilm, or a photostatic copy and, if made in the regular course of business, is admissible in evidence. Similarly, Rule 1001 of the Ohio Uniform Rules of Evidence defines a "duplicate" as a counterpart produced by the same impression as the original, or from the same matrix, or by means of photography, including enlargements and miniatures, or by mechanical or electronic re-recording or by chemical reproduction, or by other equivalent techniques that accurately reproduce the original. Under Rule 1003, a duplicate is admissible unless a genuine question arises as to the authenticity of the original or it would be unfair to admit the duplicate instead of the original.

Oklahoma

Under 67 Oklahoma Statutes § 251, "reproduction" means a reproduction or durable medium for making a reproduction obtained by any photographic, photostatic, microfilm, Microcard, miniature photographic or other process that accurately reproduces or forms a durable medium for so reproducing the original. § 253 adds that if in the regular course of business a person makes reproductions of original business records, the preservation of such reproductions constitutes compliance with any state law requiring keeping or preserving business records.

Oregon

Oregon permits photostatic, microphotographic, or photographic reproduction of records. The Oregon Evidence Code, § 40.560, provides that a duplicate is admissible in evidence to the same extent as an original unless a genuine question arises as to the authenticity of the original or, in the circumstances, it would be unfair to admit the original. § 41.930 adds that copies of hospital records are admissible to the same extent as the original would be.

Pennsylvania

Hospitals may store medical records as originals, as reproductions, or as microfilm. 28 Pennsylvania Statutes § 115.23. § 115.24 states that hospitals may microfilm medical records immediately after completion. If microfilming records off the premises, hospitals shall take precautions to ensure the confidentiality and safekeeping of the records. Hospitals shall not destroy the original of microfilmed medical records until the medical records department has had an opportunity to review the processed film for content. Further, § 115.26 authorizes the use of automation in the medical records service, provided that the process meets all statutory requirements and that the information is readily available for use in patient care. This statute expressly encourages innovations in medical record formats, compilation, and data retrieval.

42 Pennsylvania Statutes § 6109 provides that, if any business, member of a profession, and so forth in the regular course of business kept or recorded a memorandum, writing, entry, print, or representation and recorded, copied, or reproduced it by any photographic, photostatic, microfilm, Microcard, miniature photographic, or other process that accurately reproduces or forms a durable medium for reproducing the original, the entity may destroy the original in the regular course of business unless the law requires its preservation. Such reproductions are admissible in evidence.

Rhode Island

This state permits preservation of medical records either as originals or "accurate reproductions." R23–17–HOSP § 25.9. A print of a microfilm copy of an unavailable original record is admissible in evidence if made in the regular course of business. Laws § 9–19–14(A) § B authorizes the disposal of any record made in the regular course of business if the hospital has reproduced the original on microfilm and no other law prohibits its disposal.

South Carolina

Regulation No. 61–16, covering minimum standards for hospitals and institutional general infirmaries, states in Section 601.7 that facilities that microfilm before ten years have expired must film the entire record. As to records generally, Code § 19–5–610 states that, if any business, member of a profession, and so forth in the regular course of business kept or recorded a memorandum, writing, entry, print, or representation and recorded, copied, or reproduced it by any photographic, photostatic, microfilm, Microcard, miniature photographic, or other process that accurately reproduces or forms a durable medium for reproducing the original, the entity may destroy the original in the regular course of business unless it holds the record in a custodial or fiduciary capacity or unless the law requires its preservation. Such reproductions are admissible in evidence. § 39–1–40 authorizes photographic copies of business records.

South Dakota

South Dakota Rules of Evidence 19–18–1 (4) defines a "duplicate" as a "counterpart produced by the same impression as the original, or from the same matrix, or by means of photography, including enlargements and miniatures, or by mechanical or electronic re-recording, or by chemical reproduction, or by other equivalent techniques which accurately reproduce the original." Such duplicates are admissible unless a genuine question arises as to the authenticity of the original or it would be unfair to admit the duplicate instead of the original. § 19–18–3. § 19–7–12 provides that, if any business or member of a profession during the regular course of business reproduces a record by a photographic, photostatic, microfilm, Microcard, miniature photographic, or other process that accurately reproduces or forms a durable medium for reproducing the original, the entity may destroy the original in the regular course of business unless the entity holds the record in a custodial or fiduciary capacity or unless the law requires its preservation. Such reproduction is admissible in evidence.

Tennessee

Tennessee permits transfer upon photographic film of convenient size, such as microfilm, photograph, or photostat, for the purposes of medical research, professional education, or administrative convenience any or all of the original files and records of any such hospital dealing with case history, physical examination, and daily hospital records of the individual patients thereof, including any miscellaneous documents, papers, and correspondence. Tennessee Code § 53-1324.

For business records, § 24-7-111 provides that, if any business, member of a profession, and so forth, in the regular course of business kept or recorded a memorandum, writing, entry, print, or representation and recorded, copied, or reproduced it by any photographic, photostatic, microfilm, Microcard, miniature photographic, or other process that accurately reproduces or forms a durable medium for reproducing the original, the entity may destroy the original in the regular course of business unless the law requires its preservation. Such reproductions are admissible in evidence.

Texas

A hospital may microfilm for retention all medical records and any other records the hospital considers necessary to preserve. Standard 1-22.1.4.

Concerning business records, Texas Statutes Article 3731b(2) allows photographing, photostating, microfilming, or other process that accurately reproduces or forms a durable medium for reproducing the record and allows such reproductions in evidence.

Utah

Utah Code § 78-25-16 provides that, if any business or member of a profession during the regular course of business reproduces a record by a photographic, photostatic, microfilm, Microcard, miniature photographic, or other process that accurately reproduces or forms a durable medium for reproducing the original, the entity may destroy the original in the regular course of business unless the entity holds the record in a custodial or fiduciary capacity or unless the law requires its preservation. Such reproductions are admissible in evidence.

Vermont

12 Vermont Statutes § 1701 specifies that, if any business or member of a profession during the regular course of business reproduces a record by a photographic, photostatic, microfilm, Microcard, miniature photographic, or other process that accurately reproduces or forms a durable medium for reproducing the original, the entity may destroy the original in the regular course of business unless the entity holds the record in a custodial or fiduciary capacity or unless the law requires its preservation. Such reproductions are admissible in evidence.

Virginia

Virginia permits hospitals to preserve records as either originals or accurate reproductions, presumably allowing any media that result in an accurate copy. Rules and Regulations for the Licensure of Hospitals 208.8, for Nursing Homes, 24.5. Code § 8.01–413 makes microphotographic copies of hospital records admissible in evidence.

Concerning business records, § 8.01–391 defines copies to include photographs, microphotographs, photostats, microfilm, Microcard, printouts or other reproductions of electronically stored data, or any other reproduction of an original from a process that forms a durable medium for its recording, storing, and reproducing. Such copies made in the regular course of business are admissible in evidence.

Washington

Hospitals may file originals or "durable, legible, direct copies" of originals of reports in patients' individual medical records. Washington Department of Social and Health Services Hospital Rules and Regulations WAC 248–18–440. Hospitals may store computer entries on magnetic tapes, disks, or other devices suited to the storage of data.

Washington Code § 5.46.010 governs business records and specifies that, if any business or member of a profession during the regular course of business reproduces a record by a photographic, photostatic, microfilm, Microcard, miniature photographic, or other process that accurately reproduces or forms a durable medium for reproducing the original, the entity may destroy the original in the regular course of business unless the entity holds the record in a custodial or fiduciary capacity or unless the law requires its preservation. Such reproductions are admissible in evidence.

West Virginia

West Virginia's healthcare regulations provide for preservation in the original form or by microfilm or electronic data process. Part VI, Section C, Regulation 603.1(b) 2.

Code § 31A–4–35 specifies that, if any business or member of a profession during the regular course of business reproduces a record by a photographic, photostatic, microfilm, Microcard, miniature photographic, or other process that accurately reproduces or forms a durable medium for reproducing the original, the entity may destroy the original in the regular course of business unless the entity holds the record in a custodial or fiduciary capacity or unless the law requires its preservation. Such reproductions are admissible in evidence.

Wisconsin

Hospitals may retain medical records either as originals or in the form of microfiche. HSS 124.14 (2) (c).

As to records generally, Wisconsin's Rules of Evidence define a "duplicate" as a counterpart produced by the same impression as the original, from the same matrix, by means of photography, including enlargements and miniatures, by mechanical or electronic re-recording, by chemical reproduction, or by other equivalent technique that accurately reproduces the original. Rule 908.03. Rule 910.03 makes a duplicate admissible to the same extent as the original unless a genuine question arises as to the authenticity of the original or it would be unfair to admit the duplicate in lieu of the original.

Wyoming

"Public records" include the original and all copies of any paper, correspondence, form, book, photograph, photostat, film, microfilm, sound recording, map, drawing, or other document, regardless of physical form or characteristics, that the state, a political subdivision, or an agency of the state has made or received in transacting public business. Thus, apparently, healthcare facilities may use any of the above methods to preserve their records because such methods are acceptable to the state for public records.

5

How to Store Records

Storage Generally

Two major concerns should determine how you store your records: utility and security.

Storing records in such a manner that no one can use them is not very efficient. Many state laws and regulations provide, for example, that healthcare facilities must maintain their medical records in a manner providing easy retrievability. See Connecticut's State Department of Health Regulation § 19–13–D3 (d) (1). Similarly, Code of Maryland Regulations 10.07.02.20 G states that hospitals shall maintain adequate space and equipment, conveniently located, to provide for efficient processing of medical records (reviewing, indexing, filing, and prompt retrieval). Also, see appendix A for Health Care Financing Administration guidelines.

You must also consider the security of your records, especially your medical records. Obviously, the loss of information contained in vital financial, personnel, or medical records could have catastrophic consequences. You must protect against loss, damage, destruction, or unauthorized access or release. To do this effectively, you must consider personnel security, physical security, and system security. California and Colorado have very detailed storage specifications that you may want to look at to help you plan for security of your records.

Personnel Security

Probably the most effective way to ensure the security of your records is to make certain the people who work with your records safeguard them. First, a careful screening of employees who have access to critical or confidential records is a must. Once you are certain that you have responsible employees handling your records, you should promote security consciousness on the part of your staff by orienting new employees and refreshing old ones about the principles of records security and confidentiality. You should stress their responsibility for records in their possession and their duty not to disclose confidential information (see part IV). Your staff should sign an agreement verifying their understanding of your policies and procedures concerning records retention, security, and disclosure, that they will adhere to your policies and procedures, and that they understand that they face disciplinary action if they fail to. See the accompanying "Medical Records Oath of Confidentiality" used in California as an example. You should provide for periodic refreshers in records security to emphasize staff accountability for information security.

You should also require your staff to have to show identification, preferably photo identification badges, to gain access to your records. Computer security with appropriate access and passwords is also crucial. Of course, you must have a system to recover keys and badges and delete computer access codes when your personnel no longer work for you. Your staff is more likely to remember the rules on access to and disclosure of records if you clearly mark records with warnings about any special requirements.

**Medical Records
Oath of Confidentiality**

I, _____ do hereby swear and affirm that I will not discuss, reveal, copy or in any manner disclose the contents of the medical record of any patient who has received or is receiving health care services from _____ unless an appropriate and properly executed "Authorization for Release of Medical Information" form is received and it is determined that the records are to be released to a person with a legitimate interest.

I understand that medical records are confidential; that the information in a medical record is protected by both Federal and California state laws and regulations and that reading, discussing or otherwise utilizing the information within the record for other than legitimate health care purposes is grounds for immediate dismissal and possible legal action.

Sworn before me this _____ day of _____ 19_____
at _____, California.

_____
Signature of Administrator of Oath

_____
Signature of Employee

Physical Security

Physical security is probably easier to accomplish than personnel security is. Obviously, you will need to store your records in fireproof or fire-resistant storage facilities with a sprinkler system. In fact, many state regulations require that you store records in fireproof or fire-resistant facilities.

You should also consider whether you need to maintain a certain temperature and humidity to prevent the records from deteriorating. Generally, a temperature of about 70 degrees and humidity between 50 and 60 percent will be safe for most records. Finally, you need to consider how to limit access. You should store confidential and critical records in a secure area that you keep locked unless a records custodian is actually present. California has very specific requirements for off-site storage, discussed below, that you may wish to review to help you consider how to keep your records secure.

System Security

System security relates to both personnel and physical security. Having a security-conscious staff and good physical security will not prevent loss, damage, destruction, or unauthorized disclosure of records if you do not have a good system to control access to and disclosure of your records. You need to implement a requisition and charge-out system for critical records, especially medical records. Users should requisition records. Requisitions help records custodians ensure that the requester has authorization for access to the record and that the request is a proper one. Your requisition procedure should require countersignatures by supervisors of individuals, such as student nurses, who would not normally have access.

Once records custodians have proper requisitions, they should require requesters to sign out the records, either on the requisition documents or on separate forms. Custodians must maintain the sign-out forms, which should contain the name of the requester, an identification of the record, the date, and the location of the file. Your policy should require requesters who have signed out records to notify their custodians of any changes in the records' location, as by use of a records transfer form.

You should also consider the security aspects of transferring records and reproducing them. Loose reproduction procedures may, for example, lead to unauthorized disclosure of confidential information.

Your procedures should also cover how your staff ensures that the release of records to other parties, such as patients, is proper. Comparing signatures on patient requests to the signatures on admission documents, for example, ensures that the patients themselves are making the requests, not someone else. Your staff must check the credentials or authorization of others who request records or information and specify any restrictions, such as nondisclosure to any other party, on the use of the record. You can require any third party who receives a record to sign a nondisclosure agreement.

Finally, proper destruction of records (see chapter 16) is the final step in ensuring confidentiality.

State Laws

Alabama

Alabama's regulations require you to make provision for the safe storage of records. "This shall mean that records are handled in such manner as to assure safety from water or fire damage and are safeguarded from unauthorized use." 420–5–7.07 (b), Rules of Alabama State Board of Health Division of Licensure and Certification.

Alaska

Alaskan Health and Social Services Regulations provide that a facility must maintain procedures to protect the information in medical records from loss, defacement, tampering, or access by unauthorized persons. 7 AAC 12.425(c), 7 AAC 12.770(d).

Arizona

Arizona regulations note that a hospital may store records it does not currently need in a responsible warehouse that protects the confidentiality and safety of the records.

Arkansas

Arkansas requires that hospitals keep patient records in a room or area that is as fire-resistant as possible.

California

California requires hospitals to store records in an easily accessible manner in the hospital or an approved medical record storage facility off the hospital premises. Title 22 California Administrative Code § 70751 (f). The hospital must safeguard records against loss, defacement, tampering, or use by unauthorized persons. § 70751 (b).

California has the following guidelines for off-site storage of medical records:

- Physical plant:
    - Concrete block structure with loading dock and adequate parking for vehicle maneuvering.
    - Record storage center should be the sole occupant.
    - Open-faced shelving with vertically adjusted shelves: Maximum height should be 147 inches with seismic bracing to meet uniform building codes. Bracing should be adequate to meet a static load of 3,325 pounds and to withstand an impact load of 40 pounds from a height of 18 inches.
- Protection from fire, flood, intrusion:
    - Sprinkler system with at least 18 inches beneath the sprinkler head and the top of the files.
    - Fire/smoke alarm systems.
    - Four-hour fire walls with all openings protected by Class "A" firedoors.
    - Disaster plan for flood or water damage from sprinklered rooms.
    - Protection from material carried in overhead pipes.
- Ambient environment:
    - Temperature maintained between 65 and 75 degrees Fahrenheit.
    - Relative humidity between 50 and 55 percent.

- Ventilation system of fresh forced air.
- Fluorescent lights filtered to remove ultraviolet radiation. Protect records against exposure to direct sunlight.
- Minimum standards for illumination are three feet above the storage area, at least 25 foot-candles of illumination. For office space, at least 50 foot-candles.
- Policies and procedures:
  - Retrieval:
    —Records are accessible 24 hours a day, seven days a week.
    —Turnaround time for Stat patient use: 0–1 year—20 minutes; 1–5 years—40 minutes; 5–7 years—60 minutes; 7 plus years—2 hours.
    —Turnaround time for administrative/subpoena use: 0–7 years—24 hours; 7 plus years—3 days.
  - Confidentiality:
    —In-service training of personnel.
    —Document individual employee orientation to facility policies and procedures.
  - Retention:
    —Describe the age of files in storage.
    —Identify destruction dates.
    —Identify records destroyed, including name of patient, date of last treatment, date of birth, and date of destruction.
    —Destroy by shredding or burning or in a commercial land fill. If personnel other than facility employees with training in confidentiality destroy the records, have a supervisor with such training observe. Obtain a certificate of destruction from a commercial firm.
- Access and transport:
  - Specify in policy functional titles of persons authorized to request records.
  - Specify in policy functional titles of persons authorized access to the storage facility.
  - Describe procedures for retrieval and transport, such as in sealed envelopes hand-delivered to authorized users.
- Inventory control and indexing:
  - Policies describe use of a master patient index.
  - File organization specified.
  - Method to audit records in storage to determine current location and user with procedures to locate misfiles.
- Physical environment:
  - Service aisles allow for passage of loading carts or vehicles. Files terminate at least 18 inches from a wall with no deadend aisles.
  - Adequate work space for employees in the storage area.

Colorado

Colorado has one of the more detailed requirements for medical record rooms. Generally, each hospital shall have an adequate medical record room or other suitable facility with adequate supplies and equipment and should store records to provide protection from loss, damage, and unauthorized use. 6 CCR 1011-1 § 4.1.

Under § 4.1.1, new hospitals or those modifying an existing hospital facility shall have a medical record department and other medical record facilities with supplies and equipment for medical record functions and services, including the following elements:

- Active record storage area.
- Record review and dictating room for physicians.
- Work area for sorting, recording, typing, filing, and other assigned medical record functions shall be separate from the record review and dictating room. Consider isolating noisy equipment. Provide accommodations for conducting medical record business with hospital paramedical personnel or public individuals for legitimate access to medical records.
- Medical record storage area within the department.
- Inactive medical record storage area (may omit if facility uses microfilming).

The medical record department shall be located in an area of the hospital that is convenient to most of the professional staff. § 4.1.2. Facilities shall maintain security measures by mechanical means in the absence of medical record supervision to preserve confidentiality and to provide protection from loss, damage, and unauthorized use of the medical records.

Note that Colorado Criminal Code § 18-4-412 makes it a class 5 felony for anyone, without proper authorization, to obtain, to steal or disclose, or to copy a medical record.

Connecticut

The State Department of Health Regulations merely say to store medical records in a manner providing easy retrievability. Medical record departments must have adequate space and equipment. § 19-13-D3 (d) (1) and (6).

Florida

Florida simply says that hospitals shall provide space for active and inactive record storage and clerical staff. 10D-28.81 (8).

Illinois

Hospitals shall maintain suitable record facilities with adequate supplies and equipment and provide for safe storage of medical records. Safe storage means to assure safety from water seepage or fire damage and to safeguard the records from unauthorized use. § 250.1510 (a).

Indiana

The hospital must keep medical records on the nursing unit during the patient's hospitalization but may store inactive records in a fire-resistive structure, preferably fire-resistive cabinets or shelves, in such a way as to maintain confidentiality. 410 IAC 15-1-9(2) (a) and (c).

Kansas

The medical records department shall be properly equipped to enable its personnel to function in an effective manner and to maintain medical records in such a manner that the records are readily accessible and secure from unauthorized use. Regulations 28-34-9a (c).

Kentucky

The hospital is responsible for safeguarding the record and its information against loss, defacement, and tampering and particularly against damage by fire or water. 902 KAR 20:016 Section 3 (11) 3.

Maryland

Code of Maryland Regulations 10.07.02.20 G states that hospitals shall maintain adequate space and equipment, conveniently located, to provide for efficient processing of medical records (reviewing, indexing, filing, and prompt retrieval). H states that hospitals shall file closed or inactive records in a safe place that provides for confidentiality and, when necessary, retrieval.

Michigan

Michigan's rules only provide that hospitals may preserve medical records as originals, abstracts, microfilms, or otherwise so as to afford a basis for a complete audit of professional information without specifying the means of storing them. Department of Public Health Rule 325.1028 (5).

Minnesota

Minnesota's Hospital Licensing and Operation regulations, § 4640.1000, Subpart 2., requires hospitals to provide space and equipment for recording and completion of the record by the physician and for indexing, filing, and safe storage of medical records.

Mississippi

Mississippi Regulations § 41-9-63 simply states that all hospitals must prepare and maintain hospital records in accordance with the minimum standards adopted by the licensing agency.

Missouri

Hospitals must store records in such a manner as to safeguard them from loss, defacement, and tampering and to prevent damage from fire and water. Hospitals must keep medical records in the permanent file in the original or on microfilm (13 CSR 50–20 (D) 16) and maintain them so as to facilitate rapid retrieval and use by authorized personnel.

Montana

Administrative Rule 16.32.308(1) of Chapter 32 requires healthcare facilities to maintain medical records by storing them in a safe manner and in a safe location. Chapter 23–4.1B of the Montana Hospital Association Manual amplifies this guidance by suggesting that storage be in a responsible warehouse that protects the security and safety of the records.

New Hampshire

As to hospitals, this state only specifies that "provision shall be made for storage of all records required by these regulations." He-P 802.11(b). Its rules for other facilities are a little more specific. Sheltered care facilities must store resident records in a fireproof cabinet. He-P 804.04 (b). In addition to the fireproof cabinet, He-P 805.05 requires sheltered care facilities with nursing units to protect records against loss, destruction, or unauthorized use, as does He-P 806.10 for outpatient clinics. Finally, He–P 809.07 requires home healthcare providers to safeguard records against loss or unauthorized use.

New Jersey

Hospitals' medical record departments must be conveniently located and adequate in size and equipment to enable physicians to properly complete medical records. The filing equipment and storage space must be adequate to accommodate all records and to facilitate retrieval. The facility shall keep records confidential and inaccessible to unauthorized persons. § 8:43B–7.1. Hospitals must safeguard cardiac diagnostic or surgical medical records against loss, destruction, or unauthorized use. § 8:43B–17.10 (c).

New York

The New York Department of Health requires, in § 405.10 (a) (1) of Memorandum H–40, only that hospitals properly file and retain records and make them accessible and ensure the confidentiality of medical records.

North Carolina

North Carolina Administrative Code T10:03C.1403(e) places the responsibility on the hospital to safeguard the information in medical records against loss, tampering, or use by an unauthorized person. 1401 adds that the medical records department shall be conveniently located and adequate in size and equipment, that the hospital must provide for safe storage of all medical records, and that, if they are stored in a separate building, it shall be of fire-resistive construction.

For nursing homes, § 10 NCAC 3H .0606 requires locating medical record work space to assure that records are protected from unauthorized disclosure. The facility must store records in a protected or supervised environment.

Oregon

Oregon Administrative Rules 333-70-055 (10) states that hospitals must protect medical records against unauthorized access, fire, water, and theft.

Pennsylvania

Facilities must store medical records in such a manner as to provide protection from loss, damage, and unauthorized access. 28 Pennsylvania Statutes § 115.22.

Rhode Island

Rhode Island's Rules and Regulations for the Licensing of Hospitals, R23-17-HOSP, § 25.8, requires hospitals to make provisions for the safe storage of medical records in accordance with the standards in "Protection of Records," of the National Fire Protection Association.

South Carolina

Regulation No. 61-16, governing hospitals and institutional general infirmaries, requires that the institution make provision for storing medical records in an environment that will prevent unauthorized access and deterioration. Section 601.7.A. Intermediate care facilities must keep records in a safe storage area, Section 504.1, Regulation No. 61-14, as must nursing care facilities, Section 704.1, Regulation No. 61-17.

South Dakota

The medical records units of hospitals and nursing homes must include the following areas: active record storage area; record review and dictating area; work area for sorting, recording, or microfilming; and inactive record storage area, which the facility may omit if it uses microfilming. 44:04:14:14. Supervised personal care facilities must have written policies to safeguard the residents' records against destruction, loss, and unauthorized use.

Texas

Standard 7-21 of the Hospital Licensing Standards states that the medical records unit shall have the following elements: medical records administrator/technician office or space; review and dictating room(s) or spaces; work area for sorting, recording, or microfilming records; and storage area for records. Its standard for special care facilities requires that such facilities store records in a lockable area during nonuse and after the resident's discharge.

Utah

Utah requires that facilities have sufficient space and equipment to enable medical records personnel to function effectively and make provision for filing, safe storage, and easy accessibility of medical records. Facilities must safeguard the records and their contents against loss, defacement, tampering, fires, floods, and unauthorized access. Health Facility Licensure Rules 7.402.

Vermont

The only reference to record storage standards for Vermont hospitals requires that storage facilities for X-ray films shall be in accordance with the requirements of the National Board of Fire Underwriters and the state fire marshal. Hospital Licensing Procedure 3–964 (c) (6).

Vermont's Residential Care Home Licensing Regulations for Level III and Level IV Facilities require such facilities to store records in an orderly manner so that they are readily available for reference. Regulation 9. c. The regulations for nursing homes have a similar provision, adding that nursing homes shall provide separate file folders for each resident, employee, and administrative report. 3–29.

Virginia

Hospitals shall provide for safe storage of medical records or accurate and legible reproductions in accordance with "Protection of Records," of the National Fire Protection Association. Rules 208.7.

Washington

Hospitals must store medical records and other patient personal and medical data so that they are not accessible to unauthorized persons, are protected from undue deterioration or destruction, and are easily retrievable. Title 248 Washington Administrative Code 248–18–440.

Wisconsin

Wisconsin's rules only specify that filing equipment and space must be adequate to maintain the records and facilitate retrieval. If records must leave the hospital, as under subpoena, the hospital must take measures to protect the records from loss, defacement, tampering, and unauthorized access. HSS 124.14 (2)) (b) 2.

6

Correcting Records

What Do You Do If a Record Is Inaccurate?

What do you do if you find out that a record is inaccurate? Certainly you can and should correct an inaccurate record. But you must be careful to make the change properly—by noting the change in the record in the proper chronological order and by noting that it is an addition or a correction.

You should not alter the original record in any way, such as by trying to erase, remove, or change the information contained therein. You must leave the original record in its original condition. Why? If it appears that you have tampered with a record, such as a medical record, the tampering can result in losing a malpractice case, even when the medical care was proper, because of the loss of credibility inherent in such an improper alteration. Modern technology can easily detect tampering. Further, if a judge or jury members believe that the defendant tried to tamper with the evidence, they may increase the damages in addition to imposing other penalties, such as an indictment for forgery or obstruction of justice.

Altering a medical record to avoid liability for malpractice is especially foolhardy because not all errors in treatment amount to the negligence that results in malpractice liability. And you may void your malpractice liability insurance if you alter any pertinent records.

What you should do if you find it necessary to correct a record is to leave the original record intact. Draw a line through the incorrect matter, being careful to ensure that it is still legible. Make a notation in the margin indicating that the entry was erroneous and enter the correction in the record in the proper order at the time noted.

Only a few states have specific statutory or regulatory rules concerning altering medical records. Some laws, such as Florida's, make it a crime to alter, deface, or falsify a medical record; some, such as New Mexico's, specify how to correct an erroneous record; and some, like Maryland's, specify procedures for patients who want their records corrected.

Federal Laws

The Privacy Act, 5 U.S.C. § 552, gives people access to records the federal government maintains on them or any information pertaining to them that the system maintains and gives them the opportunity to request that the government amend their records to correct any errors. The statute also provides people a procedure, including a possible lawsuit, to contest a government agency's refusal to amend their records.

State Laws

Florida

Statute § 395.0165 provides that any person who fraudulently alters, defaces, or falsifies a medical record or causes or procures these offenses is guilty of a second degree misdemeanor.

Georgia

In Georgia, any person who, with intent to conceal any material fact relating to a potential claim or cause of action (facts upon which the plaintiff may base a lawsuit), knowingly and willfully destroys, alters, or falsifies any record shall be guilty of a misdemeanor. Georgia Code § 16–10–94.1 (b).

Indiana

A person who intentionally destroys or falsifies records of health facilities is guilty of a class D felony. Indiana Code § 16–10–4–23.

Kentucky

Kentucky Administrative Regulations, 902 KAR 20:016, Section 3 (11) 3, places the responsibility on the hospital to safeguard records and their contents from tampering.

Maryland

Maryland Code § 4–303 makes it a misdemeanor for a healthcare provider to knowingly or willfully destroy, damage, alter, obliterate, or otherwise obscure a medical record, hospital report, X-ray report, or other information about a patient in an effort to conceal the information from use as evidence in an administrative, civil, or criminal proceeding.

Maryland Code § 4–302 (c) establishes a procedure by which a person in interest may request an addition to or other correction of a medical record. If the facility does not make the requested change, it must give the person in interest written notice of the refusal, specify the reason therefor, explain the procedure for review of the refusal, and permit the person in interest to insert a concise statement of disagreement in the record. The facility must provide a notice of a change or the statement of disagreement to every person to whom they previously disclosed inaccurate, incomplete, or disputed information and whom the person in interest designates to receive such notice.

New Mexico

The New Mexico Hospital Association Legal Handbook suggests you make corrections carefully so as to preserve the original. Do not obliterate, erase, or destroy errors. Instead, draw a line through a mistake and make a correction clearly. Chapter 5A.1 c and d, New Mexico Hospital Association Legal Handbook.

New York

§ 405.10 (a) (6) of the Department of Health, Health Facilities Series H-40, notes that hospitals shall allow patients and other qualified persons to obtain access to their medical records and to add brief written statements that challenge the accuracy of the medical record documentation to become a permanent part of the medical record.

Oklahoma

Oklahoma Statutes § 165.080 makes criminal falsifying with the intent to defraud business records by making false entries or altering, erasing, obliterating, deleting, removing, or destroying a true entry.

Wisconsin

The Wisconsin Administrative Code HSS 92 (4) provides rules for modifying treatment records of patients treated for mental illness, developmental disabilities, or alcoholism or drug abuse other than by private practitioners. Modification before the patient's inspection is to be as minimal as possible. Upon granting a request to correct a record, the facility shall correct immediately. Challenged information that is completely false, irrelevant, or untimely shall be marked through and specified as incorrect. If investigation casts doubt on the information, but a clear determination cannot be made, the investigator's doubts and both the challenge and expression of doubt shall become part of a record. If the request is denied, the denial will include notice to the patient that the patient has a right to insert a statement in the record challenging the accuracy or completeness of the challenged information in the record. Statements that give a diagnosis are judgments based on professional expertise and are not open to challenge.

Part **III**

When Can You Disclose Information?

When must you disclose information? The simple answer is this: when the government requires you to. Such an answer is overly simplistic, however. For example, you should not release a confidential record solely on the basis of a request by a law enforcement officer. Rather, you should require the officer to subpoena the record unless the law requires disclosure, such as in the case of child abuse.

The Fifth Amendment privilege against compulsory self-incrimination does not protect records that the government requires you to keep. Official records are the property of the government, and consequently, you have to produce them upon demand. Similarly, even private records that the government requires you to keep are not within the scope of the Fifth Amendment privilege, so you must produce them on demand. Thus, if a law or regulation requires you to keep a record, it becomes a "public" record, and you may not rely upon the privilege against self-incrimination to keep from disclosing it.

Thus, state and federal law may require you to disclose information concerning child, adult, or patient abuse (see chapter 7), drug abuse (see chapter 8), communicable diseases (see chapter 9), during inspections and for credentialing (see chapter 10), and pursuant to a court order or subpoena (see chapter 11). You may also disclose information for research purposes (see chapter 12) or upon request (see chapter 13).

7

Reporting Child and Other Forms of Abuse

Reporting Generally

Most states require healthcare providers to report cases of child abuse, whether actual or suspected, and protect personnel who make such reports from liability for improper disclosure of confidential information so long as they made the report in good faith. Failure to so report may subject the healthcare provider to a criminal penalty and/or liability for any further injuries the child suffers.

State Laws

Alabama

§ 26-14-3(a) of the Alabama code provides that all hospitals, clinics, sanitariums, doctors, physicians, surgeons, medical examiners, coroners, dentists, osteopaths, mental health professionals, or any other person called upon to provide aid or medical assistance to any child, when such child is known or suspected to be a victim of child abuse or neglect, must report or cause a report to be made of the same, orally, either by telephone or direct communication immediately, followed by a written report, to a duly constituted authority.

Alaska

§§ 47.17.010 through .070, Alaska Statute, require practitioners of the healing arts and others who, in the performance of their professional duties, have cause to believe that a child has suffered harm as a result of abuse or neglect to immediately report the harm to the nearest office of the department. Anyone who makes such a report in good faith is immune from any criminal or civil liability for so doing. The physician-patient privilege does not apply to child abuse cases. Anyone who fails to file a report is guilty of a misdemeanor.

Arizona

§ 13–3613 (A) of the Arizona Criminal Code states that any physician, hospital intern or resident, surgeon, dentist, osteopath, psychologist, or any other person having responsibility for the care or treatment of children whose observation or examination of any minor discloses reasonable grounds to believe that a minor is or has been the victim of injury, sexual molestation, death, abuse, or physical neglect that appears to be inflicted upon such minor by other than accidental means or that is not explained by the available medical history as being accidental in nature or who has reasonable grounds to believe there has been a denial or deprivation of necessary medical treatment or surgical care or nourishment with the intent to cause or allow the death of an infant protected under § 36–2281 shall immediately report or cause reports to be made of such information to a peace officer or to the protective services of the department of economic security. People must make reports immediately by telephone or in person and must follow up by a written report within 72 hours, which must contain the following information:

- Names and addresses of the minor and the minor's parents or person having custody of such minor, if known.
- Minor's age and nature and extent of the minor's injuries or physical neglect, including any evidence of previous injuries or physical neglect.
- Any other information that such person believes might be helpful in establishing the cause of the injury or physical neglect.

A person having custody or control of medical records of a minor for whom a report is required or authorized under this section shall make such records or a copy of such records available to a peace officer or child protective services worker investigating the minor's neglect or abuse on written request for the records signed by the peace officer or child protective services worker. Records disclosed pursuant to this subsection are confidential and may be used only in judicial or administrative proceeding or investigation resulting from a report required or authorized under this section.

A person furnishing a report, information, or records required or authorized under this section or a person participating in a judicial or administrative proceeding or investigation resulting from a report, information, or record required under this section shall be immune from any civil or criminal liability by reason of such action unless such person acted with malice or unless such person has been charged with or is suspected of abusing or neglecting the child or children in question. The physician-patient privilege or any privilege except the attorney-client privilege provided for by professions shall not pertain in any civil or criminal litigation or administrative proceeding in which a child's neglect, dependency, abuse, or abandonment is an issue or in any judicial or administrative proceeding resulting from a report, information, or records submitted pursuant to this section or in any investigation of a child's abuse or neglect.

Arkansas

When any physician or other healthcare practitioner engaged in admission, examination, care, or treatment has reasonable cause to suspect that a child has been subjected to abuse, sexual abuse, or neglect or observes the child being subjected to conditions that would reasonably result in such abuse, the practitioner shall immediately report to the Department of Human Services. The individual may report to the person in charge of the medical institution, who is then responsible for making the report. Statutes § 12-12-504. Those persons must also report deaths from such abuse. § 12-12-505. Reports must be made immediately by telephone, followed by a written report in 48 hours if requested by the receiving agency. § 12-12-507. Anyone making such a report in good faith is immune from any liability, but failure to report subjects the offender to a fine of $100 and up to five days in jail and to civil liability for damages caused by such failure. § 12-12-503. Knowingly making a false report is also punishable by the same criminal penalties. The physician-patient privilege does not apply to such abuse cases. § 12-12-511.

California

California Penal Code § 1543 requires mandatory release of medical information if there is reason to believe that a crime was committed by or to the patient. In addition, you may release the identity, diagnosis, prognosis, or treatment of any patient if you have the patient's prior written consent or a court order (not a subpoena) or pursuant to a search warrant. You may release the patient's name, address, age, and sex, a general description of the reason for treatment, and the patient's general description without the patient's consent unless the patient has expressly specified that you not release such information.

California Penal Code § 1543 requires mandatory release of medical information if there is reason to believe that a crime was committed by or to the patient, presumably including child abuse. In addition, Title 1, Control of Crimes and Criminals § 11161.8, requires every person, firm, or corporation conducting any hospital in the state, or its managing agent or any person in charge of any ward or part of such hospital, who receives a patient transferred from a health facility or from a community care facility, who exhibits a physical injury or condition that, in the opinion of the attending physician, reasonably appears to be the result of neglect or abuse, to report such fact by telephone and in writing, within 36 hours, to both the local police authority having jurisdiction and the county health department. Any registered nurse, licensed vocational nurse, or licensed clinical social worker employed at such hospital may also make a report under this section if, in the opinion of such person, a patient exhibits a physical injury or condition that reasonably appears to be the result of neglect or abuse. Physicians and surgeons must make such reports. No employee may be discharged, suspended, disciplined, or harassed for making such a report, nor does such an employee incur any civil or criminal liability for making such a report.

Colorado

Colorado's Child Abuse and Neglect statute is in article § 19–10–104, which provides, in (1), that any person specified in subsection (2) of this section who has reasonable cause to know or suspect that a child has been subjected to abuse or neglect or has observed the child being subjected to circumstances or conditions that would reasonably result in abuse or neglect shall immediately report or cause a report to be made of such fact to the county department or local law enforcement agency.

§ 19–10–104(2) requires, among others, physicians or surgeons (including physicians in training), dentists, osteopaths, registered nurses, hospital personnel engaged in the admission, care, or treatment of patients, and mental health professionals to report such abuse or neglect or the circumstances or conditions that might reasonably result in abuse or neglect. In addition to persons specifically required by this section to report, any other person may make such a report.

§ 19–10–104(4)(a) and (b) provides that any person who willfully violates subsection (1) of this section commits a misdemeanor and shall also be liable for damages proximately caused thereby.

§19–10–108(1)-(4) explain who, when, what, and how to report. Reports of known or suspected child abuse or neglect shall be made immediately to the county department, which will forward the report to the district attorney's office and to the local law enforcement agency, or directly to the local law enforcement agency, and shall be followed by a written report prepared by those persons required to report. Such reports, when possible, shall include the following information:

- Name, address, sex, age, and race of the child.
- Name and address of the responsible person.
- Nature and extent of the child's injuries, including any evidence of previous known or suspected abuse to the child or to the child's siblings.
- Names and addresses of the persons responsible for the suspected abuse or neglect, if known.
- Family composition.
- Source of the report and name, address, and occupation of the person making the report.
- Any action taken by the reporting source.
- Any other information that the person making the report believes may be helpful in furthering the purposes of this article.

A written report from persons or officials required to report known or suspected child abuse or neglect shall be admissible as evidence in any proceeding subject to the limitations of § 19–10–115 (confidentiality).

§ 19–10–110 provides immunity from liability, both civil and criminal, for the above specified persons. For the purpose of any proceedings, civil or criminal, the good faith of any such person reporting child abuse, any such person taking photographs or X rays, and any person who has legal authority to place a child in protective custody shall be presumed.

§19-10-115(1) provides for confidentiality. Except as provided in this section, reports of child abuse or neglect and the name and address of any child, family, or informant or any other identifying information contained in such reports shall be confidential and shall not be public information. Disclosure of the name and address of the child and family and other identifying information shall be permitted only when authorized by a court for good cause. Such disclosure shall not be prohibited when there is a death of a suspected victim of child abuse or neglect and the death becomes a matter of public record, the subject of an arrest by a law enforcement agency, and the subject of the filing of a formal charge by a law enforcement agency. Any person who violates any provision of subsection (1) is guilty of a class 2 petty offense and, upon conviction, shall be punished by fine of not more than $300.

Connecticut

Physicians, surgeons, nurses, medical examiners, dentists, psychologists, osteopaths, optometrists, chiropractors, podiatrists, mental health professionals, and others who have reasonable cause to suspect or believe that a child under the age of 18 has had physical injury or injuries inflicted upon him by other than accidental means or injuries that are at variance with the history given of them or is in a condition that is the result of maltreatment, such as malnutrition, sexual molestation, deprivation of necessities, or cruel punishment, or is in danger of being abused must report immediately by telephone or otherwise to the state welfare commissioner or the local police department and follow up with a written report within 72 hours. Any one making such a report in good faith is exempt from any civil or criminal liability as a result. Failure to make such a report, however, is punishable by a fine of not more than $500. Title 17 Connecticut Statutes § 17-38.

Delaware

Title 16 § 903 of the Delaware code provides that any physician and any other person in the healing arts, including any person licensed to provide services in medicine, osteopathy, or dentistry, any intern, resident, nurse, school employee, social worker, psychologist, and medical examiner, or any other person who knows or reasonably suspects child abuse or neglect shall make a report in accordance with § 904 of this title.

§ 904 specifies that any report required to be made under this chapter shall be made to the division of Child Protective Services of the Department of Services for Children, Youth and Their Families. An immediate oral report shall be made by telephone or otherwise. Reports and the contents thereof, including a written report, if requested, shall be made in accordance with the rules and regulations adopted by the Division.

According to § 906, anyone participating in good faith in the making of a report pursuant to this chapter shall have immunity from any liability, civil or criminal, that might otherwise exist, and such immunity shall extend to participation in any judicial proceeding resulting from such report.

§ 908 provides that the physician-patient privilege, husband-wife privilege, or any privilege except the attorney-client privilege provided for by the professions, such as social work or nursing, covered by law or a code of ethics regarding practitioner-client confidences, both as they relate to the competency of the witness and to the exclusion of evidence, shall not pertain in any civil or criminal litigation in which a person's neglect, abuse, dependency, exploitation, or abandonment is in issue nor in any judicial proceeding resulting from a report submitted pursuant to this chapter.

Florida

§ 415.503 of Title 30 specifies that any person, including, but not limited to, any physician, osteopath, medical examiner, chiropractor, nurse, or hospital personnel engaged in the admission, examination, or treatment of persons, or any other health or mental professional, who knows or has reasonable cause to suspect that a child is an abused or neglected child shall report such knowledge or suspicion to the department. Each report of known or suspected child abuse or neglect pursuant to this section shall be made immediately to the department's central abuse registry and tracking system on a statewide toll-free number. Each report shall be confirmed in writing to the local office of the department designated by the central abuse registry and tracking system within 48 hours of the initial report. Reports involving known or suspected institutional abuse or neglect shall be made and received in the same manner as all other reports made pursuant to this section. Any person required to make a report or investigate cases of suspected child abuse or neglect who has reasonable cause to suspect that a child died as a result of child abuse or neglect shall report that suspicion to the appropriate examiner.

§ 415.511 provides that any person, official, or institution participating in good faith in reporting such abuse shall be immune from any civil or criminal liability that might otherwise result by reason of such action.

According to § 415.512, no privilege except that between attorney and client or the privilege provided in § 90.505 shall apply to any situation involving known or suspected child abuse or neglect and shall not constitute grounds for failure to report such abuse, failure to cooperate with the department in its activities, or failure to give evidence in any judicial proceeding relating to child abuse or neglect.

Under § 415.111, you must also report cases of abuse, neglect, or exploitation of an aged or disabled person.

Georgia

Any physician, any other hospital or medical personnel, dentist, psychologist, podiatrist, nursing personnel, and any others having reasonable cause to believe that a child under age 18 has had physical injury or injuries inflicted upon him by a parent or caretaker other than by accidental means, has been neglected or exploited, or has been sexually assaulted or exploited shall make an oral report by telephone or otherwise as soon as possible, followed by a report in writing, to a child welfare agency providing protective services or, in the absence of such an agency, to a police authority or district attorney. Anyone making such a report in good faith is immune from criminal or civil liability for so doing. Failure to make such a report, however, is a misdemeanor. § 19-7-5 Georgia Statutes.

Hawaii

Notwithstanding any other state law concerning confidentiality to the contrary (including the physician-patient privilege), healthcare professionals and others who, in their professional or official capacity, have reason to believe that child abuse or neglect has occurred or there is a substantial risk such may occur shall immediately report to the Department of Human Services or the police. They shall follow up the initial oral report as soon as possible with a written report. Any person required to make such a report, upon demand of the Department or the police, must provide all information related to the alleged abuse or neglect, including medical records and reports. Nonreporting is a petty misdemeanor, but anyone who makes a report in good faith is immune from civil or criminal liability for so doing. Hawaii Statutes Chapter 350 §§ 350-1 through -5.

Idaho

Any physician, resident, intern, nurse, coroner, or others having reasonable cause to believe that a child under age 18 has been abused or who observes the child being subjected to conditions that would reasonably result in abuse shall report such to the proper law enforcement agency or the Department of Health and Welfare or its authorized representative within 24 hours. Idaho Statutes § 16-1619. Anyone doing so in good faith is immune from civil or criminal liability for so reporting. § 16-1620. The physician-patient privilege or any other privilege except the lawyer-client privilege does not apply to child abuse.

Illinois

Any physician, resident, intern, hospital, hospital administrator, personnel engaged in examination, care, and treatment of persons, surgeon, dentist, dental hygienist, osteopath, chiropractor, podiatrist, coroner, emergency medical technician, registered nurse, psychologist, psychiatrist, and others having reasonable cause to believe that a child known to them in their professional capacity may be abused or neglected shall immediately report to the Department of Children and Family Services. Anyone who knowingly submits a false report commits the offense of disorderly conduct. Any person who knowingly and willfully violates the reporting requirement is guilty of a class A misdemeanor. 23 Illinois Statutes § 2054.

Indiana

Staff members of medical or other public or private institutions shall immediately notify the person in charge of the institution or the designated agent, who then becomes responsible to report cases of child abuse or neglect to the local child protection service or law enforcement agency. Medical practitioners who are required to make such reports should also take photographs of the area of trauma and, if medically indicated, order a radiological examination and send copies of the reports, photographs, and X rays to the local child protection service. The photographs and X rays will be available to the county department, prosecutor, or law enforcement agency. A person performing these functions in good faith is immune from civil or criminal liability. The statute waives the physician-patient privilege in child abuse or neglect cases. Failure to make a required report is a crime under Indiana Statutes §§ 31-6-11-1 through 21.

Iowa

Iowa has a central registry for child abuse information within the Department of Human Services. The registry has a toll-free telephone number that anyone may use to report cases of suspected child abuse. Health practitioners who are examining, attending, or treating a child may, upon written request unless the information is needed immediately, have access to child abuse information in the registry, notwithstanding its confidential nature. A practitioner receiving such information may not disseminate it except as necessary pursuant to professional responsibilities. Acts 235A.12 through .19.

Kentucky

Kentucky law requires health facility personnel to report child or adult abuse to the Department of Human Resources immediately by phone or otherwise, followed up by a written report within 48 hours. No professional/patient privilege prevents such reporting.

Louisiana

§ 14:403 of the Louisiana Revised Statutes provides that health practitioners, that is, individuals who provide healthcare services, including a physician, surgeon, physical therapist, dentist, intern, resident, hospital staff member, podiatrist, chiropractor, licensed nurse, nursing aide, dental hygienist, any emergency medical technician, paramedic, optometrist, medical examiner, or coroner, where they have cause to believe that a child's physical or mental health or welfare is endangered as a result of abuse or neglect or sexual abuse, shall make an immediate report to the child protection unit of the Department of Social Services. Where the abuse is believed to be made by someone other than the caretaker and the victim's caretaker is not believed to have any responsibility for the abuse, neglect, or sexual abuse, a report shall be made immediately to the law enforcement agency.

§ 14:403 D (2) specifies that the report shall contain the following information if known:

- Name, address, age, sex, and race of the child.
- Nature, cause, and extent of the child's injuries or endangered condition, including any previous known or suspected abuse to this child or the child's siblings.
- Name and address of the child's parents or caretaker.
- Child's family composition.
- Name and address of the reporter.
- Account of how this child came to the reporter's attention.
- Any explanation of the cause of the child's injury or condition offered by the child, the caretaker, or any other person.
- Any other information that the reporter believes may be important or relevant.

According to § 14:403 D (3), the report may also name the person or persons who are thought to have caused or contributed to the child's condition.

§ 14:403 D (4) specifies that, if the initial report was in oral form by a mandatory reporter, it shall be followed by a written report made within five days to the local child protection unit of the department or, if necessary, to the local law enforcement agency.

§ 14:403 E provides that there shall exist no cause of action against any person who in good faith makes a report, cooperates in the investigation by any agency, or participates in judicial proceedings authorized under the provisions of this section and that such person shall have immunity from civil or criminal liability that otherwise might be incurred or imposed. This immunity does not extend to the following people:

- Any alleged principal, conspirator, or accessory to an offense involving the abuse or neglect or sexual exploitation of a child.
- Any person who makes a report known to be false or with reckless disregard for the truth of the report.

§ 14:403 F suspends the operation of any professional-patient privilege to exclude evidence in any proceeding concerning the abuse or neglect or sexual abuse of a child or the cause of such condition.

Maine

Under Title 22 § 3477, healthcare practitioners must, upon suspecting that an adult has been abused, neglected, or exploited, immediately report to the Department and follow up with a written report within 48 hours. Such person does not have to report, however, in the following situations:

- Factual basis for knowing or suspecting abuse, neglect, or exploitation of an adult covered under this subchapter derives from the professional's treatment of the individual suspected of causing the abuse, neglect, or exploitation.
- Treatment was sought by the individual for a problem relating to the abuse, neglect, or exploitation.
- In the opinion of the person required to report, the abused, neglected, or exploited adult's life or health is not immediately threatened.

A report made in good faith immunizes the reporter from civil liability.

When, while acting in a professional capacity, a healthcare provider knows or has reasonable cause to suspect that a child has been or is likely to be abused or neglected, that person shall immediately make a report to the Department of Human Services. Staff may report to the person in charge of the institution, who must then report to the Department. If the abuse was by a person not responsible for the child, the report should be made to the appropriate district attorney. A written report should follow the immediate report within 48 hours. Title 22 § 1012. § 4013 mandates reporting to the medical examiner when a child dies as a result of abuse or neglect. Anyone who so reports in good faith is immune from civil or criminal liability. § 4014. The physician-patient and psychotherapist-patient privileges do not apply to child abuse situations except that statements to a licensed mental health professional in the course of counseling, therapy, or evaluation may not be used against the patient in a criminal proceeding except to rebut the client's testimony contradicting those statements. § 4015.

Maryland

Notwithstanding any law on privileged communication, any health practitioner who contacts, examines, attends, or treats a child and has reason to believe that the child has been subject to abuse shall notify the local department of Human Services (§ 5–901) or the appropriate law enforcement agency and, if a staff member of a hospital or public health agency, immediately notify and give all information to the head of the institution or designee. The individual reporting the abuse shall follow the oral report, by telephone or direct communication, with a written report to the local Department, with a copy to the local State's Attorney within 48 hours after learning of the abuse. Maryland Code § 5–903.

Massachusetts

119 Statutes 51A requires physicians, interns, hospital personnel engaged in patient care, medical examiners, emergency medical technicians, dentists, nurses, chiropractors, podiatrists, osteopaths, and others to report to the department of public health when they have reasonable cause to believe that a child under age 18 is suffering serious physical or emotional injury resulting from abuse, including sexual abuse, or from neglect, including malnutrition, or is dependent on an addictive drug at birth by oral report, followed up within 48 hours by a written report. Failure to do so is punishable by a fine of not more than $1,000. No privilege relating to confidential communications prevents the filing of such reports.

Michigan

Various individuals, including physicians, coroners, dentists, medical examiners, nurses, emergency medical care providers, audiologists, psychologists, and others who have reasonable cause to suspect child abuse or neglect shall make immediately, by telephone or otherwise, an oral report to the Department of Social Services, followed, within 72 hours, by a written report. The identity of a reporting person is confidential, and such person reporting in good faith is immune from liability, civil or criminal. Laws §§ 722.601 through .628.

Minnesota

Persons who know or have reason to believe that a child is being neglected or physically or sexually abused or has been neglected, including professionals or their delegates who are engaged in the healing arts, shall immediately report the information to the local welfare agency, police department, or county sheriff. Within a licensed facility, the person required to report shall report to the agency responsible for licensing the facility. Persons so reporting in good faith are immune from civil or criminal liability. The statute also prohibits the employer from retaliating against anyone who reports such abuse. A false report, however, subjects its maker to civil suit for actual and punitive damages, and failure to report is a misdemeanor offense. § 626.556.

Mississippi

Mississippi requires a person who is "a professional or his delegate who is engaged in the practice of the healing arts, social services, hospital administration, psychological or psychiatric treatment, child care, education, or law enforcement" who knows or has reason to believe a child is being neglected or physically or sexually abused or has been within the past three years to immediately report, by telephone or otherwise, the information to the local welfare agency, police department, or county sheriff. A suspected death from abuse must be reported to a medical examiner or coroner. An oral report should be followed by a written report. Persons doing so in good faith are immune from any civil or criminal liability for making such a report, but a false report subjects the maker to liability for actual and punitive damages. Failure to report is a misdemeanor. § 626.556.

Missouri

Under § 210.115 of Missouri's Child Protection and Reformation law, any healthcare practitioner who has reasonable cause to believe that a child has been or may be subject to abuse or neglect must immediately report or cause a report to be made to the Missouri Division of Family Services. Whenever practitioners must report in their official capacity as staff members of medical institutions, whether public or private, they shall immediately notify the physician in charge or designee, who shall then have color photographs taken of physical trauma and shall, if medically indicated, have X rays taken of the child who is the subject of the report.

§ 198.070 requires reporting of neglect or abuse of residents of convalescent, nursing, and boarding homes.

164   Healthcare Records

Montana

Professionals engaged in the admission, examination, care, or treatment of persons, including physicians or hospital staff members, nurses, osteopaths, chiropractors, podiatrists, medical examiners, coroners, dentists, optometrists, or other health or mental health professionals must report to the Department of Family Services when they know or have reasonable cause to suspect that a child known to them in their professional or official capacity is an abused or neglected child. No privilege, such as the physician-patient privilege, prevents making the required report. Anyone so reporting is immune from criminal or civil liability unless they acted in bad faith or with malicious purpose. Failure to report subjects the offender to liability for any damages caused by such failure and also to criminal liability (a misdemeanor). § 41–3–201 through 208.

Nevada

Medical personnel listed in § 432B.220, including any "other person providing medical services licensed or certified in this state" must immediately report to an agency that provides protective services or to a law enforcement agency when there is reason to believe that a child has been abused or neglected. Anyone who makes such a report in good faith is immune from civil or criminal liability. § 432B.220. No person required to report may invoke a privilege to avoid reporting. § 432B.250.

New Hampshire

Any physician, surgeon, county medical referee, psychiatrist, resident, intern, dentist, osteopath, optometrist, chiropractor, psychologist, therapist, registered nurse, hospital personnel (engaged in admission, examination, care, or treatment of persons), and others having reason to suspect that a child under the age of 18 has been abused or neglected must report the same to the Bureau of Child and Family Services, Department of Health and Welfare, immediately by telephone or otherwise. A follow-up written report is due within 48 hours. Anyone making such a report in good faith is immune from any civil or criminal liability for so doing. No privilege, except the attorney-client privilege, is ground for excluding evidence of the abuse or neglect of a child. Failure to make the required report is a misdemeanor. Statutes §§ 169:38–:45.

New Jersey

Hospital facilities must establish and implement written policies and procedures for reporting all diagnosed and/or suspected cases of child abuse or neglect in compliance with New Jersey Statute Annotated 9:6–1. That statute requires that any person who has a reasonable cause to believe that a child has been subjected to child abuse shall report the same immediately to the Division of Youth and Family Services by telephone or otherwise. Such reports are confidential. A person making such a report in good faith is immune from civil or criminal liability. § 9:6–8.13.

New Mexico

New Mexico statute 32–1–15 establishes a duty on the part of physicians, nurses, and others to report knowledge or suspicion of child abuse or neglect to the district attorney, the county social services office, or the probation services office.

New York

Department of Health Memorandum, Health Facilities Series H–40, requires hospitals to provide for the identification, assessment, reporting, and management of cases of suspected child abuse and maltreatment and to designate a staff member to report such cases to the New York State Central Register of Child Abuse and Maltreatment and to comply with Article 6, Title 6 of the State Social Service Law. § 405.9 (d). § (c) similarly requires the hospital to provide for the maintenance of evidence of sexual offenses. The memorandum contains specific procedures for the release of this evidence, which is privileged in certain circumstances.

North Carolina

§ 17–38 of the North Carolina Child Welfare Law requires hospital personnel to report suspected child abuse to the state welfare commissioner or representative or local or state police. The individual reporting must make an immediate oral report by telephone or otherwise and follow it up with a written report to the welfare commissioner. Failure to report subjects the healthcare provider to a fine of not more than $500.

North Dakota

North Dakota Statutes Chapter 50 25.1 requires physicians, nurses, dentists, optometrists, medical examiners, any other medical health professionals, and others having knowledge or reasonable cause to suspect that a child coming before them in their official or professional capacity is abused or neglected shall report to the Department of Human Services or its designee. Failure to do so is a misdemeanor. Records and reports under this statute are confidential. § 50–25.1–11.

Ohio

Physicians, dentists, podiatrists, nurses, other healthcare professionals, psychologists, speech pathologists, coroners, and others must report alleged child abuse or neglect on penalty of committing a misdemeanor under § 2151.421 of the Revised Code. Ohio Administrative Code § 5101:2–34–04.

Oklahoma

Every physician or surgeon, including dentists and osteopaths, and every registered nurse attending or treating a child under age 18 and every other person having reason to believe that such child has had physical injuries inflicted upon him by other than accidental means when the injuries seem to have been caused by abuse or neglect shall report the matter promptly to the county office of the Department of Human Services. Failure to do so constitutes a misdemeanor. All records concerning child abuse are confidential. 21 Oklahoma Statutes § 846. Under § 847, any person making a good faith report and exercising due care in the making of the report is immune from any civil or criminal liability for so doing.

Oregon

Oregon Statutes § 418.750 requires any public or private official having reasonable cause to believe that any child with whom the official comes in contact in an official capacity has suffered abuse to report to law enforcement agencies and the local Children's Services Division office immediately. A psychiatrist or psychologist need not report if the communication is privileged under Statutes 40.225 to 40.295.

Pennsylvania

11 Pennsylvania Statutes § 2204 requires any persons who in the course of their employment, occupation, or practice of their profession come into contact with children who have reason to believe, on the basis of their medical, professional, or other training and experience, that a child coming before them in their professional capacity is an abused child must report such to the Department of Public Welfare. Medical reports or X rays may be sent to the child protective service with the written report. Anyone making such a report in good faith is immune from any criminal or civil liability for making such a report, § 2211, but failure to do so is a summary offense under § 2212.

Rhode Island

Physicians, nurses, nurse's aides, orderlies, medical examiners, dentists, optometrists, opticians, chiropractors, podiatrists, coroners, social workers, physical and occupational therapists, or others who have reasonable cause to believe that a patient or resident in a healthcare facility has been abused, mistreated, or neglected shall make a report to the director of the department of health within 24 hours. Failure to report is a misdemeanor punishable by a fine of not more than $500. Any person who reports such abuse in good faith is immune from criminal or civil liability for so doing. No professional privilege concerning confidential communications prevents making such reports. Statutes § 23–17.8–2 through .6.

§ 40–11–6 (1) of Rhode Island General Laws states that when physicians have cause to suspect that a child brought to them for examination, care, or treatment is an abused or neglected child or when they determine that a child under the age of 12 years is suffering from any sexually transmitted disease, they shall report such incident or cause a report to be made to the Department for Children and Their Families.

§ 40–11–6 (2) states that the physician or other person making the report should make an immediate oral report by telephone or otherwise to both the department and the law enforcement agency and shall follow it up with a report in writing to the department and the law enforcement agency explaining the extent and nature of the abuse or neglect the child allegedly suffered.

§ 40–11–6.1 provides that persons required to report incidents of child abuse who either fail to make or prevent any person acting reasonably from making the required report shall be guilty of a misdemeanor and, in addition, shall be civilly liable for the damages proximately caused by such failure.

Finally, § 40–11–11 abrogates the professional-patient privilege in situations involving known or suspected child abuse or neglect. Moreover, in any family court proceeding relating to child abuse or neglect, no privilege of confidentiality may be invoked with respect to any illness, trauma, incompetency, addiction to drugs, or alcoholism of any parent.

South Dakota

In South Dakota, hospitals must have a written policy on reporting of child abuse and neglect and report such to the state's attorney or the police department. Hospital personnel also have an individual duty to make such reports if they have reasonable cause to suspect child abuse. Failure to make a required report is a misdemeanor. Such reports are confidential and may only be released to those performing official functions relating to child abuse or neglect or pursuant to court order. Statutes 26–10–10. The report shall be made orally and immediately by telephone or otherwise to the state's attorney of the county in which the child resides or is present, to the Department of Social Services, to the county sheriff, or to the city police.

26–16–15 provides that the physician-patient privilege may not be claimed in any judicial proceeding involving child abuse or neglect or resulting from the giving of any report concerning a child's injury or neglect or the cause thereof.

Tennessee

Any person having knowledge of or called upon to aid a child suffering from or having sustained a wound, an injury, a disability, or a physical or mental condition that is of such a nature as to reasonably indicate that it was caused by brutality, abuse, or neglect or on the basis of available information reasonably appears to have been so caused shall report such harm immediately by telephone or otherwise to the judge having juvenile jurisdiction, to the county office of the Department of Human Services, or to the office of the sheriff or chief law enforcement officer of the municipality where the child resides. Code § 37–1–403.

Texas

Any person having cause to believe that a child's physical or mental health or welfare has been or may be adversely affected by abuse or neglect shall report to the Department of Human Services. An oral report must be made immediately. Professionals, including doctors and nurses, must make an oral report not later than 48 hours after the hour they first suspect the abuse or neglect, followed up by a written report in five days. Persons making such reports are immune from criminal or civil liability unless they made the reports in bad faith or with malice. No privilege, except the attorney-client privilege, prevents making such a report. Chapter 34.01 through .08.

Utah

Persons licensed under the Medical Practice or Nurse Practice Acts who have reason to believe that a child has been subjected to incest, molestation, sexual exploitation, sexual abuse, physical abuse, or neglect or who observe a child being subjected to conditions that would reasonably result in abuse or neglect shall immediately notify the nearest peace officer or law enforcement agency or the Division of Family Services. 62A–4–503. 62A–4–508 provides that such reports shall be followed by a written report within 48 hours if requested by the Division of Family Services. Finally, 62A–4–510 immunizes persons who participate in good faith in the making of such a report from civil or criminal liability.

Vermont

Any physicians, hospital administrators, nurses, medical examiners, dentists, psychologists, or others having reasonable cause to suspect that a child has been abused or neglected must report to the Commissioner of Social and Rehabilitative Services or designee orally and follow up with a written report. Violation of the reporting requirement may result in a $500 fine, but anyone who makes a report in good faith is immune from any civil or criminal liability for making such a report. Chapter 14 Vermont Statutes §§ 683–84.

Virginia

Any persons licensed to practice medicine or any of the healing arts, any nurses, or any mental health professionals who have reason to suspect that a child is an abused or neglected child shall report the matter immediately to the local department of the State Department of Social Services. They must make such reports immediately by telephone to the local state department child protective service agency and follow up with a written report within 48 hours if requested by the receiving agency. Failure to make a report can result in a fine of not more than $500. Any person making such a report, however, is immune from civil or criminal liability unless he acted with malicious intent. §§ 63.1–248.3 through .5.

Washington

Practitioners, including nurses, physicians and their assistants, podiatrists, optometrists, chiropractors, dentists, social workers, psychologists, and pharmacists must report, within 48 hours, suspected instances of nonaccidental injury, neglect, sexual abuse, or cruelty to a child, dependent adult, or developmentally disabled person by a person who appears to be legally responsible for that individual's welfare to a law enforcement agency or the Department of Social and Health Services. Hospitals must orient practitioners as to their reporting responsibilities, post notices, including police and department phone numbers, state the reporting requirements, and annotate medical records of the person who may have been abused, reflecting that the practitioner made the required report. Revised Code of Washington § 26.44.030, Washington Administrative Code § 248-18-202.

West Virginia

West Virginia Statutes § 49-6A-2 requires any medical, dental, or mental health professionals or emergency medical services personnel who have reasonable cause to suspect that a child is neglected or abused or observe the child being subjected to conditions that are likely to result in abuse or neglect to immediately report to the state department of human services. If such personnel are members of the staff of public or private institutions, they shall notify the person in charge, who shall report. Failure to report child abuse or neglect is a misdemeanor.

Wisconsin

Wisconsin law requires any therapist to whom a victim of sexual exploitation by another therapist reports and expresses that she wants to make such a report to report the matter to the Department of Regulation and Licensing. Failure to make a report is a misdemeanor. Such reports are confidential. § 940.22 (4) of the Wisconsin Criminal Code.

Wisconsin also requires reporting elder abuse or neglect to the county agency. § 46.90 (4).

A physician, coroner, medical examiner, nurse, dentist, chiropractor, optometrist, or other medical or mental health professional, physical therapist, occupational therapist, speech therapist, emergency medical technician, ambulance attendant, or anyone else who has reasonable cause to suspect that a child seen in the course of professional duties has been abused or neglected or threatened with the same shall report immediately by telephone or in person to the county department, the sheriff, or the city police department. Intentional failure to make such a report is punishable by a fine of not more than $1,000 or imprisonment for not more than six months or both. Anyone making such a report in good faith, however, is immune from civil or criminal liability for so doing. All such reports are confidential and may be released only in limited circumstances. § 48.981 of the Wisconsin Children's Code.

The physician-patient privilege does not apply in cases where the examination of an abused or injured child creates a reasonable ground for an opinion that the condition was other than accidentally caused. Wisconsin Evidence Code § 905.4 (4) (c).

Wyoming

Any person who knows or has reasonable cause to believe or suspect that a child has been abused or neglected or who observes any child being subjected to conditions or circumstances that would reasonably result in abuse or neglect shall immediately report it to the child protective agency or law enforcement agency and follow up the oral report with a written report. Any person examining or treating suspected abuse shall photograph or x ray areas of trauma. § 14–3–205.

8

Drug and Alcohol Abuse Records and Reports

Introduction

Your state may require you to identify patients who obtain controlled substances, to report crimes involving drugs or alcohol, or to have specific rules about disclosing information in medical records involving drug and alcohol abuse patients.

Federal Laws

The Comprehensive Alcohol Abuse and Alcoholism Prevention, Treatment, and Rehabilitation Act of 1970, 42 U.S.C. § 242(a) and 21 U.S.C. § 872(e) as amended, prohibits discrimination in the admission of alcohol abusers to any hospital or outpatient facility that receives federal funding. A similar provision of the Drug Office Abuse and Treatment Act of 1972, 21 U.S.C. § 1175(b) (2) (c), prohibits discrimination in the admission of drug abusers to hospitals that receive federal funding. Both statutes establish standards for disclosure of medical records of drug abusers. Violating patients' confidentiality may result in a criminal penalty. Under either statute, unless you have the patient's express consent, you may only disclose patient records to medical personnel as needed to meet an emergency, to qualified personnel conducting medical research if you delete any patient identifiers, or by authority of a court order based on a showing of good cause. Written consent must include the date, the name of the patient and the facility, the name of the party to whom the information may be disclosed, the purpose of the disclosure, the precise nature of the information to be disclosed, and the length of time the authorization is valid.

42 Code of Federal Regulations Part 2 requires public, nonprofit, and for-profit private entities conducting, regulating, or assisting alcohol or drug abuse programs to maintain records showing patient consent to disclosure and documenting disclosure to medical personnel in a medical emergency from confidential alcohol and drug abuse patient records. The regulation does not specify a retention period.

Part 2a of 42 CFR requires alcohol, drug abuse, and mental health researchers to maintain confidentiality certificates showing that the secretary has authorized the researcher to withhold the identity of research subjects in legal proceedings to compel the disclosure of the identity of research subjects, again without specifying a retention period.

State Laws

Alaska

Alaska Revised Statute § 11.71.040 makes it a felony to furnish false or fraudulent information in or to omit any material information from any report or other required document concerning controlled substances. Similarly, failure to make, keep, or furnish any required record required by Alaska Statute § 17.30, which covers record-keeping requirements for controlled substances, is a misdemeanor. § 11.71.050.

Arizona

Persons registered to manufacture, distribute, or dispense controlled substances shall keep records and maintain inventories in conformance with federal and state law. These records and inventories are open to inspection by peace officers in the performance of their duties. § 36-2523B. The pharmacist must maintain a bound record book for dispensing of controlled substances that shall contain the name and address of the purchaser, the name and quantity of the controlled substance purchased, the date of each purchase, and the name or initials of the pharmacist or pharmacy intern who dispensed the substance. § 36-2525F.4. See § 36-2523 for specific record-keeping requirements.

Medical records of patients of substance abuse units are confidential and may not be released except as noted in chapter 14 of this guide.

Arkansas

The record of any person committed for treatment, guidance, or rehabilitation for alcohol abuse is confidential and may not be divulged except on court order. § 20-64-716.

California

California Penal Code § 1543 requires mandatory release of medical information if there is reason to believe that a crime was committed by or to the patient, presumably including drug abuse.

§ 1795.18 states that the division shall not require a healthcare provider to permit inspection or provide copies of alcohol and drug abuse records where or in a manner prohibited by § 408 of the federal drug laws or regulations.

Colorado

Community health treatment facilities must promptly furnish a record of all applicants for enrollment and enrolled patients in a program for drug-dependent persons to the commissioner of mental health. Such reports shall also be available to the commissioner of health services for informational and statistical purposes only. Otherwise, such reports are confidential except that they may be used in a criminal proceeding for establishing fraudulent efforts to enroll at two or more facilities. § 19a-373. In addition, § 19a-382 specifies that no hospital shall report or disclose the name of a person who requests treatment and rehabilitation for drug dependence. If the patients are minors, their requests for treatment or their treatment shall not be disclosed to their parents or guardians without their consent.

Florida

Notwithstanding confidentiality of medical records, hospitals shall release evidence relating to the alcoholic content of the blood or the presence of chemical substances to a court, prosecuting attorney, defense attorney, or law enforcement official. Florida Statutes 88-82. Records of alcohol testing should not be released without a written request from the state assuring that it is pursuing a drinking violation.

Georgia

Georgia permits the Department of Human Resources to require each licensee to furnish copies of complete records of each drug-dependent person treated or advised pursuant to a program. § 25-5-12.

Idaho

Every physician who provides treatment or rehabilitation services to a person addicted to or dependent upon drugs shall make a statistical report to the Director of the Mental Health Division of the Department of Health and Welfare each quarter of the year. The physician shall not report the name of the person treated. § 37-3105. No physician or person acting under the physician's supervision may report or disclose the names of persons who request treatment or rehabilitation for addiction or dependency on any drug.

Indiana

A physician or person acting under the physician's direction who obtains a blood, urine, or bodily fluid sample for diagnostic purposes or at the request of a law enforcement officer in motor vehicle intoxication cases shall deliver the sample or disclose the results to a law enforcement officer who requests it as part of a criminal investigation even if the person has not consented. Nor does the physician-patient privilege apply to such information. Motor Vehicles Code 9-11-4-6.

Iowa

§ 204.507 provides that medical practitioners or researchers shall neither be required to furnish the name or identity of a patient or research subject to the board or department nor be compelled to furnish the name or identity of such an individual in any proceedings.

Kansas

In Kansas, disclosing records showing treatment of drug abusers is a misdemeanor unless the patient consents, or if under age 16, the patient's guardian consents, or unless disclosure would be injurious to the patient's welfare. You may, however, legally disclose such records upon bona fide medical emergencies, for purposes of research, and upon court order. § 65-5225.

Maryland

Oral or written statements of a person who seeks counseling, treatment, or therapy for any form of drug or alcohol abuse, from a physician, psychologist, or hospital or person who is certified for counseling or treating such abuse are privileged, as are observations and conclusions that the physician, psychologist, hospital, or other person makes. Such information is not admissible in any proceeding against the individual except parole, probation, or conditional release proceedings and commitment proceedings. § 8-801. The disclosure and use of records of individuals served by alcohol and drug abuse treatment programs shall be governed by federal regulations on the confidentiality of alcohol and drug abuse patient records. § 8-801 (c).

Nevada

Nevada exempts from its physician-patient privilege any information communicated to a physician in an attempt to unlawfully obtain controlled substances. Statutes § 49.245.

§ 458.280 makes records of facilities for the treatment of alcohol and drug abuse confidential.

New Hampshire

Healthcare practitioners must keep separate records, so as not to breach the confidentiality of patient records, to show receipt and disposition of all controlled drugs. Such records are confidential and open to inspection only by law enforcement officers and officers, agents, inspectors, and representatives of the board of pharmacy, the attorney general, and all county attorneys whose duties involve enforcing controlled drug laws. Statutes § 318-B:12.

New Mexico

A court order is necessary to release drug or alcohol abuse information relating to a patient, even if the patient consents, § 43-2-11 New Mexico Statutes. A subpoena is insufficient authority to release drug or alcohol abuse information.

New York

Department of Health Memorandum, Health Facilities Series H-40, § 405.17 (c) (3), requires the pharmacy to report all abuses and losses of controlled substances to the director and to the medical staff, as appropriate, in accordance with applicable laws.

Ohio

Records or information pertaining to identity, diagnosis, or treatment of drug treatment program patients is confidential and may only be disclosed upon patient consent or to qualified personnel for research, management, audits, or program evaluation, but such personnel may not identify any individual patient in any report or otherwise disclose a patient's identify. Ohio Code § 5122.53. Likewise, under § 5122.52 (D), communications by a person seeking aid in good faith for drug dependence or danger of such dependence is confidential.

§ 5122.52 (C) requires hospitals, clinics, persons, or agencies that conduct programs for reception, treatment, care, housing, counseling, rehabilitation, or other services for drug dependent persons or those in danger of drug dependence to supply information concerning such programs to the department of mental health.

Oklahoma

43A Oklahoma Statutes § 3-422 establishes a confidentiality rule concerning treatments for alcohol and drug abuse. All written communications relating to the treatment and rehabilitation of drug-dependent persons must be in folders clearly marked "Confidential." They may be used only by persons actively involved in treatment and rehabilitation. Those persons may not testify about information relating to drug possession or dependency, nor may medical records compiled during the treatment and rehabilitation be admitted into evidence. Information in the records is confidential and privileged to the patient, but the administrator of an approved facility may make information from such records available for research into the causes and treatment of alcohol and drug abuse so long as the patient is not identified. § 3-423.

Oregon

Records of patients at a treatment facility for drug and alcohol abuse shall not be revealed to any person other than the director and the staff without the patient's consent. § 426.460 (5).

Rhode Island

§ 5-37.3-4 (4) permits disclosure of otherwise confidential healthcare information to law enforcement personnel if a patient has or is attempting to obtain narcotic drugs from the healthcare provider illegally.

South Carolina

All certificates, applications, records, and reports identifying patients hospitalized for alcohol or drug abuse are confidential and may not be disclosed except upon consent or court order, for research conducted or authorized by the State Department of Mental Health or the South Carolina Commission on Alcohol and Drug Abuse, as may be necessary to cooperate with law enforcement, health, welfare, and other state agencies, or as is necessary to carry out the provisions of state law concerning such treatments. This rule also permits disclosure, upon proper inquiry, of information as to the patient's current medical condition to his family or relatives. § 44-51-190.

South Dakota

The registration and other records of treatment facilities shall remain confidential and are privileged to the patient. § 34-20A-90. If used for research, information shall not be published as to disclose patients' names or other identifying information.

Tennessee

Every physician or other medical professional who diagnoses or treats a person enrolled in school in K through 12th grade for a drug overdose and every chief administrative officer of a hospital, clinic, or dispensary in which there is such a case shall report to public school officials under rules of the Department of Mental Health and Mental Retardation. The Department adopted such rules to ensure such reports are not in violation of federal or state laws requiring confidentiality in the treatment of drug abusers. § 33-8-301. Failure to make such a report is subject to professional discipline by the licensing agency or the employer.

Texas

Communications between a patient/client being diagnosed, evaluated, or treated for any mental or emotional disorder, including alcoholism and drug abuse, are confidential and will not be disclosed except in limited circumstances listed in Title 92, Article 5561h, § 4 (a) (4).

Utah

Persons licensed under the Medical Practice or Nurse Practice Acts must report fetal alcohol syndrome and drug dependency to the division as soon as possible. Required reports should be followed by a written report within 48 hours, if requested by the division. Anyone making such reports in good faith is immune from criminal or civil liability as a result of so doing. Failure to report subjects the offender to punishment for a misdemeanor. §§ 62A-4-501 through 514.

Wisconsin

Treatment records of individuals receiving services for alcoholism or drug dependence are confidential and privileged. They may be released only as authorized by the statute or by the informed written consent of the subject. § 51.30. § 51.30 (b) lists categories of people or entities authorized access to such records without informed written consent. (d) specifies the rules governing the individual's access to such records.

§ 140.81 establishes a drug dependence and drug abuse program that allows the department to collect data on drug abuse treatment from all treatment facilities.

9

Reporting and Release of Communicable Disease Information

Introduction

Many states require healthcare providers to provide local public health officials name, identifying information, and details of the illness of individuals with infectious diseases. Be careful, however, not to release any information other than that required. Otherwise, you may violate the patient's right to privacy.

State Laws

Alabama

Alabama Code § 22-11A-2 requires healthcare professionals, including hospital administrators, to report cases or suspected cases of notifiable diseases and health conditions as specified by the state board of health. Records of any person having such a disease must be readily available to the state health officer. Similarly, § 22-11-A-9 requires notification of tuberculosis cases to the state or the county health officer by confidential report. § 22-11A-14 requires confidential reporting of sexually transmitted diseases to the state board of health. § 22-11A-22 makes it a misdemeanor to violate the confidentiality of such records.

Arizona

Arizona R9-6-701, "Acquired Immunodeficiency Syndrome (AIDS)," requires case, suspect case, and suspect carrier reports. "Suspect carrier" means a person without clinical symptoms of disease, but who tests positive for HTLV-III/LAV by culture or antigen detection or repeatedly positive for antibodies to the virus.

Arizona R9-14-113, "Reports of Certain Contagious Diseases," specifies that the clinical laboratory director shall report to the Department findings or evidence suggestive of syphilis or tuberculosis in accordance with the provisions of R9-6-311, "Reporting of Certain Contagious Diseases by Clinical Laboratories."

Arkansas

Any person who determines by laboratory examination that a specimen from a human body yields evidence suggestive of venereal diseases shall notify the Division of Health Maintenance of such findings. § 20-16-501. Physicians have a similar duty. § 20-16-503. All such notifications, however, are confidential. § 20-16-504. Failure to notify the Division is a misdemeanor. § 20-16-506. § 20-15-401 requires physicians to report cases of Reye's syndrome to the Department of Health as promptly as possible. § 20-15-502 requires reporting of the sudden death of children between the ages of one week and one year who appeared in good health to the county coroner within 24 hours.

California

§ 3123 authorizes the State Department of Health Services to establish a list of reportable diseases. All physicians, nurses, attendants, proprietors, or others visiting any sick persons in any hotel, house, building, office, or other place where any person is ill of any infectious, contagious, or communicable disease shall promptly report that fact to the health officer. § 3125.

§ 304 requires every physician and surgeon or other person attending a newborn diagnosed as having had rhesus (Rh) isoimmunization hemolytic disease to report such condition to the State Department of Health Services.

Any physician and surgeon who knows or has reasonable cause to believe that a patient is suffering from pesticide poisoning or any disease or condition caused by a pesticide shall report that fact by telephone within 24 hours to the local health officer followed within seven days by a copy of that report. Failure to comply with this requirement can result in a civil penalty of $250. § 2950.

Colorado

All attending physicians and other persons treating a case of HIV infection in hospitals, clinics, laboratories, and so forth in Colorado must make a written report to the state or local department of health on every individual known to have a diagnosis of AIDS or HIV related illness, including death from HIV infection, within 24 hours. Good faith reports cannot constitute libel or slander or violate any right of privacy or privileged communication. Further, those who comply with this statute in good faith are immune from criminal or civil liability for so doing. § 25-4-1402. These reports are confidential and may be released only in limited circumstances. § 25-4-1404. Failure to make such a report or breaching confidentiality requirements of this law is a misdemeanor. § 25-4-1409.

Connecticut

§ 19a-215 governs reporting of communicable diseases, requiring physicians to report, in writing, each case of cholera, yellow fever, typhus fever, leprosy, smallpox, diphtheria, typhoid fever, scarlet fever, all forms and stages of syphilis, all forms and stages of gonorrhea, chancroid, or other communicable diseases occurring in their practices to the director of health of the town, city, or borough in which such case occurs.

Delaware

All physicians or other persons having knowledge of any person who is suffering from any disease dangerous to the public health that the State Board of Health requires be reported shall report the disease to the local health board or official. Local boards of health and physicians in rural districts or other localities where there are no health officials report to the State Board of Health. 16 Delaware Code § 501. § 702 requires reporting venereal diseases to the Board. § 701 similarly requires reporting sexually transmitted diseases. Information and records held by the Division of Public Health relating to known or suspected sexually transmitted diseases, including HIV infection, are confidential and may be released only in limited circumstances. §§ 711-2. Except for § 702, violations of these reporting requirements may result in a fine of between $100 and $1,000. A violation of § 702 may result in a fine of $25 to $200 under § 713.

Florida

Every person who diagnoses or treats a person with sexually transmitted disease, including AIDS, and every laboratory that has a positive test for such a disease must report the same to the department of health. Florida Statutes § 384.25. Failure to do so can result in a fine of up to $500.

Georgia

Georgia law, § 24-9-47, requires mandatory reporting of confirmed positive HIV tests to the Department of Human Resources. This section also makes AIDS information confidential and specifies the limited circumstances under which such information may be disclosed.

Idaho

§ 39-602 of the Idaho Code provides that any physician or other person who makes a diagnosis of or treats a case of venereal disease and any superintendent or manager of a hospital in which there is a case of venereal disease shall make a report of such case to the health authorities. § 39-601 states that venereal disease includes syphilis, gonorrhea, acquired immunodeficiency syndrome (AIDS), AIDS related complex (ARC), other manifestations of HIV (human immunodeficiency virus) infections, and chancroid. These diseases are declared to be infectious, communicable, and dangerous to public health.

Illinois

77 Illinois Administrative Code 690 requires reporting communicable diseases to the Department of Public Health.

Indiana

Indiana Code §16–1–9.5–2 requires physicians, hospital administrators, and directors of medical laboratories to report to the local or state health officer incidents of communicable diseases and others that are dangerous to health. Such individuals must also report to the state board each case of human immunodeficiency virus (HIV) infection, including each confirmed case of acquired immune deficiency syndrome (AIDS). Failure to report is a Class A infraction, but a person who makes such a report in good faith is immune from liability for so doing. The law waives the physician-patient privilege in such situations.

Physicians, dentists, hospitals, and medical laboratories must report all confirmed cases of cancer to the cancer registry (§ 16–4–9–4), and physicians, nurse midwives, and hospitals must report each confirmed case of a birth problem to the birth problems registry (§ 16–4–10–6). In addition, Indiana has just set up a pilot project on traumatic injuries requiring participating hospitals to report confirmed cases of traumatic injuries to the traumatic injuries registry (§ 16–4–11–7).

Iowa

In Iowa, physicians or other health practitioners, directors of clinical laboratories and directors of blood plasma centers or blood banks must report all cases of reportable disease to which they attend to the Department of Public Health. Hospitals and healthcare facilities are encouraged to do so. Iowa Administrative Code § 641–1.5(135,139,140). § 641–1.2(135,139) lists reportable diseases or conditions, including AIDS. Iowa Code § 141.8 requires any physician or practitioner who tests a person for AIDS to report to the Department if the result is a confirmed positive within seven days. The information so reported is confidential. Anyone making a report in good faith is immune from civil or criminal liability.

Kansas

A new Kansas statute specifies that whenever physicians have information that a person is suffering from or has died from AIDS, they must report that information to the secretary of health and environment. Otherwise, such information is confidential. Physicians who perform services other than the direct provision of medical services for insurance companies, health maintenance organizations, or nonprofit medical and hospital service organizations have no duty to so report.

Kansas Administrative Regulations 28–1–2 likewise require reporting infectious or contagious diseases to the secretary of health and environment, including cancer, congenital malformations in infants under one year old, Reye's syndrome, toxic shock syndrome, AIDS, and fetal alcohol syndrome. All such reports are confidential medical information.

Kentucky

Kentucky Statutes Chapter 214 and Kentucky Administrative Regulation 2:2020 require reporting communicable diseases to the health department in whose jurisdiction the disease occurs. All records in the possession of local health departments or the cabinet for human resources that concern persons infected with sexually transmitted diseases are confidential and may be released only to the physician retained by the patient, for statistical purposes as long as no individual can be identified, with consent, if necessary to enforce the rules of the cabinet for human resources relating to the control and treatment of such diseases, and to the extent necessary to protect the life or health of the named party. § 214.420.

Louisiana

Every licensed physician and every superintendent or manager of a hospital or dispensary must report every case of venereal disease to the State Board of Health within 24 hours. Statutes 40 § 1065.

§ 1299.87 requires disclosure of an abstract of a patient's records reflecting the patient's physical condition upon request of the Louisiana cancer registry.

§ 1562 establishes a requirement for any physicians or other persons reporting the death of any patient with a known or diagnosed virulent contagious disease, including AIDS, and including deceased individuals who are known carriers of any such disease, but whose death is due to other causes, to notify the coroner of such disease. In addition, they must immediately notify the coroner of any death under suspicious circumstances where the deceased did not receive medical attention within 36 hours before death.

Maine

Title 5 Maine Statutes, § 19203, provides for disclosure of the results of an HIV test to state agencies, including the Department of Corrections, the Department of Human Services, and the Department of Mental Health and Mental Retardation to the extent that they are responsible for the treatment or care of the subject. Such agencies must promulgate rules covering disclosures of test results. The statute also provides for court-ordered disclosure and disclosure to the Bureau of Health.

Maryland

Physicians with reason to suspect that a patient has an infectious or contagious disease that endangers public health shall immediately report to the local county health officer. Institutions have a similar duty. Maryland Code § 18–202. Such reports are confidential. §18–201. Other reportable diseases are cancer, § 18–203, sentinel birth defects, § 18–206, occupational diseases, § 18–204, gonococcal ophthalmia neonatorum,

§ 18–308, and rabies, § 18–316. Failure to report an occupational disease may result in a $10 fine, and failure to report an infectious or contagious disease may result in a fine of up to $100.

§18–205 requires directors of medical laboratories to submit reports to county health officers within 48 hours after an examination of a specimen shows evidence of any of the following conditions: gonorrhea; viral hepatitis A or B; hemophilus, meningococcal, streptococcus A or B, or viral meningitis; meningococcemia; typhoid or nontyphoid salmonellosis; syphilis; and tuberculosis. § 18–207 (d) requires directors of medical laboratories to make monthly reports concerning tests for human immunodeficiency virus.

Massachusetts

If a physician knows or believes that a person is infected with a disease dangerous to the public health or an infant's eyes become inflamed, swollen, and red or show an unnatural discharge within two weeks after birth, the physician must immediately notify the town board of health in writing. § 111. This requirement does not apply to tuberculosis or venereal diseases except those of eye infections of newborns. Those diseases are separately reportable under special rules and regulations of the Department of Health. § 111A requires reports to the city or town board of health when a physician or hospital medical officer attends a patient with cerebral palsy.

Nurses or other attendants must report if an infant's eyes become inflamed, swollen, and red or show an unnatural discharge within two weeks after birth within six hours to the board of health of the town where the infant is. 111 Statutes § 110. Physicians or other healthcare professionals who treat a child with Reye's syndrome must report the same to the Department of Public Health. 111 Statutes § 110B.

Minnesota

Physicians and healthcare facilities, including hospitals, nursing homes, medical clinics, medical laboratories, veterinarians, and veterinary medical laboratories must report any disease, including AIDS, listed in part 4605.7040 of the Minnesota Administrative Rules within one working day to the commissioner of health. Part 4605.7090, MAR, specifies what information such reports require.

Mississippi

§ 41–23–1 requires physicians or persons in charge of hospitals, healthcare facilities, or laboratories to report such diseases as the State Board of Health specifies to the Executive Officer of the Board, including reporting the death of any person who has been diagnosed as having AIDS or any Class One disease. Failure to make such a report is grounds for suspension of license. § 41-33-39 requires those same individuals to report tuberculosis to the Board of Health within seven days.

Missouri

Chapter 192, Missouri Statutes, requires that the Department of Health be notified concerning patients who have reportable infectious or contagious diseases.

Montana

The Administrative Rules of Montana, Chapter 28, Communicable Disease Control, lists reportable communicable diseases in Rule 16.28.202, including AIDS. Any persons, including physicians, dentists, nurses, medical examiners, other healthcare practitioners, healthcare facility administrators, or laboratories must immediately report reportable diseases to the county, city-county, or district health officer. AIDS is to be reported to the Department of Health and Environmental Sciences. Rule 16.28.201.

Nebraska

Because of the need for confidentiality and special follow-up in the case of tuberculosis and the venereal diseases (acquired immunodeficiency syndrome, chancroid, chlamydia genital infection, gonorrhea, granuloma inguinale, herpes genital infection, lymphogranuloma venereum, and syphilis), healthcare practitioners must report these diseases to the Medical Director of the Local Health Department or the State Health Department as soon as diagnosed or reasonably inspected on a morbidity report card provided by the Department. Other diseases requiring epidemiologic investigation or special handling are to be reported as well. Title 173, Chapter 1, 002.01 and .02.

Nevada

Nevada Statutes § 439.210 requires attending physicians to report communicable diseases to the state board of health. Failure to do so constitutes a misdemeanor.

§ 439.270 requires physicians to report to the health division, in writing, the name, age, and address of every person diagnosed as having epilepsy.

Chapter 457.240 of the Nevada Statutes establishes a reporting requirement for cancer, makes the records of every case of malignant neoplasms of every hospital available to the state health officer or representative, and prohibits disclosure of any patient, physician, or hospital involved in reporting cancer unless the individual consents in writing.

New Hampshire

Test results of human immunodeficiency virus samples submitted to the Division of Public Health Services, Department of Health and Human Services, shall not be disclosed except to the director or to the physician ordering the test. Statutes 141–F:7. The physician may disclose the results to the person tested or to the parent or legal guardian if the patient is less than 18 or is mentally incapable of understanding the ramifications of a positive test result. If the patient is confined to a facility pursuant to a court order, the results may be disclosed to the medical director or chief medical officer of the facility. 141–F:7 II–IV. Otherwise, the identity of the person tested may not be disclosed. All records and other information relating to persons testing for this virus shall be maintained as confidential and protected from inadvertent or unwarranted intrusion. Such information may be released, however, upon request if the patient has given written authorization or to other healthcare providers when necessary to protect the health of the patient tested. 141–F:8.

RHA 141–C requires reporting of communicable diseases to the Division of Public Health Services. He–P 808.12 (8) requires clinical laboratory directors to report to the division all laboratory findings that indicate the presumptive presence of any reportable disease.

New Jersey

§ 26:4–19 New Jersey Code requires every physician, superintendent, or other person having control or supervision over a state, county, or municipal hospital, sanatorium, or other public or private institution in which any person ill or infected with any disease required by law or the State Sanitary Code to be reported is received for care or treatment, within 24 hours after any such patient has been received into the institution, to make a written report of that fact to the health officer or other officer or employee designated to receive such reports by the local board of health having jurisdiction over the territory where the institution is.

New Mexico

§ 24–1–15 A. of the New Mexico Statutes provides that whenever any physician or other person knows that any person is sick with any disease dangerous to public health, the physician or other knowledgeable person shall promptly notify the district health officer or authorized agent.

New York

Hospitals must have an infection control officer who must maintain a log of occurrences of infections and communicable diseases. The officer must report increased incidence of infections, including nosocomial infections, to the appropriate area office of the Office of Health Systems Management in accordance with the incident reporting requirements of § 405.8. (See chapter 3.) § 405.11 (B) (4).

North Carolina

§ 19–89 of the North Carolina Public Health and Safety Law requires physicians to report in writing each case of cholera, yellow fever, typhus fever, leprosy, smallpox, diphtheria, typhoid fever, scarlet fever, all forms and stages of syphilis, all forms and stages of gonorrhea, chancroid, or other communicable diseases occurring in their practice to the director of health of the town, city, or borough in which such case occurs within twelve hours of recognizing the disease.

North Dakota

Under § 23-07-02 of the North Dakota Code, each physician and all persons who treat or administer to the sick shall report reportable diseases to the nearest health officer. The superintendent or manager of a hospital or dispensary in which there is a case of venereal disease must report such case to the nearest health officer. Also, § 23-07-07.3 requires physicians to report births and stillbirths, stating whether a blood test for syphilis was taken from the mother. § 23-07-18 states that physicians must report to the local board of health, in writing, within 24 hours, the death of any of their patients from contagious or infectious disease.

§ 23-07-01.1 requires physicians to report immediately to the state Department of Health, in writing, when there is reasonable cause to believe a person over age 14 cannot safely operate a motor vehicle because of physical or mental reasons or is diagnosed as having a disorder characterized by lapse of consciousness or gross physical or mental impairments. The physician-patient privilege does not bar such reporting.

Ohio

Chapter 3701-3 of the Ohio Administrative Code requires attending physicians or persons in charge of hospitals, dispensaries, clinics, or other institutions to report notifiable diseases to the board of health unless they have evidence that a physician has already so reported. Section 3701-3-04. When no physician is in attendance, any individual who knows of a person suffering from a disease that is communicable or suspected of being communicable will report the same to the board of health. Individuals who have a duty to report must report diseases listed as class A and B within 24 hours, except that reports of cases of inflammation of the eyes of the newborn and gonorrheal ophthalmia must be submitted within 6 hours. Class C diseases shall be reported only when there occurs any outbreak or unusual prevalence of such diseases. In such cases, the individual having knowledge of such occurrences shall report these facts immediately to the health commissioner of the health district wherein such outbreak or unusual occurrence exists. Section 3701-3-05. Section 3701-3-02 lists the Class A, B, and C diseases. AIDS and AIDS related complex are Class A diseases. Laboratories have similar reporting requirements under § 3701-3-26. Cancer must be reported to the cancer registry.

A physician who diagnoses or treats or other person who has knowledge of a sexually transmitted disease must also in addition to the report required above report the name, address, age, sex, color, and other information as will permit any person who might be suspected of harboring or acquiring a sexually transmitted disease to be located to the health commissioner. § 3701-3-25 requires the physician treating a person for a sexually transmitted disease to report to the health commissioner discontinuance of treatment if the disease is still communicable.

Any person or institution providing care or treatment to an individual suffering from a communicable disease must permit the director of health or representative to have access to the patient's medical record. Section 3701-3-08.

§ 3701-13-02 requires reporting of inflammation of the eyes of the newborn and gonorrheal ophthalmia to the health commissioner of the city or general health district.

Oklahoma

63 Oklahoma Statutes § 1-503 authorizes the State Board of Health to promulgate rules and regulations requiring physicians and clinical laboratories to report diseases as required by the Board. Failure to do so is a misdemeanor. § 1-528 adds a reporting requirement for venereal diseases. Physicians must report such diseases to the local health officer. These reports are confidential (§ 1-502 (b)) and may be released only in the circumstances enumerated in the statute. See chapter 14.

Oregon

Oregon law requires notifying the local public health administrator of reportable diseases.

Pennsylvania

Physicians and hospitals must report cases of AIDS promptly to the Department of Health, Division of Acute Infectious Disease Epidemiology, or to local health departments in Allegheny, Bucks, Chester, Erie, and Philadelphia counties and the cities of Allentown, Bethlehem, and York when the subject of the report resides there. 28 Pennsylvania Statutes § 27.32. 28 Code § 27.21 requires physicians to report reportable diseases to the local board of health or, if none, to the State Health Center of the Department of Health. § 27.31 has a similar requirement to report cancer. § 27.29 permits heads of healthcare institutions to report nonreportable diseases, and § 27.22 requires laboratories to report certain infections and conditions. § 27.25 requires other licensed healthcare practitioners to report reportable diseases other than cancer and AIDS.

Rhode Island

Rhode Island's Rules and Regulations for the Licensing of Hospitals, R23-17-HOSP, § 41.4, requires hospitals to report promptly to the Rhode Island Department of Health cases of communicable diseases designated as "reportable diseases" by the Director of Health.

South Carolina

§ 44-29-10 of the South Carolina Code specifies that in all cases of known or suspected contagious or infectious diseases occurring within the state the attending physician shall report such disease to the county health department within 24 hours, stating the name and address of the patient and the nature of the disease.

§ 44-29-70 further provides that any physician or other person who makes a diagnosis of or treats a case of a sexually transmitted disease and any superintendent or manager of a hospital, dispensary, healthcare related facility, or charitable institution in which there is a case of a sexually transmitted disease shall report it to the health authorities according to the form and manner as the Department of Health and Environmental Control directs.

South Dakota

Any physician or other person who makes a diagnosis or treats a case of venereal disease and any superintendent or manager of a hospital or dispensary in which there is a case of venereal disease shall report such case to the health authorities in the form and manner the Department of Health directs. The patient's identity is confidential. § 34-23-2.

Tennessee

Every physician or other person who diagnoses, treats, or prescribes for a sexually transmitted disease and every superintendent or manager of a clinic, hospital, laboratory, or penal institution in which there is a case of sexually transmitted disease shall report the case immediately to those persons or agencies directed by the Commissioner of Health and Environment. § 68-10-101.

Texas

Hospital Licensing Standard 12-8.7.3.1 permits disclosure of medical record information maintained by special care facilities for reporting of communicable disease information.

Utah

Utah's Communicable Disease Control Act, Title 26, Utah Code § 26-6-4, covers reporting of communicable diseases to the Department of Health. A28-02-3 of the Utah Administrative Code contains extremely detailed requirements for reporting communicable diseases. Physicians, dentists, nurses, and hospitals must make immediate reports by telephone to the State Division of Health or the local health department when a case of the following conditions is diagnosed: botulism, cholera, plague, relapsing fever (louse-borne), rubeola, smallpox, typhus (louse-borne epidemic type), and yellow fever. They must also report other diseases and outbreaks or undue prevalence of nonreportable diseases or occurrences of unusual diseases. Such reports are confidential.

Vermont

Any physicians who know or suspect that a person they have attended is sick or has died of a communicable disease dangerous to public health must immediately report to the health officer. 18 Vermont Statutes § 1004. All such reports are confidential. § 1099.

Superintendents or other officers in charge of public institutions, such as hospitals, dispensaries, clinics, and so forth, must promptly report the name, sex, nationality, race, marital status, and address of every patient suffering from venereal disease, stating the name, character, stage, and duration of the infection and, if obtainable, the date and source of contracting the same. 18 Statutes § 1101.

Physicians must report tuberculosis cases to the commissioner within one week under 18 Vermont Statutes § 1041. § 1007 requires physicians or those in charge of hospitals to immediately report to the commissioner when a quarantined patient leaves the hospital without consent.

Virginia

The hospital shall report promptly to the Virginia Department of Health, through the local health department, "reportable diseases" under the Rules and Regulations for the Reporting and Control of Diseases of the State Board of Health and any infectious diseases, including nosocomial infections. In addition, hospitals must report two or more epidemiologically related infections, including, but not limited to, staphylococcus aureus, group A beta hemolytic streptococcus, and salmonella species occurring in the obstetrical or nursery units. Rules and Regulations for the Licensure of Hospitals in Virginia § 402.3.

Washington

Washington law requires the state board of health to establish reporting requirements for sexually transmitted diseases. Chapter 70.24 Washington Code § 70.24.125.

West Virginia

West Virginia's Regulations for Hospital Licensure, 64 CSR 12, Section 10.3.3 & .4, requires licensed institutions to make communicable disease reports to the local health officer within 24 hours after the disease is discovered and to make venereal disease reports to the state director of health within 48 hours of diagnosis. 7.3.10 makes the administrator of the facility responsible for the reporting of deaths, reportable diseases, and any other reports required by state or federal law and regulations.

Wisconsin

Any healthcare provider knowing or having reason to know that a person has a communicable disease or has died from one shall report the same to the local health office. § 143.04. Physicians must also report sexually transmitted diseases to the local health officer and the Department of Health in writing. Such reports are confidential. §143.07.

Results of tests for AIDS are confidential and may be disclosed only to the person who receives a test, to healthcare providers who care for the subject, to an agent or employee of the healthcare provider who stores patient healthcare records, provides patient care, or processes specimens of bodily fluids or tissues, to blood banks, to healthcare providers processing human body parts, to the state epidemiologist for surveillance, investigation, or control of communicable disease, to a funeral director or other who prepares the body for burial or to a person who performs an autopsy, to healthcare facility staff committees or accreditation or services review organizations, under court order, to a researcher, to one who provides aid to victims of emergency if exposed to the victim, to a coroner or medical examiner if the patient is deceased, and to sheriffs or jailers, and to persons with whom the patient has had sexual contact or shared intravenous drug use paraphernalia. § 146.025 (5). The healthcare provider, blood bank, or plasma center that obtains specimens to test for HIV shall maintain a record of informed consent for testing or disclosure and maintain a record of the results. § 146.025 (4). Notwithstanding the confidentiality requirements, such persons must report positive tests results for HIV or an antibody to the state epidemiologist. § (7). Violations of this statute can result in civil liability of up to $5,000 or a criminal penalty. §§ (8) (9).

Wyoming

Every licensed physician must immediately report every case of a contagious or infectious disease to the county health officer by telephone, telegram, or the most expeditious manner and keep complete records of such cases. The name of the person suffering from the disease is confidential. Failure to report is a misdemeanor. Wyoming Statutes §§ 35-4-107 and -108. Hospitals or local health officers must report every case of Reye's syndrome to the division of health and medical services of the department of health and social services. § 35-4-111. Physicians or others who diagnose venereal disease and hospital, dispensary, and laboratory superintendents or managers must report venereal diseases to the health authorities. §§ 35-4-130 through 132.

10

Assessing Patient Care, Inspections, and Credentialing

Introduction

Whether a government or one of its agencies has statutory authority to assess patient care, to conduct inspections of healthcare facilities and their records, or to determine whether a provider should be licensed, little doubt exists that it has such powers as are necessary to fulfill its mission of ensuring that the public has quality health care. Many states, however, have laws that give state boards, licensing authorities, or facilities themselves access to medical records and other information to carry out these purposes. Often, however, they limit this authority by placing confidentiality requirements on use of the information gathered. A good starting point to an understanding of what agency can inspect your healthcare facility is to learn what express laws and regulations exist and how they apply.

Federal Laws

The Occupational Safety and Health Administration requires that facilities that expose employees to toxic substances and harmful physical agents permit immediate access to the employee medical records and analyses. 29 C.F.R. § 1910.20.

State Laws

Alabama

After noting that medical records are confidential, § 420–5–7.07 of the Rules of the Alabama State Board of Health Division of Licensure and Certification specifies that inspectors for licensure or surveyors for membership in professional organizations may review hospital records as necessary for compliance.

Arizona

32 Arizona Statutes § 32–1451.01 gives the board of medical examiners the authority to have access to and to copy any documents, reports, records, or any other physical evidence of the person being investigated or those maintained by or in the possession of hospitals, clinics, physician's offices, laboratories, pharmacies, or other public or private agencies or healthcare providers. The board may also subpoena witnesses and documents. The physician-patient privilege does not apply to the board's investigations and proceedings. But patient records, hospital records, medical staff records, medical staff review records, and testimony concerning such records and proceedings are not available to the public. Arizona Health Care Institutions Licensure R9–10–116 notes that when the regulation requires an institution to have bylaws, rules, regulations, policies, procedures, plans, job descriptions, orders, reports, minutes of meetings, records, contracts, agreements, duty schedules, or any other similar items, such requirement means written documents that are readily available for inspection by the director or director's representative.

Arizona R9–14–116, concerning reporting significant blood lead levels, requires the clinical laboratory director to report to the Department's Bureau of Sanitation all findings or evidence of levels of lead in blood samples at or above 40 micrograms of Pb/100 grams of whole blood within ten days. The report must provide the following information: name, age, sex, ethnic group, lead level, and address, and the name, address, and telephone number of the person submitting the sample.

Arkansas

Arkansas Department of Health Regulations Part Six, Section I. C. provides that medical records, although confidential, shall be available to authorized personnel from the Arkansas Department of Health to carry out the purposes of the regulations. Arkansas Statutes § 17–93–104 authorizes disclosure of confidential information in disciplinary hearings before the State Medical Board or in a trial or appeal of a Board order or to physician licensing or disciplinary authorities of other jurisdictions or to hospital committees within or outside the state or pursuant to a court order.

Under the same statute, hospitals must report in writing to the board the name of any member of the medical staff or any other physician practicing in the hospital whose hospital privileges have been revoked, limited, or terminated for any cause, including resignation, within 60 days. The proceedings, minutes, records, or reports of organized committees of hospital medical staffs or medical review committees that review the quality of care and any records compiled or accumulated by the administrative staff of the hospital in connection thereto, together with all communications or reports originating in such committees, are not subject to discovery or admissible in any legal proceeding and are absolutely privileged. Such data may, however, be disclosed to appropriate federal or state agencies that are entitled to such data by statute or regulation. Nor does this statute prevent discovery and admissibility if a practitioner subjected to disciplinary action by such a committee brings such an action. §16–4–105. A similar rule applies to peer rule committees. § 20–9–503.

Under § 5–55–104, the Arkansas Attorney General and prosecuting attorneys have access to all records of persons and Medicaid recipients under the Arkansas Medicaid Program to which the Commissioner of the Department of Human Services has access for the purpose of investigating whether any person has committed Medicaid fraud or for potential use in any legal, administrative, or judicial proceeding. Such records are confidential, however, and are not subject to any outside review or release except when used in a legal, administrative, or judicial proceeding. Anyone who fails to maintain such records is guilty of a felony if the unavailability of records impairs or obstructs the prosecution of a felony. Otherwise, the unavailability of records for such a reason is a misdemeanor.

California

The Welfare and Institutions Code §§ 5328.15(b) and 4515(o) require release of medical information if there is cause to believe that there has been a violation of law subject to the licensing board's jurisdiction.

District of Columbia

Any person in the District may transmit, upon request and if required by the provisions of § 14–307, with consent of the patient, to any medical utilization review committee or medical staff committee operating in the District, any report, note, record, or other data or other information that such person properly has possession of relating to the medical or psychological services provided to any person. No one doing so is liable for damages or equitable relief unless the information was false and the person providing it knew or had reason to believe it was false. § 32–503.

Florida

Florida law § 395.041 requires every licensed facility to have an internal risk management program. The responsible individual has free access to all establishment medical records. The facility must submit annual reports to the department of health and rehabilitative services. The report is confidential and is not available to the public and is not discoverable except in disciplinary proceedings. The reports may be available to a practitioner facing disciplinary proceedings. The facility must report to the department within three working days adverse or untoward incidents that result in the death of a patient, severe brain or spinal damage to a patient, a surgical procedure being performed on the wrong patient, or a surgical procedure unrelated to the patient's diagnosis or medical needs being performed on the patient. These reports are likewise not available to the public or discoverable except in disciplinary proceedings. The department, upon subpoena, has access to any facility records necessary to carry out its functions.

Idaho

The medical staff of any licensed acute care hospital shall promptly notify the board of medicine of all disciplinary actions and revocations or reductions of privileges imposed on physicians and surgeons licensed in Idaho. The board may request, or the hospital may provide on its own, additional files, records, and information. Such materials provided the board will be confidential and available only to the board and its staff unless the board orders otherwise or such matter becomes the subject of formal proceedings. § 39–1393.

Illinois

The Department of Public Health may make such investigations as it deems necessary. § 9, Hospital Licensing Act.

Indiana

§ 34–4–12.6–2 makes all proceedings of peer review committees confidential and privileged except in limited circumstances, such as to a disciplinary authority or the state board of registration or licensure.

Kansas

Only persons authorized by the hospital's governing body shall have access to medical records, but § 28–34–9a (5) states that such persons shall include individuals designated by the licensing agency for the purpose of verifying compliance with state or federal statutes or regulations and for disease control investigations of public health concerns.

Louisiana

Under 37 Statutes § 1278.1, notwithstanding any privilege of confidentiality, no physician or healthcare institution shall refuse to respond to a subpoena of the board for any medical information relative to any patient, provided, however, that the identity of the patient must be maintained in confidence. Any person holding a license to practice medicine shall be deemed, notwithstanding any privilege of confidentiality, to have consented to the disclosure to the board of any and all medical records and information when the board is acting on a complaint and has reasonable cause that the person's fitness and ability to practice medicine has been impaired. § 1278 B.

Maryland

Code § 4–301 (b) and (c) (2) excepts from prohibited disclosure of medical records providing information requested by or to further the purpose of a medical review committee, accreditation board, or commission.

Massachusetts

111 Statutes § 53B requires reporting any restriction, revocation, or failure to renew staff privileges or any resignation of a physician for any reason related to the physician's competence to practice medicine to the board of registration in medicine within 30 days of the reportable action. Such reports are confidential and may be used only in a disciplinary proceeding.

Minnesota

Minnesota Statutes § 147.161 Subdivision 1 requires medical disciplinary boards to keep files containing complaints filed against physicians. In cases in which the board investigates a physician, the board has access to the hospital and medical records of the patient treated by the physician under review if the patient has signed a written consent to such access. If not, the hospital or physician must delete information that identifies the patient before providing the record to the board. Subdivision 3.

Missouri

§§ 198.052.1 and 198.180, Convalescent, Nursing and Boarding Homes, permit the state auditor and the director of fraud investigations to inspect the records of such facilities.

Nebraska

Nebraska provides that even though medical records are confidential, they are subject to inspection by authorized persons. Title 175, Nebraska Department of Health, Chapter 9, § 003.04A.

Nevada

Nevada Statutes § 449.235 specifies that every licensed medical facility or facility for the dependent may be inspected at any time, with or without notice, as often as is necessary by the Health Division or by the Aging Services Division of the Department of Human Resources to investigate complaints made against the facility. § 620.061 is more specific as to records. It requires each healthcare provider to make patient healthcare records available to any authorized representative or investigator of the board of medical examiners of the state in the course of any investigation. Such records may not be used in a public hearing unless the patient consents or the patient's identity is not disclosed.

New Hampshire

The Department of Health and Human Services, Division of Public Health, may make such inspection as shall be prescribed by rules, including at least an annual inspection. § 151:6. Information other than reports relating to vital statistics received by the Department are confidential. § 151:13.

New Jersey

New Jersey Statutes § 26:2H-1 authorizes the Department of Health to inspect healthcare facilities. § 8:43B-7.4 of the Standards for Hospital Facilities makes hospital and patient records available for inspection at all times, within legal limits, to duly authorized representatives of the Department. Another section, however, prevents disclosure of information received thereby in such a way as to indicate the names of specific patients or hospital employees to whom the information belongs and notes that the public prosecutor also has access to hospital records. § 8:43B-1.10.

New Mexico

New Mexico's Medical Malpractice Act, § 41-5-15 (2), requires that an application to the Medical Review Commission by a claimant alleging malpractice must authorize the commission to obtain access to all medical and hospital records and information pertaining to the malpractice claim.

New York

Hospitals must establish a quality assurance program that may review medical records and other records to perform its function of improving the quality of patient care and preventing malpractice. § 405.6.

North Carolina

§ 131E-95 (b) of the Hospital Licensure Act makes the proceedings of medical review committees, the records and materials they produce, and the matters they consider confidential.

Ohio

§ 3727.04 permits the Director of Health to inspect any hospital if there are substantial allegations or evidence of a significant deficiency that would adversely affect the health or safety of its patients and also may inspect to enforce the licensure laws.

Any person or institution providing care or treatment to an individual suffering from a communicable disease must permit the Director of Health or representative to have access to the patient's medical record. § 3701-3-08.

§ 3701-17-18 requires nursing homes to make all records and reports available at all times for inspection by the Director or authorized representative.

§ 3701-7-23 makes the medical records of each maternity patient and newborn available for inspection by the Director of Health.

Oklahoma

76 Oklahoma Statutes § 17 requires any practitioner of the healing arts or any hospital to report to the appropriate licensing board or agency whenever a personal injury claim alleging medical malpractice is made unless their liability insurer does so.

The disposition of the case must also be reported. Failure to make a report is a misdemeanor. Such reports are privileged information.

Oregon

Oregon Administrative Rules § 333-23-190 (11) permits authorized personnel of the Health Division to review medical records.

Pennsylvania

Healthcare facilities and hospitals must report to the State Board of Medical Education and Licensure or the State Board of Osteopathic Examiners, whichever is applicable, the following occurrences, within 60 days of the occurrence: termination or curtailment of employment, association, or professional privileges of a licensed physician with a healthcare facility or hospital where there exists reasonable cause to believe malpractice or misconduct has occurred; resignation or withdrawal of association or of privileges with a facility or hospital to avoid the imposition of disciplinary measures; or receipt of written information that establishes that any physician who has a right to practice or has applied to practice at the healthcare facility or hospital has been convicted of a felony. 35 Pennsylvania Statutes § 448.806a. Such reports are confidential and may not be disclosed except on written request by an authorized public agency or judicial subpoena. Any person who makes such a report in good faith is immune from any criminal or civil liability for having made it.

Rhode Island

Healthcare providers may make confidential healthcare information available to medical peer review committees without patient authorization. Such information, however, must remain strictly confidential. The proceedings and records of such committee are not subject to discovery or introduction into evidence except if the proceedings involve restricting or revoking a physician's license or privileges or if the committee is sued for its actions, provided that use of personally identifiable confidential healthcare information requires the patient's authorization or a court order. § 5-37.3-7.

Tennessee

Medical review committees may have access to hospital records and any practitioner, healthcare employee, or hospital administrator who furnishes information to such committee is immune from liability for furnishing such in good faith and without malice. § 63-6-219.

Texas

Hospital Licensure Standard 12-8.7.3.1 states that special care facilities may allow access to medical records as allowed by state licensing agency law and rules for licensure inspection.

Persons required to keep files and records relating to dangerous drugs shall make them available for inspection by any public official or employee enforcing the dangerous drug laws, at all reasonable hours, for inspection and copying. § 4476–14 Texas Statutes.

Utah

Utah Code § 26–25–1 states that any person or health facility may, without incurring liability, provide information, interviews, reports, statements, memoranda, or other information relating to the ethical conduct of any healthcare provider to peer review committees, professional societies and associations, or any in-house staff committee to be used for purposes of intraprofessional society or association discipline. Such information is privileged.

Health Facility Licensure Rule 7.404 requires hospitals to make records readily available for authorized representatives of the Department of Health for determining compliance with licensure rules.

Vermont

18 Vermont Statutes § 107 authorizes the board to make inspections, investigations, and inquiries respecting the causes of disease and the means of preventing the same and the effect of all circumstances relating to or affecting the public health. § 3–912 of the Hospital Licensure Procedure implements this statute by providing that the hospital grounds and buildings shall be subject to inspection by representatives of the licensing agency and other legalized authorities at all times.

The licensing agency may inspect Level III and Level IV residential care homes pursuant to § VI. 3 a. of its Licensing Regulations and nursing homes pursuant to § 3–28 of the Nursing Home Regulations. The latter regulation specifically requires nursing homes to keep records current and available for review at any time by representatives of the licensing agency.

Virginia

Medical complaint investigating committees and medical practices audit committees have full power to require the production of any documents, records, or other materials that are relevant to its inquiries. §§ 54.1–2922–23 Code of Virginia.

Washington

The Department of Social and Health Services may examine records, including patient records, pertaining to services provided by a healthcare provider and reimbursed by the Department and may remove copies, but not the originals, of records on the premises of healthcare providers during the conduct of audits or investigations.

West Virginia

§ 33-25-10 (a) requires the commissioner or the commissioner's examiners to examine each healthcare corporation's financial condition and methods of doing business at least once a year. Section (b) gives the commissioner and the commissioner's employees free access to all books, records, papers, documents, and correspondence of such a corporation. The commissioner may revoke such a healthcare corporation's license if it takes any such records outside the state without the commissioner's approval.

Wisconsin

Otherwise confidential AIDS testing information may be disclosed to the state epidemiologist or designee for the purpose of providing epidemiologic surveillance or investigation or control of communicable disease and to healthcare facility staff committees or accreditation or healthcare services review organizations for the purposes of conducting program monitoring and evaluation and healthcare services reviews. § 146.025 (5).

Under HSS 92, Confidentiality of Treatment Records, however, concerning those who receive treatment for mental illness, developmental disabilities, or alcohol or drug abuse, members and committees of boards do not have access to treatment records, and in meetings, the program directors must ensure that patient identities are not revealed. HSS 92.03.

Wyoming

§ 35-2-601, Wyoming Statutes, grants access to records, data, or other information relating to the condition of patients in hospitals in the state for the purposes of supervision, discipline, admission, privileges, or control of members of such hospital's medical staff, evaluating, studying, and reporting on matters relating to the care and treatment of such patients and patients generally, research, reducing mortality, prevention and treatment of diseases, illnesses, and injuries, and determining whether hospitals or extended care facilities are being properly used. § 35-2-106 is the statutory authority for the Division of Health and Medical Services, Department of Health and Social Services, to inspect licensed healthcare facilities. § 35-2-110 makes all information received through inspections and other authorized means confidential.

11

Disclosure When a Court Orders You To

Introduction

A subpoena is a court order that commands someone to come to court. A subpoena duces tecum is a court order that commands one who has possession or custody of a record to bring it to court. If someone serves a subpoena on you, you should document its receipt in a log book and record every action you take with respect to the subpoena. You can call the attorney who sent the subpoena, verify the information requested, and ask whether you can mail the records to the court instead of appearing with the records in person. You may also want to ask the attorney to notify you if it turns out that the court does not need the record, such as if the case is settled before trial. You may also want to notify your facility's attorney and discuss what to do about the subpoena with your attorney before you do anything about it, especially if your facility doesn't receive many subpoenas. If your facility routinely receives many subpoenas, you may need to establish a written policy and procedure for dealing with them. See appendix A for Health Care Financing Administration guidelines.

State Laws

Alabama

Appendix B, Chapter 420-5-7, of the Rules of Alabama State Board of Health Division of Licensure and Certification states that when records are removed by court order, they should be accompanied by a responsible hospital employee and returned to the hospital at the end of the hearing for which they were directed to be produced or at the direction of the court.

Alaska

7 AAC 13.130 specifies that information regarding a patient may be released without consent to a person authorized by court order.

Arizona

Arizona § 12–2282 requires the following compliance with subpoena duces tecum for hospital records.

Except as provided in § 12–2285, when a subpoena duces tecum is served upon the custodian of records or other qualified witness from a hospital in an action in which the hospital is not a party and such subpoena requires the production of all or any part of the records of the hospital relating to the care or treatment of a patient in the hospital, it is sufficient compliance therewith if the custodian or other officer of the hospital, within five days after the receipt of such subpoena, delivers by registered mail or in person a true and correct copy of all the records described in such subpoena to the clerk of the court or other tribunal or if there is no clerk then to the court or tribunal, together with the affidavit described in § 12–2283.

The copy of the records shall be separately enclosed in an inner envelope or wrapper and sealed, with the title and number of the action, name of witness, and date of subpoena clearly inscribed thereon. The sealed envelope or wrapper shall then be enclosed in an outer envelope or wrapper, sealed and directed to the clerk of the court or tribunal or if there is no clerk then to the court or tribunal.

§ 12–2283 requires an affidavit accompanying records to meet the following criteria:

- The record shall be accompanied by the affidavit of the custodian or other qualified witness, stating in substance each of the following:
    - That the affiant is the duly authorized custodian of the records and has authority to certify the records.
    - That the copy is a true copy of all the records described in the subpoena.
    - That the records were prepared by the personnel of the healthcare institution or staff physicians or persons acting under the control of either in the ordinary course of healthcare institution business at or near the time of the act, condition, or event.
- If the healthcare institution has none of the records described or only part thereof, the custodian shall so state in the affidavit and deliver the affidavit and such records as are available in the manner provided in § 12–2282.

Arkansas

Title 16 of the Arkansas Code § 46–302 provides that when a subpoena duces tecum is served upon a records custodian of any hospital licensed in the state or in a proceeding in which the hospital is neither a party nor the place where any cause of action is alleged to have arisen and such a subpoena requires the production of all or any part of the records of the hospital relating to the treatment of a patient in the hospital, then compliance is satisfied if the custodian delivers by hand or by registered mail to the court clerk or the officer, court reporter, body, or tribunal issuing the subpoena or conducting the hearing, a true and correct copy of all records described in the subpoena together with an affidavit.

The requirements of the affidavit are set forth in § 16-46-305, and the affidavit must state the following information:

- That the affiant is the duly authorized custodian of the records and has authority to certify the records.
- That the copy is a true copy of all the records described in the subpoena.
- That the records were prepared by personnel of the hospital, staff physicians, or persons acting under the control of either in the ordinary course of the hospital's business at or near the time of the act, condition, or event reported therein.
  - If the hospital has none of the records described or only part of them, the custodian shall state so in the affidavit and file the affidavit and any records in the manner described in §§ 16-46-302 and 16-46-303.
  - The custodian of the records may enclose a statement of costs for copying the records, and that cost shall be borne by the party requesting the subpoena.

According to § 16-46-303, the copy of the records shall be separately enclosed in an inner envelope or wrapper and sealed, with the title and number of the action, the name of the custodian, and the date of the subpoena clearly inscribed thereon. The sealed envelope or wrapper shall be enclosed in an outer envelope or wrapper, sealed, and directed as follows:

- If the subpoena directs attendance in court, to the clerk or the judge of the court.
- If the subpoena directs attendance at a deposition, to the officer before whom the deposition is to be taken, at the place designated in the subpoena for the taking of the deposition, or at the officer's place of business.
- In other cases, to the officer, body, or tribunal conducting the hearing, at a like address.

California

A provider of health care may disclose medical information in the following circumstances: if the disclosure is compelled by a court order; by a board, commission, or administrative agency for purposes of adjudication pursuant to its lawful authority; by a party to a proceeding before a court or administrative agency pursuant to a subpoena duces tecum, notice to appear, or any provision authorizing discovery in a proceeding before a court or administrative agency; by a board, commission, or administrative agency pursuant to an investigative subpoena; by an arbitrator or arbitration panel when arbitration is lawfully requested, pursuant to a subpoena duces tecum; by a search warrant lawfully issued to a government law enforcement agency; or when otherwise specifically required by law. Confidentiality of Medical Information Act §56.10.

Connecticut

According to § 4–104, if any private hospital, public hospital society, or corporation receiving state aid is served with a subpoena issued by a competent authority directing the production of any hospital record in connection with any proceedings in any court, the hospital, society, or corporation upon which the subpoena is served may, except where such record pertains to a mentally ill patient, deliver such record or a copy thereof to the clerk of the court. Any such record or copy delivered to such clerk shall be sealed in an envelope that shall indicate the name of the patient, the name of the attorney subpoenaing the same, and the title of the case referred to in the subpoena. A subpoena for the production of hospital records shall be valid if notice of intent to subpoena is given not less than 24 hours or more than two weeks before the time of production and the subpoena itself is served not less than 24 hours before the time for production.

Florida

§ 395.017. of Title 29 provides that, upon issuance of a subpoena from a court of competent jurisdiction and proper notice by the party seeking such records to the patient or the patient's legal representative, a licensed facility shall release all patient records requested (including X rays) except progress notes and consultation report sections of a psychiatric nature concerning the care and treatment performed by the licensed facility.

Georgia

According to § 24–10–72, an institution (see Georgia Code 37–7–1) and its personnel shall be in compliance with a subpoena or order for production if it shows timely delivery of the medical records or substitutes and certificate to the clerk of the court or other authorized person by any means, including, but not limited to, certified or registered mail.

Hawaii

According to Title 33 Hawaii Code § 622.52, whenever medical records custodians receive a subpoena duces tecum requiring them to produce medical records, they may comply by delivering by messenger or by certified or registered mail a true and correct copy within five days after receipt of the subpoena to the clerk of court or the clerk's deputy authorized to receive it together with an affidavit certifying that they are the custodians and have authority to certify medical records, that the copy is a true copy, and that the records were prepared by medical facility personnel in the regular course of business at or near the time of the act, condition, or event. A notary public must notarize the certificate. § 622–53.

Idaho

A copy of medical records, certified by the custodian of the originals authorized to certify that they are true copies, may be used to satisfy a subpoena, provided that the hospital holds the originals available for inspection and comparison. Idaho Code § 9-420. Hospitals must file certified copies of the resolutions of their governing boards authorizing and identifying such employees in order to avail themselves of this procedure.

When such employees receive a subpoena duces tecum, they may comply by promptly notifying the party causing service of the subpoena and all other parties of the hospital's election to proceed under this statute and the expenses of reproducing such records. Upon payment, the employees must deliver, by mail or otherwise, a true, legible, and durable certified copy to the clerk of the court before which the proceeding is pending or to the officer, body, or tribunal, if the case is not before a court. The copies must be separately enclosed and sealed in an outer envelope or wrapper, with the title and number of the action, cause, or proceeding, the name of the hospital and its employee. The custodian must then place the sealed envelope in an outer envelope for delivery.

Personal attendance of the custodian is required if the subpoena so states. Any patient whose records are thus copied and delivered, any person acting on the patient's behalf, the hospital having custody, or any physician, nurse, or other person responsible for entries on such records, may apply to the court or other body for a protective order denying, restricting, or otherwise limiting access and use of such records.

Indiana

Indiana Code of Civil Procedure § 34-3-15.5-6 establishes detailed rules for dealing with subpoenas received by hospitals. When a subpoena or a subpoena coupled with a patient's written authorization under § 4 or a court order requiring the production of a hospital medical record is served upon any hospital employee, the hospital employee with the custody of the original medical record may elect, in lieu of personally appearing and producing the original hospital medical record, to furnish the requesting party or party's attorney a photostatic copy of the hospital medical record, certified as described below.

If the hospital has elected to so proceed, the hospital employee with custody of the original hospital medical records shall, upon receipt of payment for the reproduction of the hospital medical records, promptly deliver, by certified mail or personal delivery, copies of the records specified in the subpoena to the person specified in the subpoena.

The hospital employee's certification of the records under this section must conform to the following standards:

- Be signed by the hospital employee with custody of the records.
- Include the following information:

- Full name of the patient.
- Patient's medical record number.
- Number of pages in the hospital medical record.
- Statement in substantially the following form:

The copies of records for which this certification is made are true and complete reproductions of the original or microfilmed hospital medical records that are housed in _____ (name of hospital). The original records were made in the regular course of business and it was the regular course of business of _____ (name of hospital) to make the records at or near the time of the matter recorded. This certification is given pursuant to IC 34-3-15.5-6 by the custodian of the records in lieu of the custodian's personal appearance.

The hospital shall prepare the records this way:

- Place the copies of the hospital medical records in an envelope or wrapper.
- Write or type on the envelope or wrapper the following data:
    - The words "Confidential Medical Records."
    - Title and number of the action or proceeding.
    - Name and business telephone number of the hospital employee making the certification.

If the hospital does not have the hospital medical records or has only part of the hospital medical record specified in the subpoena, the hospital employee with custody of the original hospital medical record shall take the following actions:

- Execute an affidavit, either notarized or by affirmation, stating that the hospital does not have or has only a part of the subpoenaed hospital medical records.
- Follow the procedures in subsections (a), (b), (c), and (d) of § 34-3-15.5-6 in delivering the part of the hospital medical records that are in the possession of the hospital.

When records are confidential under 42 U.S.C. §§ 290dd-3 or ee-3 (relating to records of alcoholism patients), the hospital employee having custody of the original medical records shall take the following actions:

- Execute a verified affidavit that contains the following data:
    - Identification of the record or part of it that is confidential.
    - Statement that the confidential record or part of the record will only be provided under the federal procedure for production of the records.
- Comply with subsections (a) through (d) of § 34-3-15.5-6 in delivering the record or part of the record that is not confidential.

Subsection (g) of § 34-3-15.5-6 applies to a medical record or part of a record concerning treatment for mental illness, for which the hospital employee with custody of the original medical record shall take the following actions:

- Execute a verified affidavit that contains the following data:
  - Identification of the record or part of a record that contains the confidential information concerning the treatment of mental illness.
  - Statement that the confidential record or part of the record will only be provided under a court order after in camera review.
- Comply with subsections (a) through (d) of § 34–3–15.5–6 in delivering the record or part of the record that is not confidential.

Subsection (h) of § 34–3–15.5–6 applies to a medical record or part of a medical record that is confidential under IC 16–1–9.5–7, concerning dangerous or communicable diseases. The hospital employee with custody of such original medical record shall take the following actions:

- Execute a verified affidavit that contains the following data:
  - Identification of the record or part of the record that contains the confidential information concerning a dangerous or communicable disease.
  - Statement that the confidential record or part of the record will only be provided under a court order after in camera review under IC 16–1–9.5–7.
- Comply with subsections (a) through (d) of § 34–3–15.5–6 in delivering the record or part of the record that is not confidential under subdivision (1) of this section.

The hospital may charge a reasonable fee to cover the costs of reproducing the hospital medical records.

Kentucky

Kentucky Statute 422.300–.330 provides for mailing by certified or registered mail or by personal delivery of certified copies of the medical record to the attorney or the clerk of court, in lieu of originals and of personal appearance by the records custodian.

Louisiana

According to § 44:7 of the Louisiana code, whenever the past or present condition, sickness, or disease, physical or mental, of any patient treated in any hospital shall be at issue or relevant in any judicial proceeding, the charts, records, reports, documents, and other memoranda shall be subject to discovery, subpoena, and introduction into evidence in accordance with the general law of the state relating to discovery, subpoena, and introduction into evidence of records and documents.

Maine

Maine's Regulations for the Licensure of General and Specialty Hospitals in the State of Maine merely says that medical records generally are not to be removed from the hospital except upon subpoena. Chapter XII, A.

Maryland

Maryland exempts from its rule prohibiting disclosure of medical records providing information in response to legal process.

Massachusetts

111 Statutes § 70 provides, upon proper judicial order, that hospitals or clinics may permit inspection and copying of medical records kept by the hospital or clinic, except a hospital or clinic under the control of the department of mental health, unless the commissioner determines that a disclosure would be in the best interests of the patient, upon request and payment of a reasonable fee.

Mississippi

Mississippi permits disclosure without patient consent when pursuant to a valid court order.

§ 41-9-101 notes that hospital records that are subject to a subpoena do not include X rays, electrocardiograms, and like graphic matter unless specifically referred to in the subpoena. §§ 41-9-103 through 117 cover the procedure to comply with subpoenas. When a subpoena requires hospital records, the custodian may comply by filing with the court clerk or the officer, body, or tribunal a true and correct copy (which may be a film or other reproducing method copy) of all records described in such subpoena. The records must be separately enclosed in an inner envelope or wrapper, sealed, with the title and number of the action, name of witness, and date of subpoena written thereon, and enclosed in an outer envelope. The custodian must enclose an affidavit stating that he is the custodian and has the authority to certify the records, that the copy is a true copy of the records described in the subpoena, and that the records were prepared by hospital personnel in the ordinary course of business at or near the time of the act, condition, or event reported therein and certifying the amount of the reasonable charges for furnishing the record.

New Hampshire

§329:9-a provides that medical disciplinary boards have the power to compel, by subpoena duces tecum, the production of papers and records. Further, malpractice hearing panels may subpoena evidence, including the copies of medical records, X rays, and other documents.

New Mexico

New Mexico's Hospital Association Legal Guide simply says that hospitals must obey any subpoena to produce medical records or information unless it concerns treatment related to drug or alcohol abuse, child abuse or neglect, and certain mental health records, or if the patient is not a party to the action. If the patient is not a party and has not consented to release of the record, the hospital should notify the patient of the request and abide by the patient's wishes as to whether to comply with the subpoena. Such records must be released, however, if the hospital receives a court order to do so instead of a subpoena. A court order is necessary to release drug or alcohol abuse information relating to a patient, even if the patient consents. § 43-2-11 New Mexico Statutes. A subpoena is insufficient authority to release drug or alcohol abuse information.

New York

§ 2306(a) of Art. 23 of the New York Civil Practice Law and Rules Code provides that where a subpoena duces tecum is served upon a hospital requiring the production of records relating to the condition or treatment of a patient, a transcript or reproduction certified as correct by the superintendent or head of the hospital may be produced unless otherwise ordered by a court. Such a subpoena shall be served at least 24 hours before the time fixed for the production of the records unless otherwise ordered by a court.

§ 2306(b) further provides that where a court has designated a clerk to receive such records, delivery may be made to the clerk at or before the time fixed for their production. The clerk shall give a receipt for the records and notify the person subpoenaed when they are no longer required. The records shall be delivered in a sealed envelope indicating the title of the action, the date fixed for production, and the name and address of the attorney appearing on the subpoena. They shall be available for inspection pursuant to the rules or order of the court.

North Carolina

1A-1, Rule 45 Rules of Civil Procedure § 8-61 specifies that when a subpoena commands custodians of hospital medical records to appear for the sole purpose of producing certain records in their custody, they may, in lieu of a personal appearance, tender to the presiding judge or designee by registered mail or personal delivery certified copies together with the subpoena and an affidavit by the custodian testifying to the identity and authenticity of the records, that they are true and correct copies, and, as appropriate, that the records were made and kept in the regular course of business, and that they were made by persons having knowledge of the information set forth. If the custodians don't have such records in their custody, they should submit an affidavit to that effect.

Ohio

Ohio has no statute pertaining specifically to subpoena of medical records. Its general subpoena statute is in Rule 45 of the Ohio Rules of Civil Procedure. § 2317.422 of the Ohio Code, however, states that hospital and nursing home records may be received in evidence if their custodian endorses them, giving the mode and time of their preparation and stating that they were prepared in the regular course of business, and delivers a copy to the attorney for the adverse party not less than five days before trial.

Pennsylvania

When employees are served a subpoena requiring the production of medical records, they may comply by notifying the attorney causing service of the subpoena of the healthcare facility's intention to proceed under the statute, 42 Pennsylvania Statute § 6152, and of the estimated reasonable and actual expenses of reproducing the records. Afterward, the healthcare facility shall hold the originals available, and upon payment of the costs, deliver, by certified mail or personal delivery, within ten days, legible and durable certified copies. The certification shall be notarized and include a statement as follows:

> The copies of records for which this certification is made are true and complete reproductions of the original or microfilmed medical records which are housed in (name of healthcare facility). The original records were made in the regular course of business at or near the time of the matter recorded. This certification is given pursuant to 42 Pa.C.S. Ch 61 Subch. E (relating to medical records) by the custodian of the records in lieu of his personal appearance.

Copies shall be separately enclosed and sealed in an inner envelope or wrapper bearing the legend "Copies of Medical Records." § 6152 (d). When these records are delivered in person, the deliverer shall obtain a receipt. §6153.

Under this statute, § 6155, patients may apply for a protective order limiting access to their records.

If the healthcare facilities have none of the charts or records specified in the subpoena or only a part thereof, § 6154 instructs the custodians of the charts or records to state so in a notarized affidavit and, following notice and payment of expenses, that they will hold available the original charts or records that are in the healthcare facility's custody and specified in the subpoena and shall deliver the certified copies together with the affidavit.

§ 6155 gives any patient whose medical charts or records are copied and delivered pursuant to this subchapter, any person acting on such patient's behalf, and the healthcare facility having custody of the charts or records standing to apply to the court or other body before which the action or proceeding is pending for a protective order denying, restricting, or otherwise limiting access to and use of the copies or original charts or records.

Finally, §§ 6158 and 6159 provide that the original record or personal attendance of the custodian of records shall be required if the subpoena so specifies.

Rhode Island

Rhode Island has a comprehensive statute governing responding to legal process concerning confidential healthcare information. Such information is not subject to compulsory legal process, such as a subpoena, in any type of proceeding. A patient or the patient's representative may refuse to disclose such information in any such proceeding except the following circumstances:

- When the patient introduces the patient's physical or mental condition into evidence.
- When, during a commitment proceeding, a physician determines that the individual needs care or treatment in a facility that is appropriate for mental illness.
- When a court finds that an individual, after having been informed that the communications would not be privileged, has made communications to a psychiatrist in the course of a psychiatric examination ordered by the court, provided that the communications shall be admissible only on issues involving the individual's mental condition.
- When, in a court proceeding, the court determines that an individual's physical or mental condition endangers another.
- In actions involving insurance carriers when such information is relevant and material.
- When, in a court proceeding, the issue arises whether the individual used intoxicating liquors, toluene, or any controlled substance and such confidential healthcare information is relevant and material. In such cases, the court may issue an order compelling production of information that demonstrates the presence of alcohol in a concentration of one tenth of one percent (.1%) or more or the presence of a controlled substance as shown by chemical analysis of blood, breath, or urine, if such test was performed at the direction of a law enforcement official.

In *Bartlett v. Danti*, 503 A.2d 515 (1986), however, the court ruled that this statute was unconstitutional insofar as, in cases in which the patient did not consent to disclosure, the statute precluded litigants from introducing material evidence, thereby preventing them from effectively presenting their claims before the court. Thus, you must check with a Rhode Island attorney as to the current status of any provisions of the Confidentiality of Health Care Information Act.

Tennessee

When custodians receive a subpoena for records in an action in which the hospital is neither a party nor the place where the case arose, they can comply by, within five days, personally delivering or mailing, by certified or registered mail, to the court clerk or officer, body, or tribunal conducting the hearing, a true and correct copy (which may be reproduced) of all records described in the subpoena enclosed in a sealed inner envelope with the title and number of the action, name of the witness, and date of the subpoena written thereon, enclosed in an outer envelope and accompanied by an affidavit that the affiant is the custodian and has authority to certify the records, that they are a true copy of the records described in the subpoena, and that hospital personnel prepared them in the ordinary course of business at or near the time of the event and certifying the charges. Code §§ 68–11–401 through 408.

Texas

Special care facilities may release medical records and other information under court order. Hospital Licensing Standard 12–8.7.3.1.

Virginia

Although Virginia does not appear to have a specific statutory provision for the subpoena of medical charts and records from healthcare facilities, §§ 54.1–2922 and 54.1–2923 of the Code of Virginia do grant a subpoena power to medical complaint investigation and medical practices audit committees, respectively. This subpoena power not only extends to the person who may be the subject of a complaint and other witnesses, but also includes requirements for the production of any documents, records, or other materials that the committee may deem relevant to the inquiry.

West Virginia

West Virginia Statutes § 57–5–4b through 4i cover providing copies of hospital records in compliance with subpoenas. They provide that when records custodians receive a subpoena duces tecum in an action in which the hospital is neither a party nor the place where the action arose, they can comply by filing with the court a true copy of the records described in the subpoena. Section 4c covers sealing, identifying, and directing the records. Section 4e requires the custodian to prepare an affidavit that the records are a true copy.

Wyoming

Wyoming's Standards for Hospital Facilities states that medical records should not be removed from the hospital except upon subpoena. § 8:43–7.2.

12

Disclosure for Medical Research

Introduction

Most states allow medical staff access to patients' records for medical research. In such cases, you should be careful to delete from any research reports all information that would identify the patient unless the patient has consented to being identified.

You should have written procedures documenting your policy on use of records for research covering, for example, the following considerations: access for staff, non-physician healthcare providers, and investigators; approval authority; and security controls.

State Laws

Alaska

Alaska Administrative Code, 7 AAC 13.130 (b) (3), states that patient records and information may be released without consent for research projects authorized by the governing board, if provision is made to preserve anonymity in the reported results.

Arkansas

Arkansas Statutes § 20–9–304 covers the use of records for medical research. All information, interviews, reports, statements, memoranda, or other data of the State Board of Health, Arkansas Medical Society, allied medical societies, or in-hospital staff committees of licensed hospitals, but not the original medical records of patients used in the course of medical studies for the purpose of reducing morbidity or mortality, shall be strictly confidential and shall be used only for medical research. Any authorized person, hospital, sanatorium, nursing home, rest home or other organization may provide such information relating to the condition and treatment of any person to the entities listed above for use in the course of studies for the purpose of reducing morbidity or mortality without incurring liability for damages or other relief. In any event, however, the patient's identity is confidential and will not be released under any circumstances.

California

You may release medical information to researchers if the Director of Mental Health or Developmental Disabilities designates by regulation rules for the conduct of research and requires such research to be first reviewed by the appropriate institutional review board. The rules shall include the requirement that all researchers sign an oath of confidentiality. Welfare and Institutions Code §§ 5328 (e).

Indiana

§ 16–4–11–9 permits the state board to grant legitimate researchers access to confidential patient information obtained by the state board upon fulfillment of certain conditions.

Kansas

Kansas has a specific authorization for disclosure of patients' records for purposes of research into the causes and treatment of drug abuse. Researchers may not publish such information in any way that may disclose a patient's identity. § 65–5525 (a) and (c).

Maryland

Maryland authorizes disclosure of medical information at the request of a researcher for medical and healthcare research under a protocol approved by an institutional review board. Code § 4–301(c)(5). Each hospital should set up its own protocol for what it considers legitimate research.

Minnesota

The Department of Public Welfare must assure confidentiality to individuals who are the subject of research by the state authority or treatment by an approved treatment program unless the individual gives written permission otherwise or in proceedings related to neglect or termination of parental rights. § 144.651, Subdivision 13, provides that written, informed consent must be obtained before a patient's participation in experimental research and that both consent and refusal shall be documented in the individual care record.

New Mexico

§ 14–6–1, New Mexico Statutes, notes that statistical studies and research reports based upon confidential information may be published or released to the public as long as they do not identify individual patients either directly or indirectly or in any way violate the privileged and confidential nature of the relationship and communications between practitioner and patient.

Rhode Island

Rhode Island exempts from the general prohibition against disclosure of confidential healthcare information release to qualified personnel to conduct scientific research, provided they do not disclose patient identities. § 5-37.3-4 (b)(3).

South Carolina

§ 44-51-190, which establishes confidentiality of records that identify drug and alcohol abuse patients, permits disclosure for research conducted or authorized by the State Department of Mental Health or the South Carolina Commission on Alcohol and Drug Abuse.

Utah

Utah Code § 26-25-1 states that any person or health facility may, without incurring liability, provide information, interviews, reports, statements, memoranda, or other data relating to the condition and treatment of any person to the Department of Health, to the Division of Mental Health within the Department of Social Services, to research organizations, to peer review committees, to professional review organizations, to professional societies and associations, or to any health facility's in-house staff committee for use in any study with the purpose of reducing morbidity or mortality or for the evaluation and improvement of hospital and health care. Such information is confidential and privileged. §§ 26-25-2 and 3.

Vermont

Vermont's Bill of Rights for Hospital Patients, contained in Title 18 Vermont Statutes § 1852 (7), when talking about a patient's right to privacy, notes that medical personnel or individuals under the supervision of medical personnel researching the effectiveness of that medical treatment shall have access to the patient's medical records without the patient's consent.

Wisconsin

HSS 92.04 (3), which relates to confidentiality of treatment records of persons treated for mental illness, developmental disabilities, and alcohol or drug abuse, permits access to medical records without patient consent for authorized research.

§ 146.02 (5), which relates to confidentiality of AIDS testing information, permits use of confidential data for research if the researcher is affiliated with a healthcare provider, has obtained permission to perform the research from an institutional review board, and provides written assurance to the person disclosing the test results that use of the information is only for the purpose for which it is provided to the researcher, that the information will not be released to a person not connected with the study, and that the final research product will not reveal information that may identify the subject unless the researcher has first received informed consent for disclosure from the subject.

Wyoming

§ 35–2–601, Wyoming Statutes, grants access to records, data, or other information relating to the condition of patients in hospitals in the state for the purposes of research, reducing mortality, and prevention and treatment of diseases, illnesses, and injuries.

13

Disclosure upon Request

Introduction

Most states have statutes or administrative regulations that provide for patients and others to have access to medical records upon request. Some are quite detailed, such as California's. Others say little more than that patients are to have access to their records. If your state does not have a detailed procedure in its statutes or regulations or your licensing body does not have a detailed procedure in its rules, you should carefully consider a procedure and adopt one in your bylaws in order to allow for authorized access while maintaining confidentiality. See the discussion on security in chapter 5.

Federal Laws

The Freedom of Information Act does not apply to private facilities, but rather to federal agencies. And medical information is not covered by the act.

The Occupational Safety and Health Administration (OSHA) requires that employers provide employees access to required medical records of employees exposed to toxic substances and harmful physical agents. Upon receiving a request from an employee or designated representative, the employer must provide a copy of the record within 15 days.

State Laws

Alabama

After noting that medical records are confidential, § 420–5–7.07 of the Rules of the Alabama State Board of Health Division of Licensure and Certification specifies that access to medical records shall be determined by the hospital governing board.

Alaska

Alaska Statutes 18.23.065 provides that patients may inspect and copy any record.

Arizona

Arizona's Healthcare Institutions Licensure Rules specify that medical record information shall be released only with the written consent of the patient or the legal guardian or in accordance with law. § R9–10–221.

Arkansas

Arkansas's rules simply state that written consent of the patient or legal guardian shall be presented as authority for the release of medical information.

California

California Health and Safety Code, § 25250, provides for patients' or their representatives' access to their medical records in licensed healthcare facilities, upon payment of reasonable clerical costs. The facility must provide for patient inspection within five working days and provide copies within 15 working days of the request and payment of fees. The facility may refuse access when providing access would have a substantial risk of detrimental consequences. Minors may inspect their records only if the records cover care that a minor is lawfully able to consent to.

California's Confidentiality of Medical Information Act § 56.10 provides for disclosure of medical records upon request to the following people and groups:

- Providers of health care or other healthcare professionals or facilities for purposes of diagnosis or treatment.
- Insurer, employer, healthcare service plan, hospital service plan, employee benefit plan, governmental authority, or any other entity responsible for paying for healthcare services provided to the patient to the extent necessary to determine responsibility for payment and for payment to be made.
- Persons or entities that provide billing, claims management, medical data processing, or other administrative services for providers.
- Organized committees and agents of professional societies or medical staffs or professional standards review organizations or to those insuring, responsible for, or defending professional liability that a provider may incur if such recipients are engaged in reviewing the competence or qualifications of healthcare professionals or reviewing healthcare services with respect to medical necessity, level of care, quality of care, or justification of charges.
- Those responsible for licensing or accrediting.
- County coroner in the course of an investigation by the coroner's office.
- Public agencies, clinical investigators, healthcare research organizations, and accredited public or private nonprofit educational or healthcare institutions for

bona fide research purposes so long as no further disclosure by the recipient identifies the patient.
- Provider of health care that has created medical information as a result of employment-related healthcare services to an employee conducted at the specific prior written request and expense of the employer may disclose to the employer that part of the information which is relevant in a lawsuit, arbitration, grievance, or other claim or challenge to which the employer and employees are parties and in which the patient has placed in issue the patient's medical history, condition, or treatment and which describes functional limitations of the patient that may entitle the patient to leave from work for medical reasons or limit the patient's fitness to perform the employment.
- Unless informed in writing of an agreement to the contrary, to a sponsor, insurer, or administrator of a plan or policy that the patient seeks coverage or benefits under.
- Group practice prepayment healthcare service plan.
- Insurance institution, agent, or support organization that has complied with the requirements of the Insurance Code.

Colorado

Patients in healthcare facilities or their designated representatives may inspect their records, other than those relating to psychiatric or psychological problems or those that an independent third-party psychiatrist believes would have a significant negative effect on the patients, at reasonable times and upon reasonable notice. The patients or their representatives are also entitled to a summary of their psychiatric or psychological problems following termination of the treatment program. Following the patients' discharge, the patients are entitled, upon submission of a written authorization-request for records and payment of reasonable costs, to have copies of their records, including X rays. This statute does not require a person responsible for the diagnosis or treatment of venereal diseases or addiction to or use of drugs in the case of minors to release records of such diagnosis or treatment to a parent, guardian, or other person other than the minor or the minor's designated representative. Colorado Code § 25–1–801.

§ 25–1–802 contains virtually identical language covering patient records in the custody of individual healthcare providers.

Connecticut

Healthcare providers shall supply to patients, upon request, complete and current information possessed by that provider concerning any diagnosis, treatment, and prognosis of the patients. Upon written request, the providers, except as provided in § 4–194, shall furnish the patients a copy of their health records at a cost of not more than $.25 per page plus postage. If the providers reasonably determine that the information is detrimental to the health of the patients or would cause harm to the patient or another, they may withhold the information from the patients. They may supply it to another provider or an appropriate third party. § 20–7c. Upon written request of the patients, the providers may furnish a copy of the medical records to another provider. §20–7d.

Delaware

25 Delaware Code § 4306 gives any person that is legally liable or against whom someone has asserted a claim for compensation for injuries permission to examine the records of any association, corporation, or other institution or body maintaining a hospital in reference to the treatment, care, and maintenance of the injured person.

Florida

Florida Statutes §766.204 provides that upon request and payment of reasonable costs, copies of any medical record that is relevant to any litigation of a medical negligence claim shall be provided to claimants or defendants or their attorneys within ten days.

Georgia

Georgia Statutes §§ 31–33–2 through 6 cover furnishing records, other than psychiatric, psychological, or other mental health records, upon request. Upon receipt of a written request from the patient, you shall furnish a complete and current copy of the records to the patient, to any healthcare provider the patient designates, or to any other person the patient designates unless disclosure would be detrimental to the physical or mental health of the patient. In such cases, you need not provide the record except to healthcare providers designated by the patient. The requester is responsible for paying the costs of copying and mailing the records unless they are records requested to apply for a disability benefit. You may require payment before you provide the records. If you provide records in good faith, under this statute, you are not civilly or criminally liable for such release. Otherwise, however, the records remain confidential.

Hawaii

If a healthcare provider's patients request copies of their medical records, the facility shall make the records available unless in the opinion of the provider obtaining such records would be detrimental to the patients' health. In such cases, the provider shall advise the patients that it will make copies of the records available to the patients' attorneys upon presentation of a proper authorization signed by the patients.

If a patient's attorney requests copies of the patient's medical records and presents a proper authorization from the patient, the facility must provide complete and accurate copies within ten working days. The requester must pay reasonable costs for making copies of the records. Hawaii Evidence Code Title 33 § 622–57.

Illinois

77 Illinois Administrative Code recommends only that hospitals issue definite policies and procedures pertaining to the use of medical records and the release of medical record information. § 250.1510 (b) (5).

Indiana

Indiana Code 16–4–8, Access to Health Records, § 2(a), provides that, upon written request and reasonable notice, a provider shall supply to patients the health records possessed by that provider concerning the patients. However, § 6 specifies that information may be withheld if a provider who is a healthcare professional reasonably determines that the information requested is detrimental to the physical or mental health of the patients or is likely to cause the patients to harm themselves or others. Note: House Bill No. 1300 amends 16–4–8–7 by clarifying who may obtain a copy of the patient's health records while that patient is an inpatient and either an emancipated minor or incompetent. Under § 16–4–8–2.1, upon the patient's written request, the provider shall, upon payment of actual costs, provide to the patient or designee, access to or a copy of the patient's X rays.

Insurance companies may also obtain health records or medical information with a written consent.

The statute does not authorize patients to obtain a copy of their health records while they are inpatients. A parent, spouse, guardian, or next of kin, however, may. § 16–4–8–7.

Kentucky

Patient information shall be released only on authorization of the patient, the patient's guardian, or the executor of the patient's estate. 902 KAR 20:016 § 3 (11) (c).

Louisiana

40 Louisiana Statutes § 2144 B. states that hospital records are subject to reasonable access to the information contained therein by the patient or the patient's authorized representative. Upon written request, signed by the requester, the hospital shall, except for good cause shown, such as if medically contraindicated, furnish the records as soon as practicable and upon payment of the reasonable costs thereof. The hospital and its employees, acting in good faith, are justified in relying on the reasonable representations of the requester and may not be held liable in damages for complying or inability to comply with the request.

Maine

Maine's Regulations for the Licensure of General and Specialty Hospitals in the State of Maine state in Chapter XII A. 2. that written consent of the patient is authority for release of medical information. The state's law on release of HIV infection status is more specific, requiring that the patient elect, in writing, whether to authorize release of that portion of the record containing the HIV infection status information at or near the time the entry is made. Title 5 § 19203–D.

Maryland

Maryland Code § 4–301 (a) states that any provider of medical care who has custody of medical records may reveal specific medical information to the person on whom the record is kept or the person's agent or representative. Maryland Statutes § 4–303 (e) makes it a misdemeanor, however, to knowingly request or obtain a medical record under false pretenses or through deception.

Massachusetts

111 Statutes § 70 provides that patients or their attorneys, when authorized in writing, may inspect medical records kept by the hospital or clinic, except a hospital or clinic under the control of the department of mental health, and receive a copy upon request and payment of a reasonable fee.

Minnesota

Minnesota Statutes § 144.335 states that upon patients' written requests and payment of reasonable costs, a healthcare provider shall furnish the patients copies of their records or the pertinent part thereof or a summary. The provider may exclude written speculations about the patients' condition, except that all information necessary for informed consent must be provided. The provider may also withhold information if the information is detrimental to the physical or mental health of the patients or is likely to cause them to harm themselves or others and may supply the information to an appropriate third party or other provider who may release it to the patients. The patients may consent to release it to another healthcare provider.

§ 144.651 specifies that patients and residents of healthcare facilities may approve or refuse release of their personal and medical records to any individual outside the facility. Residents shall be notified when their records are requested and may select someone to accompany them when the records or information are the subject of a personal interview. This section does not apply to complaint investigation and inspections by the Department of Health, where required by third party payment contracts, or where otherwise provided by law.

Mississippi

Mississippi statutes provide that hospital records are the property of the hospital subject to reasonable access upon good cause shown by the patients, their personal representatives or heirs, their attending medical personnel, and their duly authorized nominees, and upon payment of any reasonable charges for such access. Statutes § 41–9–65.

Missouri

Written consent of the patients or the patients' legal representatives is required for access to or release of information, copies, or excerpts from hospital medical records to persons not otherwise authorized to receive them. 13 CSR 50-20 (D) 5.

Information held by the Missouri Department of Social Services on convalescent, nursing, and boarding home residents may be disclosed only to the following people: the department or any person or agency designated by the department; the attorney general; the department of mental health for residents placed through that department; any appropriate law enforcement agency; the resident, the resident's guardian, or any other person designated by the resident; and appropriate committees of the general assembly and the state auditor, but only to the extent of required financial records.

Inspection reports and written reports of investigations of complaints, including reports of abuse and neglect and relating to the quality of care of residents, are accessible to the public, provided that they do not identify the complainant or any particular resident. § 198.032.

Nevada

Each healthcare provider must make patients' healthcare records available for physical inspection by the patients or their representatives if the latter have written authorization from the patients. The healthcare provider must make copies available to such persons upon request and payment of copying costs, not to exceed $.60 per page for photocopies and a reasonable cost for copies of X rays and other records produced by similar processes. Statutes § 629.061.

New Hampshire

The only reference to releasing records on request in New Hampshire's administrative regulations is in He-P 806.10 (f), requiring outpatient clinics to provide for written release of information of patient/client clinical records.

New Jersey

Hospitals must require written consent of the patient for release of medical information. Standards for Hospital Facilities 8:43B-7.1 (c) 4. The facility must have policies and procedures approved by the Department of Health governing the availability, release, and provision of copies of the medical record to patients or the patient's authorized representative. The policies must include the following elements:

- Description of the procedures to protect medical information against loss, destruction, or unauthorized use.
- Schedule of fees, as established by the facility, for obtaining copies of the medical record.
- Business hours, as defined by the facility, during which the patients have access to their medical records.

- In the event that it is medically contraindicated (as documented by a physician in the patients' medical record) that the patients have access to or obtain copies of their medical records, the medical records shall be made available to the patients' authorized representatives.

The facility must ensure that it provides a patient's medical record within 30 calendar days of the written request. § 8:43B–7.4.

New Mexico

Facilities should use New Mexico Hospital Association Form 2, which, in paragraph 4, authorizes the hospital to release information in patient's records to designated individuals and entities. If others request access to or copies of records, the hospital should require that the patient sign NMHA Form 14, Consent to Access Hospital Records and Release Medical Information. The hospital and the physician may decide whether disclosure is in the patient's best interest. If not, after advising the patient and the individual requesting the records of its decision, the hospital may withhold the record unless the patient obtains a court order for release thereof.

§ 14–6–1 New Mexico Statutes provides for release of confidential health information on request to a governmental agency or its agent, a state educational institution, a duly organized state or county association of licensed physicians or dentists, a licensed health facility, or staff committees of such facilities without incurring liability for libel or slander.

New York

§ 405.10 (a) (6) of the Department of Health, Health Facilities Series H–40, notes that hospitals shall allow patients and other qualified persons to obtain access to their medical records. § (5) adds that, other than to patients, hospitals may release records only to hospital staffs involved in treating the patient and individuals permitted by federal and state law.

North Carolina

North Carolina's physician-patient communications privilege statute, §8–53, states that confidential information in medical records shall be furnished only on the authorization of the patient or, if deceased, the patient's executor, administrator, or next of kin or if ordered by a judge.

Nursing home licensure regulation § 10 NCAC 3H .0607 requires nursing homes to make provision for patients or residents or their legal guardians to have access to the information contained in their medical records unless otherwise ordered by their physicians. The facility must keep, as part of the patients' medical records, signed authorizations concerning approval or disapproval of medical information for licensure inspections.

North Dakota

North Dakota's Hospital Licensing Rules, § 33-07-01-16.2 a. through c., require that hospitals keep medical records confidential. Only authorized persons shall have access to the record, and written consent of the patient must be presented as authority for the release of medical information.

Ohio

According to Ohio Code § 3701.74 (C), patients who want to examine or obtain a copy of their medical records must submit to the hospital a signed, written request dated not more than 60 days before the date on which it is submitted and indicate whether the hospital is to send the copy to their residence or hold it at the hospital. The hospital shall permit inspection or provide the copy within a reasonable time, unless a physician determines for clearly stated treatment reasons that disclosure is likely to have an adverse effect on the patient. In that event, the hospital shall provide the record to a physician designated by the patient.

Oklahoma

Any patient is entitled, under 76 Oklahoma Statutes Section 19, to obtain access to the information in the patient's medical records and to receive copies upon payment of the costs of the copies, not to exceed ten cents per page. Access to psychiatric records, however, requires a court order upon a finding that access is in the best interest of the patient.

43A Oklahoma Statutes § 1-109 provides that privileged or confidential medical information may not be released to anyone not involved in patient treatment programs without a written release by the patient or, if the patient is a minor or if a guardian has been appointed for the patient, the guardian of the patient or a court order.

Mental health or drug and alcohol abuse patients are not entitled to personal access to the information in their psychiatric or psychological records or to copies unless the treating physician consents or a court orders access.

Oregon

Medical records departments must maintain a current written policy on the release of medical records information including patients' access to their medical records. Oregon Administrative Rules § 333-23-190.

Pennsylvania

Patients or patient designees shall be given access to or a copy of their medical records unless access thereto is specifically restricted by the attending physician for medical purposes. Upon the death of a patient, the hospital shall provide the executor or next of kin, upon request, access to all medical records of the deceased patient. The facility may charge the reasonable costs of making copies of the record. 28 Pennsylvania Code §§ 103.22(b)(15) and 115.29. 28 Pennsylvania Statutes §115.28 adds that copies of medical records may be made available for appropriate purposes, such as insurance claims and physician review, consistent with their confidential nature.

Rhode Island

Rhode Island Title 5:37.3–4 provides that healthcare providers may release confidential healthcare information upon written consent of the patients or their authorized representatives. The consent form must contain the following elements: a statement of the need for and proposed uses of the information; a statement that all information is to be released or clearly indicating the extent of that to be released; and a statement that the consent may be withdrawn at any time and is subject to revocation except where used in an application for a life or health insurance policy, in which case the authorization expires two years from the issue of the policy. Authorizations in connection with a claim for insurance benefits are valid during the pendency of the claim. Any revocations of consent must be in writing.

South Dakota

South Dakota Statute 34–12–15 specifies that hospitals or other institutions to which persons resort for treatment of disease shall provide copies of all medical records, reports, and X rays to a discharged patient or the patient's designee upon receipt of a written request signed by the patient. The facility may require that the patient pay reproduction and mailing expenses.

Tennessee

Under Tennessee law, hospitals shall provide reasonable access to the information contained in health records upon good cause shown by the patients, their personal representatives or heirs, or their attending medical personnel and upon payment of any reasonable charge for such service. Code § 68–11–304; Rules of the Board for Licensing Healthcare Facilities 1200–8–4–.03 (1) (b) (ii).

In the case of children of whom only one parent has custody, the Tennessee Child Custody Act, §36–6–103, provides that the treating physician or hospital may release a copy of the child's medical records upon written request by the noncustodial parent; in the case of joint custody, the parent with whom the child is not residing; or in the case of a child in the custody of a legal guardian, then either parent. Costs must be paid by the requesting party.

Texas

The Texas Hospital Licensing Standards' only reference to releasing medical record information upon request is in Standard 12–8.7.3.1 relating to special care facilities. It states that such facilities may allow access or release by written authorization of the resident unless the physician has documented in the record that to do so would be harmful to the physical, mental, or emotional health of the resident.

Utah

Utah's Health Facility Licensure Rule 7.404 states that medical records shall be readily available to "other persons authorized by consent forms." The rule adds that the patient or the patient's legal representative must give written consent to release medical information to unauthorized persons.

Utah's Judicial Code § 78-25-25 requires practitioners and hospitals to make patients' medical records available for inspection and copying by patients' attorneys if they present a written authorization signed by the patient and notarized, or by the parents or guardians of minors, or by the personal representatives or heirs of deceased patients. The attorneys shall pay for the costs of the copies, and the practitioners or facilities may retain possession of the actual records.

Vermont

Vermont's Bill of Rights for Hospital Patients, contained in Title 18 Vermont Statutes § 1852, states that patients have the right to expect that all communications and records pertaining to their care shall be treated as confidential. Only medical personnel or individuals under the supervision of medical personnel directly treating the patient or those persons monitoring the quality of that treatment or researching the effectiveness of that treatment shall have access to the patients' medical records. Others may have access to those records only with the patients' written authorization.

Virginia

Hospitals may release copies of patients' medical records if the patients or their legal representatives consent in writing. In the case of minors, their parents, guardians, or legal representatives may consent. § 208.6.2, Rules and Regulations for the Licensure of Hospitals in Virginia. The same rule applies to nursing homes. § 24.3.2, Rules and Regulations for the Licensure of Nursing Homes.

Washington

Washington's Administrative Regulations simply provide, in § 248-18-440, that hospitals' medical records services must have in effect current written policies and procedures that include access to and release of data in patients' individual medical records and other medical data taking into consideration their confidential nature.

West Virginia

West Virginia Statute § 16-29-1 provides that any licensed healthcare provider shall, upon patients' written request, provide patients, their authorized agents, or representatives a copy or summary of the patients' records within a reasonable time. Furnishing a copy or summary of reports of X-ray examinations is sufficient to comply with this section, and patients shall reimburse the provider for all reasonable expenses incurred in complying with this statute.

This general rule has two exceptions. First, in the case of patients receiving treatment for psychiatric or psychological problems, a summary shall be made available to the patients, their authorized agents, or authorized representatives following termination of the program. §16–29–1 (a). Second, healthcare providers treating minors for birth control, prenatal care, drug rehabilitation, or venereal disease need not, under the above rule, release such patient records to a parent or guardian without the prior written consent of the patient. § 16–29–1 (b).

Wisconsin

Written consent of the patient or the patient's legally authorized representative shall be presented as authority for release of medical information to persons not otherwise authorized to receive such information, HSS 124.14 (2) (b).

HSS 92, relating to records of patients treated for mental illness, developmental disabilities, or alcohol or drug abuse, provides that patients have access to their treatment records during treatment unless the director has reason to believe that the benefits of allowing access to a patient are outweighed by the disadvantages. HSS 92.05. After discharge, patients are allowed access, upon one working day's notice, and may have a copy of their records, subject to payment of a uniform and reasonable fee.

Part IV

When Should You Refuse to Release Records?

Deciding whether to refuse to release records involves two major concerns: the right to privacy and the physician-patient privilege. Chapter 14 discusses patients' rights to privacy. Chapter 15 discusses the physician-patient privilege and privacy and medical ethics.

14

Patients' Rights to Privacy

Definition of the Right to Privacy

The traditional legal definition of privacy is "the right to be left alone." Modern privacy laws have expanded this definition to include an individual's right to control personal information. The United States Supreme Court has recognized a constitutional right to privacy. In addition, many statutes, such as the federal Privacy Act of 1974, have expanded individuals' right to privacy. The right to privacy is not an absolute right, however. In some situations, the public's or the government's need to know may outweigh an individual's privacy rights. Please see the American Medical Association's Confidentiality Statement in appendix E.

Federal Laws

The Privacy Act allows patients access to their medical records and the information contained therein, but it does not apply to private hospitals and other private healthcare facilities. See appendix A for Health Care Financing Administration requirements.

The Comprehensive Alcohol Abuse and Alcoholism Prevention, Treatment, and Rehabilitation Act of 1970, 42 U.S.C. § 242(a) and 21 U.S.C. § 872(e) as amended, prohibits discrimination in the admission of alcohol abusers to any hospital or outpatient facility that receives federal funding. A similar provision of the Drug Office Abuse and Treatment Act of 1972, 21 U.S.C. § 1175(b) (2) (c), prohibits discrimination in the admission of drug abusers to hospitals that receive federal funding. Both statutes establish standards for disclosure of medical records of drug abusers. Violating patients' confidentiality may result in a criminal penalty. Under either statute, unless you have the patient's express consent, you may only disclose patient records to medical personnel as needed to meet an emergency, to qualified personnel conducting medical research if you delete any patient identifiers, or by authority of a court order based on a showing of good cause. Written consent must include the date, the name of the patient and the facility, the name of the party to whom the information may be disclosed, the purpose of the disclosure, the precise nature of the information to be disclosed, and the length of time the authorization is valid.

42 Code of Federal Regulations Part 2 requires public, nonprofit, and for-profit private entities conducting, regulating, or assisting alcohol or drug abuse programs to maintain records showing patient consent to disclosure and documenting disclosure to medical personnel in a medical emergency from confidential alcohol and drug abuse patient records. Part 2a of 42 C.F.R. requires alcohol, drug abuse, and mental health researchers to maintain confidentiality certificates showing that the Secretary of Health and Human Services has authorized the researcher to withhold the identity of research subjects in legal proceedings to compel the disclosure of the identity of research subjects.

State Laws

Alabama

Rules of the Alabama State Board of Health Division of Licensure and Certification Chapter 420–5–7.07 (h) states that records and information regarding patients are confidential. Access to these records shall be determined by the hospital governing board. Inspectors for licensure or surveyors for membership in professional organizations shall be permitted to review medical records as necessary for compliance.

Alaska

7 AAC 12.890 (a) (7) states that patients have the right to confidentiality of their medical records and treatments. 13.130 specifies that information regarding a patient may be released without consent only to the following people:

- Person authorized by court order.
- Healthcare providers if a medical emergency arises.
- Research projects authorized by the governing board, if provision is made to preserve anonymity in the reported results.
- Other persons to whom disclosure is required by law.

A facility may release records and information regarding a patient to the patient or to an individual for whom the patient, or legally designated representative of the patient, has given written consent to disclosure. The consent must include the following data:

- Patient's name.
- First and last dates of service authorization.
- Information to be released.
- Recipient of the information.
- Signature of the patient or the legally designated representative of the patient.

7 AAC 36.010 applies to the use or disclosure of information concerning applicants and recipients of services from the division of family and youth services and requires safeguarding of information about such clients, including medical examinations.

Arizona

Arizona Revised Statute R9–10–221 D provides that medical records information shall be released only with the written consent of the patient or the legal guardian or in accordance with law.

Arizona R9–10–221 concerning medical records services provides in E. that hospitals that have designated psychiatric or substance abuse units shall maintain confidentiality of medical records as required by A.R.S. § 36–509 and applicable regulations.

According to Arizona Revised Statutes § 36–509, concerning confidential records, all information and records obtained in the course of evaluation, examination, or treatment shall be kept confidential and not as public records, except as the requirements of a hearing pursuant to this chapter may necessitate a different procedure. Information and records may be disclosed, pursuant to rules established by the department, only to the following people or organizations:

- Physicians and providers of health, mental health, or social and welfare services involved in caring, treating, or rehabilitating the patient.
- Individuals to whom the patient has given consent to have information disclosed.
- Persons legally representing the patient and, in such case, the department's rules shall not delay complete disclosure.
- Persons authorized by a court order.
- Persons doing research or maintaining health statistics, provided that the department establishes rules for the conduct of such research as will ensure the anonymity of the patient.
- State department of corrections in cases in which prisoners confined to the state prison are patients in the state hospital on authorized transfer either by voluntary admission or by order of the court.
- Governmental or law enforcement agencies when necessary to secure the return of a patient who is on unauthorized absence from any agency where the patient was undergoing evaluation and treatment.
- Family members actively participating in the patient's care, treatment, or supervision. An agency or treating professional may only release information relating to the person's diagnosis, prognosis, need for hospitalization, anticipated length of stay, discharge plan, medication, medication side effects, and short- and long-term treatment goals.

Further, an agency shall release information pursuant to subsection A, paragraph 8, of § 36–509 only after the treating professional or designee interviews the person undergoing treatment or evaluation to determine whether release is in that person's best interests. A decision to release or withhold information is subject to review pursuant to § 36–517.01. The treating agency shall record the name of any person to whom information is given.

Arkansas

Medical records are confidential. Only personnel authorized by the administrator shall have access to the records. Written consent of the patient is necessary for authority to release medical records. Medical records cannot be removed from the hospital except upon issuance of a subpoena by a court with authority to issue such an order.

All laboratory notifications of communicable diseases are confidential and shall not be open to inspection by anyone except public health personnel. Statutes § 20–16–504. Similarly, any reports, information, or records of a physician misconduct proceeding before the Arkansas State Medical Board are strictly confidential. § 17–93–104.

In addition, § 20–15–901 provides that the identification of persons voluntarily participating in the Department of Health AIDS testing program must be kept secret.

California

California's Confidentiality of Medical Information Act confirms patients' rights to privacy in their medical records by governing the release of patient-identifiable information by healthcare providers. The Health and Safety Code § 25250 provides for patient or patient representative access upon request and payment of reasonable clerical costs. Violation of this section may result in disciplinary action by the licensing authority. The Civil Code § 5 also provides for permissive access by the following people: healthcare providers; insurers to the extent necessary to obtain payment; credentialing committees, and so forth; licensing or accrediting bodies (however, in such cases, the facility may not permit patient-identifiable information to be removed unless expressly permitted or required by law); county coroner; researchers; and employers if the medical treatment was at the prior request and payment of the employer. The code also provides for mandatory disclosure to authorized representatives of patients when the patient has executed a valid release. Violations of this statute constitute a misdemeanor if the patient is harmed by the unauthorized release. In addition, the patient may recover actual damages, punitive damages not to exceed $3,000, and attorney's fees not to exceed $1,000.

Similarly, the Welfare and Institutions Code § 5328 covers psychiatric records. In such cases, patient authorization requires the approval of a physician, psychologist, or social worker. Mandatory disclosure is required in the following cases:

- Between qualified professionals when providing services, in referrals, and in conservatorship hearings.
- To the extent necessary to make an insurance claim.
- To persons designated by the conservator.
- For research.

- To courts and law enforcement agencies as needed to protect public officials.
- To the patient's attorney.
- To probation officers.
- To county patients' rights advocates with patient authorization.
- To law enforcement officials if the patient is a victim or has committed a crime in the facility.

Permissive disclosure of information, not access to the records, is allowed to the family or persons designated by the patient or without designation if the patient is unable to give consent.

The Welfare and Institutions Code § 4514 has similar provisions for records of the developmentally disabled.

Colorado

Colorado does not permit a person responsible for the diagnosis or treatment of venereal diseases or addiction to or use of drugs in the case of minors to release records of such diagnosis or treatment to a parent, a guardian, or other person other than the minor or the minor's designated representative. Colorado Code § 25–1–801 (d). Similarly, records relating to illegitimate children may not be disclosed except as required by a court or by the department or local board of health. § 25-3-204. Finally, § 18-4-412 makes it a felony, without proper authorization, to knowingly obtain, steal, disclose to an unauthorized person, or copy a medical record or medical information. The statute defines "proper authorization" as "a written authorization signed by the patient or his duly designated representative or an appropriate order of court or authorized possession pursuant to law or regulation for claims processing, possession for medical audit or quality assurance purposes, possession by a consulting physician to the patient, or possession by hospital personnel for record-keeping and billing purposes."

Connecticut

The fact that a doctor consulted with, examined, or treated a minor for venereal disease is confidential, § 19a–216, as are records of applicants for enrollment and enrolled patients in community drug abuse treatment programs, § 19a–373, and the fact that a minor requested or received treatment and rehabilitation for drug dependence, § 19a–382.

State Department of Health Regulations § 19-13-D44 makes industrial health facilities' records confidential except for cases involving claims under the Workman's Compensation Act, as authorized by law, to responsible individuals when such disclosure is in the employee's best interest, or when authorized by the employee.

Delaware

Information and records held by the Division of Public Health relating to known or suspected sexually transmitted diseases including HIV infection are confidential and may only be released in limited circumstances, Title 16 §§ 711–2, as are reports of venereal disease cases, § 702.

§ 9113 makes health information obtained by health maintenance organizations confidential.

District of Columbia

Any publication by any medical utilization review committee, peer review committee, medical staff committee, or tissue review committee shall keep confidential the identity of any patient whose condition, care, or treatment was a part thereof. § 32–504.

Florida

Florida Statutes § 110.123 (9) makes patient medical records and medical claims records of state employees, former employees, and eligible dependents in the custody or control of the state group insurance program confidential.

Georgia

No physician and no hospital or healthcare facility shall be required to release any medical information concerning a patient except to the Department of Human Resources and its subelements, where authorized or on other waiver (see the Georgia discussion in chapter 15) or required by law, statute, or regulation, or on written authorization by the patient, the patient's parents, or guardian, or by court order or subpoena. § 24–9–40.

§ 24–9–47 makes AIDS information confidential and specifies the limited circumstances under which such information may be disclosed.

Records of medical review committees are not subject to discovery or introduction into evidence in any civil action against a healthcare provider arising out of matters that are the subject of evaluation or review by such a committee. No person who attends such a meeting is allowed to testify about what went on at such a meeting in a civil action. Code § 31–7–143.

Data concerning the diagnosis, treatment, or health of anyone enrolled in a health maintenance organization is confidential and may not be disclosed except upon consent of the enrollee or pursuant to statute or court order or in the event of a claim or litigation between the enrollee and the health maintenance organization.

The Department of Human Services shall assure confidentiality to individuals who are the subject of research by the state authority or are recipients of alcohol or drug abuse treatment from a licensed or approved program. § 254A.09.

Hawaii

Hawaii's retention of medical records statute Title 33 § 622–58 (d) speaks of retaining medical records "in a manner that will preserve the confidentiality of the information in the record."

Idaho

Idaho Code § 39-1392 establishes a privilege for all written records of interviews, all reports, statements, minutes, memoranda, charts, and the contents thereof, and all physical materials relating to research, discipline, or medical study of any in-hospital medical staff committees or medical society for the purposes of medical research or study of hospital patient cases or medical questions or problems using data and information from hospital patient cases. § 39-1392e excepts from the privilege information involved in an inquiry, a proceeding, or a disciplinary matter regarding the propriety of health care.

§ 39-1393 makes information concerning disciplinary actions taken against physicians confidential.

Idaho Code § 39-1392b makes all written records of interviews, all reports, statements, minutes, memoranda, charts and the contents thereof, and all physical materials relating to research, discipline, or medical study of any in-hospital medical staff committees or medical society confidential. This law, however, does not prohibit medical societies or hospitals from using such records for proper purposes, such as assessing patient care. § 39-1394(d) requires that the method used to destroy the record be in keeping with its confidential nature.

Illinois

77 Illinois Administrative Code recommends that hospitals issue definite policies and procedures pertaining to the use of medical records and the release of medical record information, § 250.1510 b) 5), and safeguard records from unauthorized use, § a) 2).

Indiana

A number of Indiana statutes and regulations make medical records confidential. For example, Indiana Code § 16-4-8-8, while providing that records are the property of the provider and may be used for legitimate business purposes, including insurance claims, collection of accounts, litigation defense, quality assurance, peer review, and scientific, statistical, and educational purposes, mandates that the provider must at all times protect the confidentiality of the record and may disclose the patient's identity only when essential to the provider's business use or for quality assurance and peer review. Indiana State Board of Health Hospital Licensure Rules similarly require confidentiality. 410 IAC 15-1-9 (2) requires storage or destruction to be accomplished in such a way as to maintain confidentiality. § 16-1-9.5-2 (3) specifies that case reports of HIV infection that do not involve a confirmed case of AIDS submitted to the state board that concerns individuals included in formal research projects, who have been tested anonymously at a designated site, or who were tested by a healthcare provider permitted by the state board to use a number identifier code, may not use the name or any other identifying characteristics of the individual tested. Similarly, § 16-1-10.5-21 and 9.5-9 require confidentiality in voluntary identification information of communicable disease carriers and concerning notice of bodily fluid precautions on bodies of people who died with communicable diseases. § 16–4–9–6 covers release of confidential information concerning cancer patients by the state board. § 16–4–10–9 sets forth the requirements for disclosure of information for research purposes. § 16–4–11–9 has confidentiality requirements for traumatic injury reports, and § 34–4–12.6–2 makes proceedings of peer review committees confidential.

§16–1–9.5–7 makes information involving communicable or other diseases confidential. You may not release or make public such information upon subpoena or otherwise, except in the following cases:

- You may release such medical or epidemiologic information for statistical purposes if done in a manner that does not identify any individual.
- You may release such medical or epidemiologic information with the written consent of all individuals identified in the information you want to release.
- You may release such information to the extent necessary to enforce public health laws, laws described in Indiana Code 35–38–1–7 (relating to creating an epidemiologically demonstrated risk of the transmission of human immunodeficiency virus [HIV] as an aggravating factor for sentencing in criminal cases), or to protect the health or life of a named party.

Improperly disclosing such information can subject the offender to punishment for committing a misdemeanor or discharge or other disciplinary action by the agency that employs the offender.

Iowa

Iowa provides for confidentiality of medical records in several places. Iowa Code § 22.7 makes certain public records confidential, including hospital records, medical records, and professional counselor records of the condition, diagnosis, care, or treatment of a patient or former patient or a counselee or former counselee, including outpatients.

§ 229.25 requires hospitals or other facilities treating mentally ill persons to keep records relating to the examination, custody, care, and treatment of any person in that hospital or facility confidential with the following three exceptions:

- When the information is requested by a licensed physician, attorney, or advocate who provides the facility's chief medical officer a written waiver signed by the patient.
- When the information is sought by a court order.
- When the person who is hospitalized or the person's guardian, if the person is a minor or is not legally competent, signs an informed consent release specifying the person or agency to whom the facility is to send the information.

The chief medical officers may release such records for research purposes so long as they do not disclose patients' names or identities. They may also release appropriate information to the spouse of a patient if they deem it to be in the best interests of the patient and the spouse.

Under § 39-1392, certain records of in-hospital committees and medical societies are confidential. § 141.23 makes records of AIDS testing confidential.

§ 514B.30 prohibits officers, directors, trustees, partners, and employees of health maintenance organizations from testifying to or making public disclosure of privileged communications and from releasing the names of membership lists of enrollees.

Kansas

Kansas Administrative Regulations 28-34-9a (d) (5) specifies that records shall be confidential. Only persons authorized by the hospital governing body shall have access to the records, including individuals designated by the licensing agency to verify compliance with statutes or regulations and for disease control investigations.

Kentucky

902 KAR 20:016 Section 3 (11) (c) states that only authorized personnel shall be permitted access to patient records. Patient information shall be released only on authorization of the patient, the patient's guardian, or the executor of the patient's estate.

All records in the possession of local health departments or the cabinet for human resources that concern persons infected with sexually transmitted diseases are confidential and may be released only to the physician retained by the patient, for statistical purposes as long as no individual can be identified, with consent, if necessary to enforce the rules of the cabinet for human resources relating to the control and treatment of such diseases, and to the extent necessary to protect the life or health of the named party. § 214.420.

Maine

The Regulations for the Licensure of General and Specialty Hospitals in the State of Maine, Chapter XII, A., states that the licensing standard is that only authorized personnel have access to the record, that written consent of the patient must be presented as authority for the release of medical information, and that medical records are generally not removed from the hospital except upon subpoena.

Maine has a comprehensive statute covering AIDS testing, 5 Maine Statutes §§ 19201-19208. It provides that no person, upon penalty of termination of employment or civil liability, including damages and a fine of up to $1,000 for a negligent violation and $5,000 for an intentional violation, may disclose the results of an HIV test, except as follows:

- To the subject of the test.
- To the patient's designated healthcare provider, who may further disclose the information only to other healthcare providers who are providing direct patient care to the subject.

- To others whom the subject has designated in writing.
- To healthcare providers who process donated human body parts to assure medical acceptability of the gift.
- To certain research facilities when the test is performed in a manner in which they do not reveal the subject's identity.
- To an anonymous testing site.
- To other agencies that are responsible for the treatment or care of the subject, including the Department of Corrections, the Department of Human Services, and the Department of Mental Health and Mental Retardation.
- To the Bureau of Health.
- As part of the medical records when disclosure has been authorized by the subject.
- Pursuant to court-ordered disclosure.

No medical record containing test results may be disclosed in any proceeding without the patient's consent except in the following instances:

- Proceedings under the communicable disease laws.
- Proceedings under the Adult Protective Services Act.
- Proceedings under child protection laws.
- Proceedings under mental health laws.
- Pursuant to a court order on a showing of good cause.
- In utilization reviews.

Healthcare providers with patient records containing HIV infection status must have a written policy providing for confidentiality that requires, at a minimum, termination of employment for any employee who violates the confidentiality policy.

Maryland

Maryland makes a provider of medical care who makes a prohibited disclosure liable for damages and attorney's fees. A prohibited disclosure is defined as specific medical information contained in medical records unless authorized by the individual on whom the record is kept. Code § 4–301 (b). Subsection (c), however, permits disclosure of medical information from such records when the provider is taking one of the following actions:

- Performing medical records or allied support services for or on behalf of a patient.
- Providing information requested by or to further the purpose of a medical review committee, accreditation board, or commission or in response to legal process.
- Providing information requested to conduct the proper activities of the healthcare provider.

- Providing information to a government agency performing its lawful duties as authorized by an act of the Maryland General Assembly or the United States Congress.
- Providing information at the request of a researcher for medical and healthcare research under a protocol approved by an institutional review board.
- Revealing the contents of medical records under circumstances where the identity of the patient is not disclosed to the recipient of the records.
- Providing information to an insurance company or to a defendant or the defendant's legal counsel in connection with a potential or actual malpractice claim against a provider of medical care.
- Providing information requested by another provider of medical care for the sole purpose of treating the individual on whom the record is kept.
- Providing information to a third party payor for billing purposes only.
- Providing information to a nonprofit health service plan or a Blue Cross or Blue Shield Plan to coordinate benefit payments under more than one sickness and accident, dental, or hospital and medical insurance policy other than an individual policy.
- Providing information to organ and tissue procurement personnel at the request of a physician for a patient whose organs and tissues may be donated for the purpose of evaluating the patient for possible organ and tissue donation.

Maryland Code §§ 18–201, 18–203, 18–205, and 18–206, respectively, make infectious or contagious disease reports, cancer reports, laboratory examination reports, and sentinel birth defects reports confidential. § 18–207 (d) makes required monthly reports of directors of medical laboratories concerning the identity of anyone tested for human immunodeficiency virus confidential.

Massachusetts

Every patient or resident of a hospital, institution for the care of unwed mothers, clinic, infirmary, convalescent or nursing home, or home for the aged has the right to confidentiality of all records and communications. 111 § 70E. This section does not prevent any third party reimburser from inspecting and copying, in the ordinary course of determining eligibility for or entitlement to benefits, records relating to diagnosis, treatment, or other services provided to any person for which coverage, benefit, or reimbursement is claimed so long as the policy provides for such access or in connection with any peer or utilization review. Department of Public Health Regulations 130.111 (E) states that confidential information in medical records may be provided only upon written authority of the patient or the executor of the patient's estate.

111 Statutes § 119 makes records pertaining to venereal diseases confidential. § 70F provides for confidentiality of HLTV-III tests. 112 Statutes § 12G prevents physicians, healthcare facilities, nursing homes, and any other medical provider from

disclosing information concerning the diagnosis, treatment, or condition of a patient in connection with the establishment of eligibility for certain medical benefits.

Minnesota

Information concerning illegitimate births is confidential and may not be released except to representatives of the commissioner of health or the commissioner of human services. 4640.1400, Subpart 2, Minnesota Administrative Rules.

Mississippi

According to § 41–9–67, hospital records are not public records, and patients have a privilege of confidence in them.

Missouri

13 CSR 50–20.021 (d) 7 notes that hospitals cannot release medical records or information without the written consent of the patient or the patient's legal representative.

§ 198.032 prohibits the Department of Social Services from publicly disclosing confidential medical, social, personal, or financial records of any convalescent, nursing, or boarding home resident, except in a manner that does not identify any resident or pursuant to court order. Child or nursing home resident abuse records are also confidential.

Montana

The Montana Hospital Association Manual speaks of maintaining records to protect their secrecy. Chapter 23–4.

Nebraska

Title 175, Chapter 9, 003.04A6 states that medical records are confidential, privileged, and subject to inspection by authorized persons. They may not be removed except by court order. Title 174, Chapter 5, 008, makes data obtained by the Cancer Registry confidential and gives specific guidance on use and release of such information.

Rule 30 (2) (c) xiii 8, 1 and 2, of the Regulations and Standards for Hospitals, Nebraska Department of Health, states that proceedings, records, and reports of medical staff committees or utilization review committees are privileged and may not be disclosed unless the patient waives the privilege or a court orders disclosure.

Nevada

Nevada Statutes § 449.720 specifies that all patients of medical facilities have the right to retain their privacy concerning their programs of medical care, including confidentiality of all communications and records concerning them.

Persons applying for or receiving treatment for alcohol or drug abuse have a right to confidentiality concerning any information relating thereto. § 458.055.

The health division may not disclose the identity of any patient, physician, or hospital involved in a required cancer report unless the party gives prior written consent. § 457.270.

New Hampshire

Records of residents of sheltered care facilities are confidential. He–P 804.04 (c). Clinical records of outpatient clinics, residential treatment and rehabilitation facilities, and home healthcare providers shall be safeguarded against unauthorized use. He–P 806.10, 807.07, and 809.07. Clinical laboratories must keep records and reports of tests confidential. He–P 808.12 (e).

Statutes § 318–B:12 make healthcare practitioners responsible for keeping separate records of receipt and disposition of controlled drugs, "so as not to breach the confidentiality of patient records."

Statutes § 151:13 makes information other than reports relating to vital statistics received by the Department of Health and Welfare confidential and not subject to disclosure except in licensing or revocation of license proceedings.

Neither can the identity of a person tested for the human immunodeficiency virus be disclosed. Statutes 141–F: 8. See chapter 9.

New Jersey

Facilities must develop procedures to protect medical records from unauthorized use according to § 8:43B–7.4, Standards for Hospital Facilities.

The Department of Health may not disclose information it acquires during inspections in such a way as to indicate the names of the specific patients or hospital employees to whom the information pertains. § 8:43B–1.10.

New Mexico

New Mexico Statute 43–2–11 C prohibits disclosure of the records of residents of the state who voluntarily submit themselves for treatment for alcoholism except on court order.

Statute 14–6–1A. states that all health information that identifies specific individuals as patients is strictly confidential and is not a matter of public record or accessible to the public even though it is in the custody of a governmental agent or a licensed health facility. The custodian of such information may furnish it upon request "to a governmental agency or its agent, a state educational institution, a duly organized state or county association of licensed physicians or dentists, a licensed health facility or staff committees of such facilities." 14–6–1C says that statistical studies and research reports may be published if they do not identify individual patients or otherwise violate the physician-patient privilege. Similarly, New Mexico requires authorization by the patient for release of any information relating to a mental disorder or developmental disability from which a person well acquainted with the patient might recognize the patient unless the recipient of the information is a mental health or developmental disabilities professional working with the patient when access to such information is required for the treatment, where disclosure is necessary to protect against a clear and substantial risk of death or serious injury, where, in the case of a minor, the disclosure to a parent or guardian is essential for the minor's treatment, or where the disclosure is to an insurer who is contractually obligated to pay expenses for the patient's treatment.

According to the New Mexico Hospital Association Legal Handbook, Chapter 5B, all hospitals should treat all patient information as confidential and should not divulge it to anyone other than the patient's physician without the patient's written consent. The hospital should notify the patient of any subpoena it receives concerning the patient's records in any case in which the patient is not a party and should not release the records unless the patient consents or the facility receives a court order.

New York

§ 405.10 (a) (5) of the Department of Health, Health Facilities Series H-40, notes that hospitals shall ensure the confidentiality of patient records. § 405.7, titled "Patients' Rights," specifies that one of their rights is to confidentiality of all information and records pertaining to their treatment, except as otherwise provided by law.

North Carolina

North Carolina's physician-patient communications privilege statute, § 8-53, states that confidential information in medical records shall be furnished only on the authorization of the patient or, if deceased, the patient's executor, administrator, or next of kin or if ordered by a judge. Other provisions prohibit disclosure of specific medical information, such as disclosures of cancer patients, drug abuse patients, nursing home patients, and persons identified as having the AIDS virus.

North Dakota

North Dakota's Hospital Licensing Rules, § 33-07-01-16 a through c, requires that hospitals keep medical records confidential. Only authorized persons shall have access to the record, and written consent of the patient must be presented as authority for the release of medical information. Medical records generally shall not be removed from the hospital environment except upon subpoena. § 33-07-03-13-4 specifies that all information contained in clinical records of long-term care facilities shall be treated as confidential and may be disclosed only to authorized persons.

Ohio

§§ 2305. 24 to 2305.25.1 of the Ohio Code provides for confidentiality of information utilization review committees.

§ 3727.14 prohibits disclosing the name or social security number of a patient or physician in data that § 3727.11 requires hospitals to furnish to the department of health. See chapter 3.

Oklahoma

§ 1-109 of Title 43A Oklahoma Statutes makes medical records both confidential and privileged. Such information is available only to persons or agencies actively engaged in patient treatment or related administrative work. No such information shall be released to anyone not involved in treatment without a written release by the patient or, if the patient is a minor or if a guardian has been appointed, the guardian of the patient, or a court order.

Information received by the State Commissioner of Health through inspections or otherwise is confidential and may not be disclosed except in a licensure or license revocation or suspension proceeding. Title 63 § 1-709.

All information and records that identify persons with communicable or venereal disease that is required to be reported is confidential and may not be released except in the following circumstances:

- Upon court order.
- With informed consent of the patient or the patient's parent or legal guardian.
- Release is necessary to protect the health and well-being of the public as determined by the State Department of Health.
- Release is made of medical or epidemiological information to persons who have had risk exposures.
- Release is made of medical or epidemiological information to health professionals, state agencies, or district courts to enforce laws concerning the treatment and control of communicable or venereal diseases.
- Release is made of specific medical or epidemiological information for statistical purposes in such a way that no person can be identified. § 1-502.2.

Unauthorized disclosure of such information makes the party making the disclosure liable for damages caused thereby, including punitive damages. Title 63 § 1-502.20. Similarly, birth defects information under § 1-550.2 and tumor registry information under § 1-551.1 are confidential and may only be divulged under limited circumstances. Child abuse reporting information is also confidential. 21 Oklahoma Statutes § 846.

Oregon

Oregon Administrative Rules 333-70-055 (17) requires medical records departments to maintain written policies on the release of medical record information, including patient access to medical records.

Oregon Laws, Chapter 600, Section 17 (3), states that no person shall disclose the identity of a person upon whom an HIV-related test was performed or the results of such a test in a manner that permits identification of the person unless the person authorizes the disclosure or it is required by law.

Pennsylvania

Pennsylvania Statutes, Title 28 § 115.27, requires you to treat all medical records as confidential. Only authorized personnel shall have access to the records. The written authorization of the patient shall be presented and then maintained in the original record as authority for release of medical information outside the hospital.

11 Pennsylvania Statutes § 2215 makes records of child abuse confidential and prevents disclosure except in limited circumstances.

Rhode Island

Rhode Island enacted its Confidentiality of Health Care Information Act, § 5-37. 3-2, "to establish safeguards for maintaining the integrity of confidential health care information that relates to an individual." .3-3(c) defines "confidential health care information" as "all information relating to a patient's health care history, diagnosis, condition, treatment, or evaluation obtained from a health care provider who has treated the patient." The statute goes on to require that except as otherwise specifically provided by law, you may not release a patient's confidential healthcare information without the patient's consent or the consent of the patient's authorized representative except in the following cases:

- To a physician, dentist, or other medical personnel who believes in good faith that the information is necessary to diagnose or treat the individual in a medical or dental emergency.
- To medical peer review committees or the state board of medical review.
- To qualified researchers, auditors, and so forth provided they do not identify any individual patient in any report, audit, or evaluation or otherwise disclose patient identities.
- To law enforcement personnel if someone is in danger from the patient or if the patient tries to get narcotics from the healthcare provider illegally or in child abuse and gunshot wound cases.
- For coordinating healthcare services and to educate and train within the same healthcare facility.
- To insurers to adjudicate health insurance claims.
- To malpractice insurance carriers or lawyers if the healthcare provider anticipates a medical liability action.
- To a court or lawyer or medical liability insurance carrier if a patient brings a medical liability action against the provider.
- To public health authorities in order to carry out their functions.
- To the state medical examiner in the event of a fatality that comes under the examiner's jurisdiction.

- Concerning information directly related to a claim for workers' compensation.
- To the attorneys for a healthcare provider when release is necessary to receive adequate legal representation.
- To school authorities of disease, health screening, and/or immunization information required by the school or when a school age child transfers from one school or school district to another.
- To a law enforcement agency to protect the legal interests of an insurance institution agent or insurance-support organization in preventing and prosecuting the perpetration of fraud upon it.
- To a grand jury or court pursuant to a subpoena when the information is required for the investigation or prosecution of criminal wrongdoing by a healthcare provider and the information is unavailable from any other source.
- To the state board of elections pursuant to a subpoena when required to determine the eligibility of a person to vote by mail because of illness or disability.
- To certify the nature of permanency of a person's illness or disability, the date when the patient was last examined, and that it would be an undue hardship for the person to vote at the polls so that he may obtain a mail ballot.
- To the central cancer registry.

A hospital may release the fact of patients' admission and general descriptions of their condition to their relatives, their friends, and the news media.

The statute also provides that third parties receiving a patient's confidential healthcare information must establish security procedures, including the following measures:

- Limiting access to those who have a "need to know."
- Identifying those who have responsibility for maintaining security procedures for such information.
- Providing a written statement to each employee about the necessity of maintaining the confidentiality of the information and the penalties for unauthorized disclosure.
- Taking no disciplinary action against anyone who reports a violation of these rules.

§ 5-37.3-5 establishes requirements for situations in which a patient is denied insurance, benefits, employment, and so forth and requests amending or expunging erroneous information or addition of relevant information.

South Carolina

South Carolina Department for Health and Environmental Control Regulation No. 61-16 for Minimum Standards for Licensing of Hospitals and Institutional General Infirmaries, Section 601.7, states that medical records will be treated as confidential. Regulation No. 61-13 in Section 501 states that medical records of residents of intermediate care facilities for mental retardation are confidential.

South Dakota

The Administrative Rules of South Dakota, 44:04:09:04, state that hospitals and nursing homes must have written policies and procedures pertaining to the confidentiality and safeguarding of medical records. South Dakota Statute § 34–20A–91 requires information used for research into the causes and treatment of alcohol abuse to be kept confidential and not published in a way that discloses patients' names or other identifying information. § 34–14–1 makes information procured in the course of a medical study strictly confidential and specifies that it may be used only for medical research.

Tennessee

As part of its comprehensive statutory regulation of medical records, Tennessee Code § 68–11–304 specifies that hospital records, except as otherwise provided by law, are not public records, and nothing in the medical records statutes should be considered to impair any privilege of confidentiality conferred by law on patients, their personal representatives, or their heirs.

Tennessee Code § 10–7–504 provides that the medical records of patients in state hospitals and medical facilities and those of persons receiving medical treatment in whole or in part at the expense of the state are confidential and are not open for inspection by the public. Any records containing the source of body parts for transplantation or any information concerning persons donating body parts is likewise confidential.

All records and information held by the department of health and environment or a local health department relating to known or suspected cases of sexually transmitted disease are confidential and may be released only in the limited circumstances listed in Code § 68–10–113.

Finally, information furnished to medical review committees is privileged and confidential. § 63–6–219.

Texas

Texas's Hospital Licensing Standard 12–8.7.3.1, covering special care facilities, states that such facilities shall protect medical records against loss, damage, destruction, and unauthorized use by safeguarding the confidentiality of medical record information and allowing access and/or release only in the following circumstances:

- Under court order.
- By written authorization of the resident unless the physician has documented in the record that to do so would be harmful to the physical, mental, or emotional health of the resident.
- As allowed by state licensing agency law and rules for licensure inspection purposes and reporting of communicable disease information.
- As specifically allowed by federal or state laws relating to facilities caring for residents with AIDS or related disorders.

Utah

All medical records must be kept confidential. Only authorized personnel may have access to medical records. The patient or the patient's legal representative must give written consent to release medical information to unauthorized persons. Rule 7.404.

Vermont

Vermont's Bill of Rights for Hospital Patients, contained in Title 18 Vermont Statutes § 1852, states that patients have the right to expect that all communications and records pertaining to their care shall be treated as confidential. Only medical personnel or individuals under the supervision of medical personnel directly treating the patient or those persons monitoring the quality of that treatment or researching the effectiveness of that treatment shall have access to the patient's medical records. Others may have access to those records only with the patient's written authorization. Vermont's physician-patient privilege (see chapter 15) amplifies patient's rights to confidentiality by precluding disclosure of confidential information acquired by a healthcare practitioner in a professional capacity.

Vermont law also makes child abuse and neglect reports confidential, 33 Statutes § 686, tuberculosis reports confidential, 18 Statutes § 1041, and venereal disease reports confidential, 18 Statutes § 1099.

Virginia

The Rules and Regulations for the Licensure of Hospitals in Virginia § 208.6 specifies that medical records shall be kept confidential, that only authorized personnel shall have access to the records, and that the hospital shall release copies thereof only with the written consent of the patient or the patient's legal representative or to duly authorized state or federal health authorities or others authorized by the Virginia Code or federal statutes. If the patient is a minor, the patient's parent, guardian, or legal representative must consent. Under § 208.6.3, the hospital's permanent record may be removed from the hospital's jurisdiction only in accordance with a court order, subpoena, or statute. The same rules apply to nursing homes, §§ 24.3 and 24.3.3.

Washington

Hospitals must establish policies and procedures that govern access to and release of data in patients' individual medical records and other medical data taking into consideration the confidential nature of these records. Washington Administrative Code § 248–18–440. These records and other personal or medical data on patients must be handled and stored so that they are not accessible to unauthorized persons.

No person may disclose or be forced to disclose the identity of a person who has been investigated or who has considered or requested a test or treatment for a sexually transmitted disease or upon whom such a test has been performed except to the following people:

- To the subject of the test or the subject's legal representatives, with the exception of such a representative of a minor child over 14 years of age and otherwise competent.
- To any person who secures a specific release from the subject or the subject's guardian with the exception of representatives of minors as above.
- To a public health officer or the Centers for Disease Control.
- To health facilities or providers that procure, distribute, or use human body parts or body tissues, semen, or blood specimens.
- To public health officers conducting investigations when the record was obtained as a result of court-ordered HIV testing.
- To persons allowed access to the record by court order granted upon a showing of good cause.
- To persons at risk for acquisition of the disease because of their interaction with the infected individual.
- To law enforcement officers, firemen, healthcare providers, and so forth after exposure to bodily fluids.
- To claims management personnel only when the information is solely for the prompt and accurate evaluation and payment of claims. Chapter 70.24 Washington Statutes.

West Virginia

Legislative Rule 16-5C of the Board of Health, Section 9.7, covers nursing home patients' rights to confidentiality. The rule states that patients are assured confidential treatment of their personal and healthcare records and condition, which shall not be discussed without their consent with persons not treating or caring for them. Patients have the right to refuse release of their personal or healthcare records to any individual outside the facility, except as required by law or third-party payment contracts. A specific signed release by the patient is required for all other releases. A prior executed blanket release is not acceptable.

§ 33-25A-26 states that any data or information pertaining to the diagnosis, treatment, or health of any enrollee or applicant that a health maintenance organization obtains from the person or a healthcare provider is confidential and may not be disclosed except in the following instances:

- As necessary to facilitate an assessment of the quality of care or to review the complaint system.
- Upon the express written consent of the enrollee or legally authorized representative.
- Pursuant to statute or court order.
- In the event of a claim or litigation between such person and the HMO in which such data or information is pertinent.

The HMO may claim any privileges against disclosure that the provider could claim.

§ 16–4A–3 makes laboratory reports for blood tests for syphilis of pregnant women confidential. Similarly, information received by the state department of health to enforce its rules and regulations is confidential and not to be publicly disclosed except in a proceeding concerning the issuance or revocation of a license.

Wisconsin

Under Wisconsin law, all healthcare records are confidential and may be released only upon informed consent or to the following people listed in Statutes 146.82 (2):

- To healthcare facility staff committees or accreditation or healthcare services review organizations for the purposes of conducting management and financial audits, program evaluation, healthcare services reviews, or accreditation.
- To healthcare providers to the extent their duties require access.
- To the extent that the records are needed for billing, collection, or payment of claims.
- Under lawful order of a court.
- In response to a written request of any federal or state governmental agency to perform a legally authorized function.
- For research.
- To a county agency designated under s. 46.09(2) to receive reports of elder abuse.
- To the department of health under 46.73 relating to cancer reporting.
- To staff members of the protection and advocacy agency to protect the rights of persons with developmental disabilities or mental illness.
- To persons as provided under s. 655.17(7)(b) relating to filing malpractice claims if the patient files a submission of controversy.
- To a county department or law enforcement agency to investigate child abuse.
- To school district employees when they have responsibility for health records or when access is necessary for them to comply with federal or state law.
- To persons and entities under 940.22 relating to reporting sexual exploitation by a therapist.

In addition, under Statutes 53.30, records concerning individuals who have received services for mental illness, developmental disabilities, alcoholism, or drug dependence are confidential and may be released only pursuant to informed consent or as provided for by the statute.

Patients may inspect or receive a copy of the records upon submitting a statement of informed consent and paying reasonable costs. Statutes 146.83.

Wisconsin Statutes 146.025 provides that results of a test for the presence of HIV or an HIV antibody may be disclosed, other than with the subject's consent, to the following people:

- Subject of the test.
- Healthcare providers.
- Blood banks.
- State epidemiologist.
- Funeral directors.
- Healthcare facility staff committees or accreditation or healthcare services review organizations.
- Under court order.
- Researchers.
- Anyone who gives aid to the victim of an accident if exposed thereby to the disease.
- Coroner.
- Sheriff or jail keeper.
- Those with whom the person had sexual contact or shared intravenous drug use paraphernalia, if the person is deceased.

No person to whom such test results have been disclosed may disclose it except under the same rules.

Finally, the Wisconsin Administrative Code, HSS 92, establishes further rights to privacy for patients who received treatment for mental illness, developmental disability, and alcohol and drug abuse, except those provided by individual practitioners. Under HSS 92.03, such records that in any way identify a patient are confidential and may be released only upon informed consent by the patient or in the following cases:

- For management audits, financial audits, or program monitoring and evaluation.
- For billing or collection.
- For research.
- By court order.
- For progress determination and to determine adequacy of treatment.
- Within the department.
- In medical emergencies.
- To facilities receiving an involuntarily committed person.
- To correctional facilities or probation and parole agencies.
- To counsel, guardians ad litem, counsel for the interest of the public, and court-appointed examiners.
- To correctional officers about a change in status.
- Between a social services department and a 51 Board.
- Between subunits of a human services department and between the human services department and contracted service providers.
- To law enforcement officers when necessary to return a patient on unauthorized absence from the facility.

15

The Physician-Patient Privilege

Introduction

Most states have statutes that prohibit physicians from disclosing information that they obtained as a result of a patient-physician relationship concerning the care and treatment of the patient. The purpose of this privilege is to encourage patients to disclose everything relevant to their conditions to their physicians in a full and frank manner so that physicians may treat patients properly. The privilege means that patients have a privilege to refuse to disclose and to prevent their doctors (and perhaps other professional medical personnel) from disclosing information acquired in confidence while treating the patients. The privilege covers not only information provided orally but also any information doctors obtain during the course of examination or treatment that is confidential, including test results, diagnoses, and medical advice. Incidental information, such as the patient's address, occupation, age, and so forth, is usually not privileged. The practical effect of this privilege is to prevent doctors or other healthcare professionals from disclosing confidential information gained during medical examinations or treatments in court in a civil suit unless the patients waive the privilege. The privilege is usually inapplicable in criminal trials.

Note that the privilege is the patient's, not the physician's. A court may compel a doctor to testify if the patient has waived the privilege. The guardian of an incompetent patient or the personal representative of a deceased patient may assert the privilege on the patient's behalf. Please see the American Medical Association's Confidentiality Statement in appendix E.

Federal Laws

The federal government does not recognize a physician-patient privilege except for a psychotherapist-patient privilege in Federal Rule of Evidence 504.

State Laws

Alabama

Alabama has a physician-patient privilege, which is waived, however, when any person files a claim concerning his physical, mental, or emotional conditions. § 15–23–11. This state also has a psychologist/psychiatrist-client privilege. § 34–26–2.

Alaska

Patients have a privilege to refuse to disclose and to prevent others from disclosing confidential communications made for the purpose of diagnosis or treatment among themselves, their physicians or psychotherapists, and persons participating in the diagnosis or treatment under their direction. Alaska Uniform Rules of Evidence Rule 503 provides the following seven exceptions:

- Where the communication is relevant to an element of the claim or defense.
- If the physician's or psychotherapist's services were sought or used to commit or plan a crime or a fraud.
- If relevant to an issue of breach of duty on the part of the physician or psychotherapist.
- If the communication is relevant to an issue in proceedings to hospitalize the patient.
- If the provider is required to report to a public employee or office.
- If the examination was pursuant to the order of a judge.
- For the physician-patient privilege only, in criminal proceedings.

The physician-patient privilege does not apply in child abuse cases. § 47:17.060.

Arizona

Arizona has a physician-patient privilege, but the privilege does not apply to investigations or proceedings conducted by the board of medical examiners. § 32–1451.01 E.

Arkansas

Patients may refuse to disclose and may prevent any other person from disclosing confidential communications made for the purpose of diagnosis or treatment of their physical, mental, or emotional conditions, including alcohol or drug addiction, among themselves, their physicians, and persons who are participating in the diagnosis and treatment. The privilege does not exist, however, if relevant to an issue in proceedings to hospitalize the patients for mental illness, if the patients were examined by court order, or if their conditions are elements of their claims or defenses. Nor is there a privilege in any judicial proceedings regarding injuries to children, incompetents, or disabled persons or in any criminal prosecutions involving any injury to such persons or the willful failure to report such injuries. Arkansas Uniform Rules of Evidence Rule 503.

California

Under § 994 of the Evidence Code, the patient, whether or not a party to an action, has a privilege to refuse to disclose and to prevent another from disclosing, a confidential communication between the patient and the patient's physician. The physician must claim the privilege on the patient's behalf unless the patient has raised an issue concerning the patient's condition in an action. §§ 995–6. Nor does this privilege exist if the services of the physician were sought or obtained to help anyone commit or plan a crime or a tort or to escape detection or apprehension after committing a crime or a tort. § 997. Neither does the privilege apply in a criminal proceeding, § 998, in malpractice cases, § 1001, or in commitment proceedings, § 1004, or those to establish competence, § 1005. Among other exceptions are required reports, § 1006, and proceedings to terminate licenses or privileges, § 1007. California also has a psychotherapist-patient privilege, generally with the same exceptions as the physician-patient privilege has. §§ 1010–1026.

Colorado

Colorado has a physician-, surgeon-, or registered nurse-patient privilege as to information acquired in attending the patient that was necessary to enable the professional to prescribe or act for the patient with a number of exceptions, such as a malpractice lawsuit or a peer, governing board, or similar review. This state also has a psychologist-patient privilege. § 13-90-107.

Connecticut

§ 52-146c establishes a psychologist-patient privilege, and § 52-146d establishes a psychiatrist-patient privilege.

Delaware

Patients may refuse to disclose and may prevent any other person from disclosing confidential communications made for the purpose of diagnosis or treatment of their physical, mental, or emotional conditions, including alcohol or drug addiction, among themselves, their physicians or psychotherapists, and persons who are participating in the diagnosis and treatment. The privilege does not exist, however, in proceedings concerning whether to hospitalize the patient for mental illness, in court-ordered examinations, where the patient's condition is an element of the patient's claim or a defense, or in proceedings brought for appointment of a guardian in child abuse cases. Rule 503, Delaware Uniform Rules of Evidence.

District of Columbia

The District has a physician-patient privilege, § 14–307, but any information communicated to a physician in an attempt to unlawfully procure controlled substances is not privileged, § 33–566. Nor does the privilege apply in criminal cases in which the accused is charged with causing the death of or inflicting injuries on a human being or to evidence relating to the mental competency or sanity of the accused in criminal trials in which the accused raises the defense of insanity or in which a question arises concerning the patient's mental condition.

Florida

Florida makes communications between any professional person and the professional's patient and client privileged, but not in cases involving abuse, neglect, or exploitation of aged or disabled persons, § 425.109, or child abuse or neglect, § 415.512.

Georgia

Georgia's evidence code in § 24-9-40 states that no physician may be compelled to release any medical information concerning a patient except on written authorization or other waiver by the patient, or by the patient's parents or guardian ad litem in the case of a minor, or on appropriate court order or subpoena. However, patients waive this privilege to the extent that they place their care and treatment or the nature and extent of their injuries at issue in any civil or criminal proceeding.

Hawaii

A patient has a privilege to refuse to disclose and to prevent others from disclosing confidential communications made for the purpose of diagnosis or treatment of the patient's physical, mental, or emotional condition, including alcohol and drug addiction, except in the following circumstances:

- Proceedings for hospitalization of the patient for mental illness or substance abuse.
- Court-ordered examination, where the communication relates to the patient's condition that is an element of a claim or defenses.
- Proceedings against the physician. Rule 504, Hawaii Rules of Evidence.

Hawaii has a similar psychologist-client privilege. Rule 504.1.

Idaho

Idaho Code § 39-1392 (b) establishes a privilege for all written records of interviews, all reports, statements, minutes, memoranda, charts and the contents thereof, and all physical materials relating to research, discipline, or medical study of any in-hospital medical staff committees or medical society for the purposes of medical research or study of hospital patient cases or medical questions or problems using data and information from hospital patient cases. § 39-1392e excepts from the privilege information involved in an inquiry, a proceeding, or a disciplinary matter regarding the propriety of health care.

Illinois

Under Illinois Code of Civil Procedure 110 para. 8–802, no physicians or surgeons are permitted to disclose any information they acquired in attending any patient in a professional character necessary to enable them to serve such patient except in the following circumstances:

- In trials for homicide when the disclosure relates directly to the fact or immediate circumstances of the homicide.
- In malpractice actions against the physician.
- With the consent of the patient, the patient's personal representative, or other person authorized to sue for the patient or a beneficiary of an insurance policy on the patient.
- In actions brought by or against the patient wherein the patient's physical or mental condition is at issue.
- Concerning the validity of the patient's will.
- In a criminal action in which the charge is murder by abortion, attempted abortion, or abortion.
- In actions arising from filing a child abuse or neglect report.
- To any department, agency, institution, or facility that has custody of the patient pursuant to state statute or court order of commitment.

The statute adds that in the event of a conflict between the application of this law and the Mental Health and Developmental Disabilities Confidentiality Act, 91 1/2 Statutes Paragraph 5–100A, which requires confidentiality for medical records or confidential communications of recipients of treatment for mental health problems or developmental disabilities, the latter controls.

Indiana

In Indiana, physicians may not testify as to matters communicated to them, as physicians, in the course of their professional business.

Iowa

Patients may refuse to disclose and may prevent any other person from disclosing confidential communications made for the purpose of diagnosis or treatment of their physical, mental, or emotional conditions, including alcohol or drug addiction, among themselves, their physicians or psychotherapists, and persons who are participating in the diagnosis and treatment. The privilege does not exist, however, if relevant to an issue in proceedings to hospitalize the patient for mental illness, if the patient was examined by court order, of if the patient's condition is an element of the patient's claim or defense. Iowa Uniform Rules of Evidence Rule 503.

Kansas

Kansas's Code of Civil Procedure contains in § 60–427 a physician-patient privilege provision except in commitment proceedings, competency actions, concerning the validity of a will, in cases in which the condition of the patient is an element of a claim or defense, as to information that is required by law, and in actions to recover damages on account of the patient's conduct that constitutes a serious criminal offense, and if the services of the physician were sought or obtained to enlist or help anyone to commit or to plan to commit a crime or a tort, or to escape detection or apprehension after commission of a crime or a tort.

Kentucky

Kentucky does not have a physician-patient privilege except with regard to reports required to be filed with the Bureau of Vital Statistics, between psychiatrists or psychologists and their patients, and in compliance with federal regulations concerning the confidentiality of records of drug and alcohol abuse patients.

Louisiana

Under Louisiana law, no physicians are permitted, except with their patients' consent, to disclose any communication made to them by the patients or the result of any investigation made into the patients' physical or mental conditions, except court ordered investigations. 15 Statutes § 476.

Maine

Patients may refuse to disclose and may prevent any other person from disclosing confidential communications made for the purpose of diagnosis or treatment of their physical, mental, or emotional conditions, including alcohol or drug addiction, among themselves, their physicians or psychotherapists, and persons who are participating in the diagnosis and treatment. The privilege does not exist, however, if relevant to an issue in proceedings to hospitalize the patient for mental illness, if the patient was examined by court order, or if the patient's condition is an element of the patient's claim or defense. Maine Uniform Rules of Evidence Rule 503.

The physician-patient and psychotherapist-patient privileges do not apply in child abuse cases. Title 22 § 4021.

Maryland

Maryland has a patient-psychiatrist/psychologist privilege. Patients or their representatives have a privilege to refuse to disclose and to prevent a witness from disclosing communications relating to diagnosis or treatment of their mental or emotional disorders.

Oral or written statements of people who seek counseling, treatment, or therapy for any form of drug or alcohol abuse, from a physician, psychologist, or hospital or person who is certified for counseling or treating such abuse, are privileged, as are observations and conclusions that the physician, psychologist, hospital personnel, or other person makes. Such information is not admissible in any proceeding against the individual except parole, probation, or conditional release proceedings or commitment proceedings. § 8-801.

Massachusetts

A patient has the privilege of refusing to disclose and preventing a witness from disclosing any communication between the patient and a psychotherapist relative to the diagnosis and treatment of the patient's mental or emotional condition, with six exceptions discussed in considerable detail in 233 Statutes § 20B.

Michigan

Michigan has a physician-patient privilege, but it does not apply to an investigation or proceeding by a board or the Department of Health.

Minnesota

Physicians, surgeons, dentists, or chiropractors shall not, without their patients' consent, be allowed to disclose any information or opinion based thereon that they acquired in attending the patients in a professional capacity that was necessary to enable them to act in that capacity. After the decease of the patient, in an action to recover insurance benefits, in which the insurance has been in existence two years or more, the beneficiaries shall be deemed to be the personal representatives of the deceased for the purpose of waiving this privilege, and no oral or written waiver shall have any effect except when made upon the trial or examination in which the evidence is offered. § 595.02 1. (d). Subsection (g) states that nurses, psychologists, or consulting psychologists shall not, without their clients' consent, be allowed to disclose any information or opinion based thereon acquired in attending the patients in a professional capacity and that was necessary to enable them to act in that capacity.

Mississippi

Mississippi's Evidence Code § 13-1-21 makes all communications made to physicians or surgeons by patients under their charge or by ones seeking professional advice privileged except at the instance of the patients or their heirs, or if the validity of the patient's will is in question. Waiver of the medical privilege of cancer patients in regard to information required to be reported to the cancer registry is implied. Mississippi also has a psychologist-client privilege. § 73-31-29.

Missouri

Under Missouri's Evidence Code, § 491.060, physicians, psychologists, or dentists may not testify concerning any information that they may have acquired from patients while attending them in a professional character and that was necessary to enable them to prescribe and provide treatment for such patients.

Montana

§ 26-1-805 establishes a physician-patient privilege; § 26-1-807, a psychologist-patient privilege; and § 26-1-806, a speech-language pathologist, audiologist-client privilege.

Nebraska

Patients may refuse to disclose and may prevent any other person from disclosing confidential communications made for the purpose of diagnosis or treatment of their physical, mental, or emotional conditions, including alcohol or drug addiction, among themselves, their physicians, and persons who are participating in the diagnosis and treatment. The privilege does not exist, however, if relevant to an issue in proceedings to hospitalize the patient for mental illness, if the patient was examined by court order, or if the patient's condition is an element of the patient's claim or defense. Nor is there a privilege in any judicial proceedings regarding injuries to children, incompetents, or disabled persons or in any criminal prosecutions involving any injury to such persons or the willful failure to report such injuries. Nebraska Uniform Rules of Evidence Rule 503.

Nevada

In Nevada, patients have a privilege to refuse to disclose and to prevent others from disclosing confidential information among themselves, their doctors, or persons who are participating in the diagnosis or treatment under the doctor's direction. Statutes § 49.225. § 49.245 contains a number of exceptions:

- Communications relevant to an issue in proceedings to hospitalize the patient for mental illness.
- Communications made in the course of a court-ordered examination.
- Communications relevant to an issue of the condition of the patient in any proceeding in which the condition is an element of the claim or defense.
- In prosecutions under chapter 441 of the Nevada Revised Statutes concerning the prohibitions against exposing others to venereal infection or engaging in an occupation in which the disease may be transmitted to others.
- As to any information communicated to a physician in an effort to illegally obtain controlled substances.
- As to communications placed in healthcare records that are furnished in accordance with NRS 629.061, making records available for inspection by the patient or the board of health.
- In a review before a medical malpractice screening panel pursuant to NRS 41A.003 to .069.

New Hampshire

The confidential relations and communications between physicians or surgeons and their patients are placed on the same basis as those provided by law between attorneys and clients, and except as otherwise provided by law, no such physicians or surgeons shall be required to disclose such privileged communications. The same rule applies to those working under the supervision of physicians. Further, the same rule applies to communications between psychologists and those working under their supervision and their clients. Rule 503 New Hampshire Rules of Evidence.

New Jersey

People have a privilege to refuse to disclose and to prevent a witness from disclosing confidential communications between them and their physicians that were necessary or helpful to enable the physicians to make diagnoses of the patients' conditions or to provide treatment. New Jersey Rules of Evidence 2A:84A-22.2.

New Mexico

New Mexico does not appear to have a physician-patient statute; however, Rule 11-504 of its Rules of Evidence contains a psychotherapist-patient privilege.

New York

Physicians may not disclose information that they acquired in attending patients in a professional capacity that was necessary to act in that capacity unless the patients waive the privilege. Dentists, however, may be required to disclose information necessary to identify patients, and physicians, dentists, and nurses may disclose information indicating that patients under age 16 were crime victims. Physicians or nurses may also be required to disclose information as to the condition of deceased patients except in the following instances:

- That which tends to disgrace the patient's memory.
- When the privilege has been waived by the patient's personal representative.
- In litigation in which the interests of the patient's personal representative are adverse to the decedent's estate, by any party in interest.
- If the patient's will's validity is in dispute, by the executor, the surviving spouse, or any heir, any of the next of kin, or any other party in interest. § 4504.

North Carolina

North Carolina Statutes § 8-53 prohibits disclosure of any information doctors acquire in a professional character that was necessary for them to treat patients unless the patients consent. Other North Carolina statutes waive this privilege for certain reasons, such as investigation of health hazards. In the context of judicial proceedings (whether criminal, civil, or juvenile) concerning a juvenile's abuse or neglect, however, § 7A–551 provides that the physician-patient privilege shall not be grounds for excluding evidence of such abuse or neglect.

North Dakota

Patients may refuse to disclose and may prevent any other person from disclosing confidential communications made for the purpose of diagnosis or treatment of their physical, mental, or emotional conditions, including alcohol or drug addiction, among themselves, their physicians or psychotherapists, and persons who are participating in the diagnosis and treatment. The privilege does not exist, however, if relevant to an issue in proceedings to hospitalize the patient for mental illness, if the patient was examined by court order, or if the patient's condition is an element of the patient's claim or defense. North Dakota Uniform Rules of Evidence Rule 503.

Ohio

Physicians may not testify concerning communications made to them by their patients in relation to their advice to their patients unless the patients or, if deceased, the patient's surviving spouse, executor, or administrator consents, or if any of those persons files a claim against the physician. Ohio Rules of Evidence § 2317.02 (B).

Oklahoma

Patients have a privilege to refuse to disclose and to prevent others from disclosing confidential communications made for the purpose of diagnosis or treatment of their physical, mental, or emotional conditions, including alcohol or drug addiction, among themselves, their physicians or psychotherapists, and persons who are participating in the diagnosis or treatment under the direction of physicians or psychotherapists. The privilege does not exist in proceedings to determine whether the patients should be hospitalized for mental illness, if the examinations were court ordered, or in cases involving claims for personal injury or death against a healthcare practitioner or hospital in which people place their or others' physical or mental conditions in issue. 12 Oklahoma Statutes § 2503. See also 76 Statutes § 19 B.

Oregon

Patients have a privilege to refuse to disclose and to prevent any other person from disclosing confidential communications in a civil action to physicians or others participating in the diagnosis or treatment under the direction of the physicians. If the judge orders an examination of the physical condition of the patient, communications made in the course thereof are not privileged with respect to the particular purpose for which the examination is ordered unless the judge orders otherwise. Rule 504–1. Oregon also has a psychiatrist/psychologist-patient privilege. Rule 504.

Pennsylvania

42 Pennsylvania Statutes § 5929 establishes a limited physician-patient privilege for civil matters. No physicians shall be allowed in any civil matter to disclose any information that they acquired in attending patients in a professional capacity and that was necessary to enable them to act in that capacity, that shall tend to blacken the character of the patients, without their consent, except in civil actions brought by the patients for damages for personal injuries. This privilege does not apply to situations involving child abuse and may not constitute grounds for failure to report such. 55 Statutes § 3490.14.

Rhode Island

Rhode Island's Confidentiality of Health Care Information Act establishes a very broad patient-physician privilege (see the discussion in chapter 14). Also, Rhode Island Statute § 9–17–24 prohibits healthcare providers from disclosing information obtained about patients, submitting documentary evidence, or giving testimony disclosing confidential communications or healthcare information without the consent of the patients, their legal guardians, or, if deceased, their next of kin, executors, or administrators. § 23–17.8–6 notes that these privileges do not prevent or excuse failure to report abuse.

South Carolina

South Carolina does not have a physician-patient privilege. *Aakjer v. Spagnoli*, 352 S.E. 2d 503 (S.C. App. 1987).

South Dakota

§ 19–13–7 establishes that patients have a privilege to refuse to disclose and to prevent any other person from disclosing confidential communications made for the purpose of diagnosis or treatment of their physical, mental, or emotional conditions, including alcohol or drug addiction, among themselves, physicians or psychotherapists, and persons who are participating in the diagnosis or treatment under the direction of the physicians or psychotherapists, including members of the patients' families.

§ 19–2–3 waives the physician-patient privilege when the physical or mental health of a person is at issue in any action or proceeding or quasi-judicial administrative proceeding.

Tennessee

Tennessee has only a psychiatrist-patient privilege. § 24–1–207.

Texas

Confidential communications between physicians and patients relative to or in connection with any professional services provided by physicians to the patients, records of the identity, diagnosis, evaluation, or treatment of patients by physicians that are created or maintained by physicians are confidential and privileged and may not be disclosed, with the following eight exceptions:

- When the patient sues the physician or in license revocation proceedings when the patient is a complaining witness and in which disclosure is relevant to the claims or defense of a physician.
- When the patient or someone authorized to act on the patient's behalf submits a written consent.
- When the purpose of the proceedings is to substantiate and collect on a claim for medical services provided to the patient.
- In proceedings to recover monetary damages for any physical or mental condition, including death of the patient.
- In disciplinary investigations or proceedings of a physician, provided that the board protects the identity of the patient.
- When the disclosure is relevant in any suit involving the parent-child relationship.
- When the disclosure is relevant to an involuntary civil commitment or hospitalization proceeding.
- In any proceeding involving the abuse or neglect of an institutional resident.

Utah

Physicians or surgeons cannot, without their patients' consent, be questioned in a civil action as to any information they acquired in attending the patients that was necessary to enable them to prescribe or act for the patients. Patients, however, waive this privilege when they place their medical conditions at issue in an action as an element of or a defense to that action. Utah Code § 78-24-8.

Vermont

According to Title 12, Vermont Statutes § 1612, unless patients waive the privilege or the law waives it, people authorized to practice medicine or dentistry, nurses, or mental health professionals are not allowed to disclose any information that they acquired in attending the patients in a professional capacity and that was necessary to enable them to act in that capacity. Exceptions include the following circumstances:

- Dentists may be required to disclose information necessary for identification of a patient.
- Physicians, dentists, or nurses may be required to disclose information that a person under age 16 has been a crime victim or as to the mental or physical condition of a deceased patient, such as where the validity of the patient's will is in question.

Virginia

Except at the request of, or with the consent of, the patients, no licensed practitioners of the healing arts may testify, in any civil action, respecting any information they acquired in attending, examining, or treating the patients in a professional capacity if such information was necessary to enable them to furnish professional care to the patients. If, however, the physical or mental condition of the patients is at issue, the judge may require disclosure. An effort to unlawfully procure a narcotic drug is not privileged.

Washington

Physicians or surgeons or osteopathic physicians or surgeons shall not, without the consent of the patients, testify in a civil action as to any information acquired in attending such patients that was necessary to enable them to prescribe to and act for the patients except in cases of child or sexual abuse and in personal injury actions. Title 5, Evidence, Chapter 5.60.060 (4). 18.83.110 establishes a client and psychologist privilege. Under 71.05.250, both privileges do not apply in probable cause hearings concerning mental illness.

West Virginia

West Virginia Statute § 49–6A–7 does away with the privilege between any professional persons and their patients, except attorneys and clients, in situations involving child abuse and neglect.

Wisconsin

Wisconsin Rules of Evidence 905.04, titled "Physician-Patient, Registered Nurse-Patient, Chiropractor-Patient or Psychologist-Patient Privilege," states that a communication or information is confidential if it is not intended to be disclosed to third persons other than those present to further the interest of the patient in the consultation, examination, or interview, or persons reasonably necessary for the transmission of the communication or information or persons who are participating in the diagnosis or treatment under the direction of the healthcare professionals listed in the title. Patients have a privilege to refuse to disclose or prevent others from disclosing such confidential information. The rule excepts information necessary to determine whether to hospitalize a patient for mental illness, judge-ordered examination, information that concerns the physical, mental, or emotional condition of the patient in a proceeding in which the patient relies on the condition as an element of the claim or defense, in homicide trials, in child abuse cases, in tests for intoxication, and in paternity proceedings, and information contained in required gunshot reports.

Wyoming

According to Wyoming Statutes § 1–12–101, physicians shall not testify concerning communications made to them by their patients in that relation except by express consent of the patients or, if the patients voluntarily testify, the physicians may testify on the same subject. Nor is child abuse information privileged. § 14–3–210.

§ 1–12–116 makes communications between victims of family violence or sexual assault and their advocates confidential.

Medical Ethics and Privacy

Even if the law did not recognize a right to privacy, the medical profession has long recognized that patients have such a right. The Hippocratic Oath states, "Whatever, in connection with my profession, or not in connection with it, I may see or hear in the lives of men which ought not be spoken abroad I will not divulge as reckoning that all should be kept secret." The American Medical Association's ethical principles reflect a similar concern for patients' privacy interests:

> A physician shall respect the rights of patients, of colleagues, and of other health professionals, and shall safeguard patient confidences within the constraints of the law.[1]

---

[1]Principles of Medical Ethics of the American Medical Association, 1980. Reprinted with permission.

Part V

How Do You Dispose of Your Records?

You may have to dispose of your records in one or both of two situations. The more common way is pursuant to a proper records retention schedule as discussed in chapter 3. Chapter 16 tells you how to accomplish the actual destruction of records to avoid any legal pitfalls. Chapter 17 discusses the rarer, although more recently prevalent, situation of disposing of records during mergers, acquisitions, and closings.

16

How Do You Destroy Your Records?

Introduction

You may destroy records in one of two situations: pursuant to your records retention plan or on a one-time basis. The latter is often necessary to eliminate old, worthless records that are not covered by your retention program. Because courts look upon any records destruction that is not part of a records retention plan with suspicion, you must be certain that you conduct such a one-time destruction properly.

When it is time to destroy records, you can't just take them out and throw them away. A lot more is involved. If you are conducting a one-time destruction of a group of records, rather than destroying records pursuant to your records retention program destruction schedule, you must first review the records to make certain that you really want to destroy them. An excellent technique is to send out notices to interested parties, such as your hospital directors, staff attorney, and the like, that you are going to destroy the named records, telling them that if they do not respond within a certain time, you will destroy the records. If your records are on computer media, such as floppy disks, you should print out a hard copy for you and others to review. Then you should destroy both the printout and the electronic media—the tape, disk, or the like—of the records you decide to destroy. Upon your review, take out any records that you should retain, like minors' records, records involved with litigation or government investigation or audit, and records that someone has requested. Also, you should not destroy any records during a one-time destruction that should be retained under your retention schedule.

State or federal statutes or regulations will normally prescribe how you must destroy records, usually by burning or shredding. Often, the controlling law will require you to create an abstract of any pertinent data in medical records before destroying the record.

If you use a commercial document destruction company, you should do so under a contract that sets forth how to destroy the records, how to avoid breaching confidentiality, including indemnification from loss due to unauthorized disclosure, and how to provide documentary proof of the destruction.

Regardless of whether you destroy records yourself or hire someone else to do it, you must be certain that the records are completely destroyed and keep dated certificates of destruction of the records permanently. These certificates may be used as evidence in court or before a government agency to show that you destroyed the records in the regular course of business instead of to hide something or to gain an advantage in a litigation. Make certain that you destroy all records according to your usual procedure. In a malpractice case, for example, the judge might allow the jury to think that your destroying records in some way other than your usual procedures would show malpractice.

Federal Laws

44 U.S.C. §§ 3301–3303a and 3308–3314, contain detailed provisions as to how the federal government disposes of federal records. §§ 3304 and 3307 have been repealed. Federal laws do not, however, seem to provide detailed instructions on the destruction of healthcare records in general.

State Laws

Alaska

Alaska has repealed 7 AAC 12.010 (f) (2) (H), which had specified that a hospital could not dispose of any records without the approval of the Department of Health and Social Services.

Arizona

Arizona's Department of Health Services suggests that when you destroy records, you keep a careful report, including the date of destruction, the name of the person or organization doing the destruction, and a list of the names of the patients' records destroyed.

Arkansas

After the ten-year retention period, you may destroy medical records, provided you retain the following records for 99 years: basic information, including dates of admission and discharge; name of physician(s); record of diagnosis and/or operations performed; operative reports; tissue (pathology) reports; discharge summaries for all admissions. Arkansas Register Part 6, Section III E.

California

The California Department of Health Services approves destruction by shredding, recycling, incineration, and even disposal in land fills upon acceptance of an approved plan. The Department retains the right to approve unusual methods of destruction.

Colorado

Colorado Administrative Regulations, 6 CCR 1011-1 § 4.2.2, requires healthcare facilities to establish procedures to notify patients whose records are to be destroyed before actually destroying such records.

Connecticut

The draft Record Retention and Disposition Schedule of the Connecticut State Library's Medical Records/Case Files User Committee states that agencies may destroy records only after receiving approval in the form of a signed "Records Disposal Authorization" from the Department of Health Services. If the institution is not subject to inspection by the Department, it may destroy records after notification of compliance from the Joint Commission on Accreditation of Healthcare Organizations.

Hawaii

Hawaii Code Title 33, § 622-58 (d), specifies that medical records may be destroyed after the seven-year retention period or after reproduction in miniature form (minification) in a manner that will preserve the confidentiality of the information in the record, provided that the healthcare provider retains basic information from the records (defined in chapter 1). The provider or its successor must retain this basic information for 25 years after the last entry or for the period of minority of a minor patient plus 25 years.

Idaho

Hospitals may destroy records relating to patient care after the retention period by burning, shredding, or other effective method in keeping with the confidential nature of their contents, provided that destruction must be in the ordinary course of business and that no record may be destroyed on an individual basis. Idaho Code § 39-1394(d).

Indiana

Before microfilming and destruction of original records, the facility shall prepare and keep on file a written program for microfilming and destruction of original records that assures that the program maintains the confidential nature of the records, that the responsibility for destruction is retained by the hospital, that given records can be obtained on short notice when out of files for microfilming, and that the microfilmed records are readily available for reference and can be furnished when needed. 410 IAC 15-1-9 (2) (c).

Kansas

Kansas regulations require hospitals to maintain a summary of medical records that have been destroyed on file for at least 25 years. According to 28–34–9a (d) (3), such a summary must contain the following data:

- Name, age, and date of birth of patient.
- Name of nearest relative.
- Name of attending and consulting physicians.
- Surgical procedure and date, if applicable.
- Final diagnosis.

Maryland

Maryland Code § 4–305 covers destruction of medical records. It prohibits destruction, except for minor patients, unless the patients are notified, of medical records, laboratory reports, or X-ray reports for five years after the record is made. Minor patient records may not be destroyed until the patients reach the age of majority plus three years or for five years, whichever is later, unless the parents or guardians are notified or unless the minors are notified when their care was provided under § 20–102(c) or § 20–103(c) of the Health-General Article. Notice must be by first class mail sent to the patient's last known address and must include a statement that the record or a synopsis thereof may be retrieved at a designated location within 30 days of the proposed date of destruction.

If a sole practitioner dies, the practitioner's administrator must forward the required notice before destroying or transferring medical records to the last known address and publish a notice in a daily newspaper with local circulation for two consecutive weeks.

Massachusetts

Statutes 111 § 70 provides that whenever preexisting records have been photographed or microphotographed, indexed, and filed, a hospital or clinic may destroy the original upon notifying the supervisor of public records.

Minnesota

The superintendent or other chief administrative officer of a public or private hospital, with the consent of the board of directors or other governing body, may divest the files and records of that hospital of any individual case records bearing dates more than three years before the date of the divestiture and destroy them, provided they have first been recorded on photographic film of convenient size for preservation as evidence.

In Minnesota, however, the commissioner of health defines what comprises an individual permanent medical record, which must be maintained permanently. Code § 145.32. In 1988, the commissioner issued a revised rule specifying that an individual's permanent medical record must consist of all the following elements of the hospital record that are applicable to that patient:

- Identification data that include the patient's name, address, date of birth, sex, and, if available, the patient's social security number.
- Medical history that includes details of the present illness, the chief complaint, relevant social and family history, and provisional diagnosis. For obstetrical patients, the medical history shall include prenatal information when available. For newborns, a birth history consisting of a physical examination report and delivery record as it pertains to the newborn must be included.
- Physical examination report.
- Report of operations that includes preoperative diagnosis, names of all surgeons and assistants, anesthetic agent, description of the specimens removed with pathological findings, description of the surgical findings, technical procedures used, and postoperative diagnosis.
- Discharge summary that includes reason for hospitalization, summary of clinical observations, procedures performed, treatment provided, significant findings (such as pertinent laboratory, X-ray, and test results), and condition at discharge. For newborns or others for whom no discharge summary is available, a final progress note must be included.
- Autopsy findings.

This rule sets out the minimum information that the hospital must retain if it chooses to destroy a portion of the patient's medical record.

Mississippi

The Mississippi Code has comprehensive provisions for early retirement and destruction of hospital records.

Any hospital may, in its discretion, retire a record before the expiration of the retention period if the patient and the physician consent in writing. If the physician is no longer alive, the patient's consent is sufficient. In no event is such consent valid, however, if given within one year from the date of discharge. § 41-9-71. § 41-9-61 defines "retirement" as "the withdrawal from current files of hospital records, business records or parts thereof on or after the expiration of the applicable minimum period of retention." No such record, however, is subject to retirement if otherwise required by law to be kept as a permanent record.

Upon retiring any record or part thereof, the hospital shall make an abstract of any pertinent data if so required by the rules of the licensing agency or as the hospital finds proper. The record so retired will be destroyed or otherwise disposed of by burning, shredding, or other effective method in keeping with its confidential nature. § 41-9-75.

A hospital may also, in its discretion, reproduce any hospital record on film or other material and, after three years from the patient's discharge, retire the originals. § 41-9-77.

Missouri

Missouri's County/District Hospitals Record Manual states that selling of nonconfidential or valueless records as waste is permissible. But you should destroy confidential data under the supervision of a competent person(s) designated or appointed to see that no records fall into unauthorized hands. Record the disposition of records in some permanently preserved document, including description and quantity of the record series disposed of, manner of destruction, inclusive dates covered, and date of destruction.

Missouri Statute § 109.156 authorizes a business to destroy the original after it has microfilmed or otherwise reproduced a record.

Montana

The Montana Hospital Association notes that when you destroy records, you should keep a careful report of the date and the name of the organization or person performing the destruction and the list of the names of the patients' records destroyed and a summary card prepared. The fully completed face sheet of the patient's record may be substituted for the summary card. Montana Hospital Association Manual, Chapter 23–7.

Nebraska

Title 175, Chapter 9, Section 003.04A6, provides that records may be destroyed only when they are more than ten years old. In order to ensure the patient's right of confidentiality, licensed hospitals must destroy medical records by shredding, mutilation, burning, or other equally effective protective measures.

New Hampshire

New Hampshire Licensure Rules of the Department of Health and Human Services simply require that each hospital have a written policy in regard to the disposition of records. He–P 802.11 (c).

New Mexico

New Mexico law provides that any time after the retention period specified in the statute, a hospital may, without thereby incurring liability, destroy medical records by burning, shredding, or other effective method in keeping with the confidential nature of their contents, provided that the destruction is in the ordinary course of business and that no record is destroyed on an individual basis, 14–6–2. D, New Mexico Statutes Annotated.

North Carolina

Nursing homes must have plans for destruction of medical records, identifying information to be retained and the manner of destruction to ensure confidentiality. 10 NCAC 3H .0607 (c).

Pennsylvania

Before destruction, public notice must be provided to permit former patients or their representatives to claim their records. The notice must be both legal notice and display advertisement in a newspaper of general circulation. 28 Pennsylvania Statutes § 115.24. If the facility wants to destroy the original records after microfilming them, it may not do so until the medical records department has had an opportunity to review the processed film for content. § 115.23 (c).

South Carolina

Hospitals may destroy medical records after ten years except those of minors, which must be retained until after the expiration of the period of election following achievement of majority as prescribed by statute (one year, § 15-3-40), so long as the hospital retains an index, a register, or summary cards providing such basic information as dates of admission and discharge, name of responsible physicians, and record of diagnoses and operations for all records so destroyed. Regulation no. 61-16, Section 601.7 A.

Tennessee

Upon retirement of the records, the facility may destroy records by burning, shredding, or other effective method in keeping with the confidential nature of their contents. The facility must destroy records in the ordinary course of business and may not destroy any record on an individual basis. Tennessee Code § 68-11-305 (c). § 68-11-302 defines "retirement" as "the withdrawal from current files of hospital records, business records, or parts thereof on or after the expiration of the applicable period of retention." Tennessee's Department of Health and Environment, Board for Licensing Health Care Facilities, Rules § 1200-8-4-.03 (f) 1., adds that records shall not be destroyed except by shredding or incineration. When you destroy records, you must record the date and time of such destruction and make an entry on the patient index card.

Texas

Texas's Hospital Licensure Rules do not specify how to destroy records, but provide that the facility may not destroy medical records that relate to any matter that is involved in litigation if the hospital knows the litigation has not been finally resolved. Standards 1-221.3.

Utah

Before destroying a medical record, you must make a summary to be retained. The summary must include the following data: patient's name, medical record number; dates of birth, admission, and discharge; nearest relative, if available; attending physician; final diagnosis; surgical procedure or procedures; and pathological findings. Destroy the medical record completely to maintain confidentiality. Rule 7.406.

Washington

During final disposal of records, each hospital shall prevent retrieval and subsequent use of any data permitting identification of individuals in relation to personal or medical information. Chapter 248, Washington Administrative Code 18-440 (11) (h).

Wyoming

The Wyoming Public Hospital Records Management Manual requires that you extract and maintain permanent medical information (see chapter 1) from patient medical records before the hospital administrator or records officer may authorize their destruction. You should shred or burn confidential records authorized for destruction.

17

Disposing of Records During Acquisitions, Mergers, and Closings

Introduction

What do you do with your records when your healthcare facility ceases operation because another facility acquires your facility, you merge with another facility, or you close your facility?

Some states have statutory or regulatory guidelines that tell you what to do if your facility closes or merges with another facility. If not, you may want to review the guidance other states provide listed below. Most states specify that if one healthcare facility takes over another, the new operator will maintain the old facility's records as if there had been no change of ownership. In the case of a merger, the new entity should merge the old entity's active records with its records and prepare a retention schedule for inactive records so as to maintain them as required by law, regulations, or necessity (see chapter 3) and destroy them as indicated by the retention schedule. You should include a provision in your merger or other agreement detailing which party is responsible for records.

State laws vary more concerning disposition of records during closings. Some states, such as Arizona, require the closing provider to store the records for the required period. Other states, such as Indiana, require the hospital to turn over records to other hospitals or to a health authority in the vicinity. Still others, such as Mississippi, require the facility to turn over its records to the licensing authority. Regardless of the appropriate recipient of such records, many states require you to either inform the licensing agency or get its permission to dispose of your records in a particular way upon an acquisition, a merger, or a closing. If your state does not have any rules concerning disposition of records in such circumstances, you should arrange for the safe retention of those that should not be destroyed and the proper destruction of those that may be destroyed (see chapter 16) and ask your licensing authority whether your arrangements are satisfactory.

280 Healthcare Records

State Laws

Alabama

Rule 420–5–7.07 of the Alabama State Board of Health Division of Licensure and Certification states that when a hospital ceases to operate as a hospital, the medical records shall be disposed of as directed by the State Board of Health.

Alaska

Alaska Statutes § 18.20.085 (c) provides that if a hospital ceases operation, it shall make immediate arrangements, as approved by the Department of Health and Social Services, for the preservation of its records. Likewise, 7 AAC 43.030 requires healthcare providers to Medicaid recipients to notify the department so as to receive instructions as to the disposition of Medicaid records. 7 AAC 12.040 (i) (2) requires nursing homes that close or transfer ownership to apply to the department for instructions as to the disposition of their admission and death records.

Arizona

Arizona R9–10–221. R provides that if a facility ceases operation, the facility shall arrange for preservation of records to ensure compliance with these regulations. The department shall be notified, in writing, concerning the arrangements.

California

Title 22, § 70751 (d), states that if a hospital ceases operation, it shall notify the Department of Health within 48 hours of the arrangements made for safe preservation of patient records. If the hospital changes ownership, both the previous and the new licensee shall, before the change of ownership, provide the department written documentation that the new licensee will have custody of patient records, provide for safe preservation of the records, and make the records available to both the new and former licensees and other authorized persons. § 70751 (e).

Hawaii

Hawaii law notes that healthcare provider successor providers are liable for the preservation of basic information (defined in chapter 1) from the medical record for 25 years after the last entry, except in the case of minors, for which they are responsible for retention for the period of minority plus 25 years. If a healthcare provider is succeeded by another entity, the burden of compliance with this law rests with the successor. Before a provider ceases operations, it shall make immediate arrangements, subject to the approval of the Department of Health, for the retention and preservation of its medical records. Title 33 § 622–58 (e).

Indiana

The Hospital Licensure Rules of the Indiana State Board of Health 410 IAC 15-1-9 (2) requires that, upon closure of a hospital, the facility transfer the microfilmed medical records, when possible, to a local public health department or public hospital in the same geographic area. When the facility cannot do so, it should send the microfilmed records to the Board of Health.

Kansas

Under Kansas regulations, if a hospital discontinues operation, it shall inform the licensing agency as to the location of its records. 28-34-9a (d) (1).

Kentucky

Kentucky Administrative Regulations, 902 KAR 20:016 Section 3 (11) 3., state that hospitals shall provide for written designation of special locations for the storage of medical records in the event the hospital ceases to operate because of disaster or for any other reason.

Massachusetts

Massachusetts Statutes 111 § 70 provides that in the event of a transfer of ownership of a hospital, an institution for unwed mothers, or a clinic, the new owner shall maintain all medical records as if there were no change in ownership. In the event of a permanent closing, the institution will arrange for preservation of such medical records for the 30-year retention period.

Mississippi

As part of its comprehensive statutory scheme for regulating hospital records, Mississippi Code § 41-9-79 provides that when a hospital is closed, it must turn over its hospital records to any other hospital or hospitals in the vicinity willing to accept and retain them. If there is no such hospital, the closing hospital shall deliver properly indexed records to the licensing agency.

Missouri

Missouri's only reference to mergers, acquisitions, or closings is in § 198.052, relating to convalescent, nursing, and boarding homes. It requires new operators of such facilities to retain the original medical records of residents.

Nebraska

Nebraska law provides that in cases in which a hospital ceases operation, all medical records shall be transferred to the licensed hospital or other licensed healthcare facility to which the patient is transferred. All other records shall be disposed of. Title 175, Chapter 9, 003.04A6.

New Hampshire

Administrative regulation He–P 806.10 states that in the event an outpatient clinic ceases operation, it must provide for the safe preservation of clinical records as does He–P 807.07 for residential treatment and rehabilitation facilities and He–P 809.07 for home health service providers.

New Jersey

If a hospital discontinues operations for any reason, the governing authority must, before closing, notify the Department of Health, in writing, where it will store and service its medical records. § 8:34B–7.4 (b).

North Carolina

Nursing homes' policies with regard to retention of medical records shall assure that either the original or a copy of each patient's or resident's medical record is kept in the facility regardless of a change of ownership or administrator in accordance with state statutes of limitations for both adults and minors. § 10 NCASC 3H .0607 (b).

Oregon

Oregon Administrative Rules 333–70–055 (13) provides that, if a hospital or related institution changes ownership, its medical records must remain therein and become the responsibility of the new owner. (14) states that if a hospital is closed, its medical records may be turned over to any other hospital or hospitals in the vicinity willing to accept and keep them.

Pennsylvania

If a hospital discontinues operation, it shall inform the Department of Health where its records are stored. The storage facility must offer retrieval services for at least five years after the closure date. Before destruction, public notice must be provided to permit former patients or their representatives to claim their records. The notice must be both legal notice and display advertisement in a newspaper of general circulation. 28 Pennsylvania Statutes § 115.24.

South Carolina

The South Carolina Department of Health and Environmental Control's regulations specify what to do if the facility changes ownership or ceases operations. According to Regulation No. 61–16, hospitals and institutional general infirmaries must transfer all medical records to the new owners in the event of a change of ownership. If the hospital closes, it must arrange for preservation of the records and notify the Department, in writing, of its arrangements therefor. § 601.7 D.

Regulation No. 61–14 is similar, except that it states that upon the closing of an intermediate care facility, the medical records "will be kept intact or legally disposed of." § 504.3.

No. 61–17, governing nursing care facilities, has language identical to that of 61–14.

No. 61–13, covering mental retardation facilities, states that upon closure of a facility, the licensee must maintain the health records and all other required records. § 503.

Tennessee

Tennessee Code § 68–11–308 states that if any hospital closes, it shall deliver and turn over its hospital records, in good order and properly indexed, to the Department of Health and Environment.

Texas

Texas Hospital Licensing Standards do not discuss changes of ownership of hospitals, but Standard 1–22.1.6 notes that if a hospital closes, it shall notify the licensing agency of the disposition of medical records, including the location of records storage and the identity of the custodian of the records. Standard 12–8.7.6 states that in the event of change of ownership of special facilities, the new management will maintain proof of the medical information required for the continuity of services of residents.

Utah

In Utah, when a hospital ceases operation, it must provide for appropriate safe storage and prompt retrieval of all medical records, patient indexes, and discharges for the ten-year retention period of Rule 7.406 A. The hospital may arrange for storage with another hospital or may return patient medical records to the attending physicians if they are still in the community. In any event, the facility will notify the Department of Health in writing within three business days of closure detailing the provisions for the safe storage of the records and their location and publish the location of all hospital medical records in the local newspaper. 7.406 D.

Virginia

Virginia's regulations do not specify what a hospital must do with its medical records upon closing, but its Rules and Regulations for the Licensure of Nursing Homes 24.7 states that nursing home records should be transferred with the patient if the patient is transferred to another licensed healthcare facility. Otherwise, the owners shall make provisions for the safeguarding and confidentiality of all medical records. When a nursing home changes ownership, it must make adequate provision for the orderly transfer of all medical records.

Washington

If any hospital ceases operations, it shall make immediate arrangements as approved by the Department of Social and Health Services for preservation of its records. Title 70 Revised Code of Washington § 70.41.90.

Washington's administrative code amplifies the statutory guidance by providing that in the event of transfer of ownership of a hospital, the hospital shall keep patients' medical records, registers, indexes, and analyses of hospital services in the hospital to be retained and preserved by the new owner in accordance with state statutes and regulations. If the hospital ceases operation, the hospital shall make immediate arrangements for preservation of its medical records and other records of or reports on patient care data in accordance with applicable state statutes and regulations and obtain approval of the department for the planned arrangements before the cessation of operation. § 248-18-440.

Appendix A

Condition of Participation: Medical Records Services Health Care Financing Administration 42 CFR, Chapter IV, Section 482.24

The hospital must have a medical record service that has administrative responsibility for medical records. A medical record must be maintained for every individual evaluated or treated in the hospital.

(a) Standard: Organization and staffing. The organization of the medical record service must be appropriate to the scope and complexity of the services performed. The hospital must employ adequate personnel to ensure prompt completion, filing, and retrieval of records.

(b) Standard: Form and retention of record. The hospital must maintain a medical record for each inpatient and outpatient. Medical records must be accurately written, promptly completed, properly filed and retained, and accessible. The hospital must use a system of author identification and record maintenance that ensures the integrity of the authentication and protects the security of all record entries.

  (1) Medical records must be retained in their original or legally reproduced form for a period of at least five years.
  (2) The hospital must have a system of coding and indexing medical records. The system must allow for timely retrieval by diagnosis and procedure, in order to support medical care evaluation studies.
  (3) The hospital must have a procedure for ensuring the confidentiality of patient records. Information from or copies of records may be released only to authorized individuals, and the hospital must ensure that unauthorized individuals cannot gain access to or alter patient records. Original medical records must be released by the hospital only in accordance with Federal or State laws, court orders, or subpoenas.

(c) Standard: Content of record. The medical record must contain information to justify admission and continued hospitalization, support for the diagnosis, and describe the patient's progress and response to medications and services.
  (1) All entries must be legible and complete, and must be authenticated and dated promptly by the person (identified by name and discipline) who is responsible for ordering, providing, or evaluating the service furnished.
     (i) The author of each entry must be identified and must authenticate his or her entry.
     (ii) Authentication may include signatures, written initials, or computer entry.
  (2) All records must document the following, as appropriate:
     (i) Evidence of a physical examination, including a health history, performed no more than seven days prior to admission or within 48 hours after admission.
     (ii) Admitting diagnosis.
     (iii) Results of all consultative evaluations of the patient and appropriate findings by clinical and other staff involved in the care of the patient.
     (iv) Documentation of complications, hospital acquired infections, and unfavorable reactions to drugs and anesthesia.
     (v) Properly executed informed consent forms for procedures and treatments specified by the medical staff, or by Federal or State law if applicable, to acquire written patient consent.
     (vi) All practitioners' orders, nursing notes, reports of treatment, medication records, radiology, and laboratory reports, and vital signs and other information necessary to monitor the patient's condition.
     (vii) Discharge summary with outcome of hospitalization, disposition of care, and provisions for follow-up care.
     (viii) Final diagnosis with completion of medical records within 30 days following discharge.

Appendix B

State Statutes of Limitations

State	Contracts[a]	Wrongful Death	Medical Malpractice
Alabama	2 years § 6–5–482	2 years § 6–2–38	2 years § 6–5–482
Alaska	6 years § 09.10.050	2 years § 09.55.580	2 years § 9.10.070
Arizona	3 years § 12–543	2 years § 12–542	2 years § 12–551
Arkansas	3 years[b] § 37–206	3 years § 27–907	2 years § 34–2616
California	2 years § 339[c]	3 years § 340.45	3 years § 340.5
Colorado	2 years § 13–80–102	2 years § 13–80–102	2 years § 13–80–102
Connecticut	3 years § 52–581	2 years § 52–555	2 years § 52–584
Delaware	2 years Tit. 10 § 8121	2 years Tit. 18 § 6856	2 years § 6856
District of Columbia	3 years § 12–301(7)	1 year § 16–2702	3 years § 12–301(8)
Florida	4 years § 95.11	2 years § 95.11	2 years § 95.11
Georgia	4 years § 9–3–25	2 years § 9–3–71	2 years § 9–3–71
Hawaii	6 years § 657.1	2 years § 657–7.3	2 years § 657–7.3
Idaho	5 years[d] § 5–217	2 years § 5–219	2 years § 5–219

[a] States may have different statutes of limitations for sales contracts and for oral as opposed to written contracts.
[b] For oral contracts.
[c] California Civil Procedure Code.
[d] Oral contracts have a four-year statute of limitations.

Healthcare Records

State	Contracts	Wrongful Death	Medical Malpractice
Illinois	2 years Ch. 110 § 13–215	2 years § 13–215	2 years § 13–215
Indiana	10 years[e] § 16-9.5-3-1	2 years § 34-1-1-2	2 years § 16-9.5-3-1
Iowa	2 years § 614.1(2)	2–6 years[f] § 614.1(9)	2–6 years[f] § 614.1(9)
Kansas	3 years § 60–512	2 years § 60–513(a)(5)	2 years § 60–513(a)(5)
Kentucky	1 year § 413.245	1 year § 413.180	1 year § 413.245
Louisiana	1 year Tit. 40:1299.41C	1 year Ch. 9 § 5628	1 year Ch. 9§ 5628
Maine	6 years[g] Tit. 14 § 752	3 years[h] Tit. 24 § 2902	3 years § 2902
Maryland	3 years § 5–101	3 years § 3–904	5 years[i] § 5–109
Massachusetts	3 years Ch. 260 § 4	3 years Ch. 260 § 4	3 years Ch. 260 § 4
Michigan	3 years § 600.5805(8)	3 years[j] § 600.5805(8)	2 years § 600.5805(4)
Minnesota	2 years § 541.07(1)	3 years[k] § 573.02	2 years § 541.07(1)
Mississippi	3 years § 15–1–29	2 years § 15–1–36	2 years § 15–1–36
Missouri	5 years § 516.120	3 years § 537.100	2 years § 516.105
Montana	3 years § 27–2–205	3 years § 27–2–204 & 205	3 years § 27–2–205

[e]Oral contracts have a six-year statute of limitations. But no claim, whether in contract or tort, may be brought against a health care provider based upon professional services or care rendered unless filed within two years from the date of the alleged act, omission, or neglect.

[f]The action must begin within two years after the claimant knew, or through the exercise of reasonable diligence should have known, or received notice in writing of the existence of the injury or death for which damages are sought in the action, whichever comes first, but in no event shall any action begin later than six years from the date on which the action or omission occurred.

[g]All civil action must begin within 6 years, 14 § 752. § 751 provides for a twenty-year statute of limitations on personal actions on contracts, promissory notes, and the like.

[h]Wrongful death actions other than as a result of professional actions must begin within ten years, Title 18A § 2–804.

[i]After the injury or three years after discovery of the injury.

[j]Several Michigan cases, however, hold that where medical malpractice causes the wrongful death, the statute of limitations is two years.

[k]Wrongful death actions resulting from professional negligence, however, have a two-year statute of limitations under § 541.07.

Appendices

State	Contracts	Wrongful Death	Medical Malpractice
Nebraska	2 years § 25-222	2 years § 30-810	2 years § 25-222
Nevada	4 years § 11.190(2)	4 years[l] § 41A.097	4 years[l] § 41A.097
New Hampshire	2 years § 507-C:1	2 years[m] § 507-C:4	2 years § 507-C:4
New Jersey	6 years § 2A:14-1	2 years § 2A:31-3	2 years § 2A:14-2
New Mexico	3 years § 41-5-22	3 years § 41-5-22	3 years § 41-5-22
New York	6 years Civ. Prac. § 213	2 years § 208 Est. Powers & Trusts	2 1/2 years § 5-4.1
North Carolina	3 years § 1-52(1)	2 years § 153(4)	3 years § 1-15
North Dakota	6 years § 28-01-16(1)	2 years § 28-01-18(4)	2 years § 28-01-18(3)
Ohio	6 years § 2305.07	2 years § 2125(D)	1 year § 2305.11
Oklahoma	2 years Tit. 76 § 18	2 years Tit. 76 § 18	2 years Tit. 76 § 18
Oregon	6 years § 12.080	3 years § 30.020(1)	2 years § 12.110(4)
Pennsylvania	4 years Tit. 42 § 5525	2 years § 5524	2 years § 5524
Rhode Island	10 years § 9-1-13	3 years § 10-7-2	3 years § 9-1-14.1
South Carolina	3 years § 15-3-350 (1)	3 years § 15-3-350(6)	3 years § 15-3-545(A)
South Dakota	2 years § 15-2-14.1	3 years § 21-5-3	2 years § 15-2-14.1
Tennessee	1 year —§§ 28-3-104, 29-26-116—	1 year	1 year § 29-26-116
Texas	2 years —Tit. 71, art. 4590i, § 10.01—	2 years	2 years
Utah	2 years § 78-14-3(29)	2 years § 78-14-3(29)	2 years § 78-14-3(29)

[l]After the date of injury or two years after the plaintiff discovers or through reasonable diligence should have discovered the injury, whichever occurs first.
[m]The general wrongful death period of limitations is six years.

State	Contracts	Wrongful Death	Medical Malpractice
Vermont	6 years Tit. 12 § 511	2 years Tit. 14 § 1492(a)	3 years Tit. 12 § 521
Virginia	2 years § 8.01–230	2 years § 8.01–244	2 years § 8.01–230
Washington	3 years § 4.16.080	2 years § 4.16.130	3 years § 4.16.350
West Virginia	5 years § 55–2–6	2 years § 55–7–6	2 years[n] § 55–2–12
Wisconsin	3 years § 893.55	3 years § 893.54	3 years § 893.55
Wyoming	10 years[o] § 1–3–105(a)	2 years § 1–38–102	2 years § 1–3–107

[n] After the right to bring the action accrued if it was for personal injuries.
[o] Eight years for oral contracts.

Appendix C

Administrative Rules of Montana 16.32.138–142 Annual Reports by Healthcare Facilities

Administrative Rules of Montana

16.32.138 ANNUAL REPORTS BY HOSPITALS Every hospital shall submit an annual report to the department no later than January 31 of each year on forms provided by the department. The annual reports must be signed by the hospital administrator and must include the following information:

(1) whether the hospital has received JCAH accreditation, and if so, for what period;
(2) beginning and ending dates of the hospital's reporting period, and whether the facility has been in operation for 12 full months at the end of the most recent reporting period;
(3) a discussion of the organizational aspects of the project, including the following information:
  (a) the type of organization or entity responsible for the day-to-day operation of the hospital (e.g., state, country, city, federal, hospital district, church related, nonprofit corporation, individual, partnership, business corporation);
  (b) whether the controlling organization leases the physical plant from another organization. If so, the name and type of organization that owns the plant;
  (c) (i) any changes in the ownership, board of directors or articles of incorporation during the past year;
      (ii) the name of the current chairman of the board of directors;
  (d) if the controlling organization has placed responsibility for the administration of the hospital with another organization, the name and type of organization that manages the facility. A copy of the latest management agreement must be provided;

(e) if the hospital is operated as a part of a multi-facility system (e.g., medical center, chain of hospitals owned by a religious order, etc.) the name and address of the parent organization;
(4) whether the hospital provides primarily general medical/surgical services, or specialty services (specify);
(5) specific facilities and services provided by the hospital, bed capacities for each service (where applicable), and whether such services are provided full or part-time, by hospital personnel, or by contracting providers;
(6) newborn nursery statistics, including:
　(a) number of bassinets set up and staffed;
　(b) total number of births;
　(c) total newborn days;
　(d) neonatal intensive care admissions and inpatient days;
(7) surgery statistics, including:
　(a) number of inpatient and outpatient surgery suites;
　(b) number of inpatient and outpatient operations performed;
　(c) number of adult and pediatric open-heart surgical operations performed;
　(d) total adult and pediatric cardiac catheterization and intracardiac and/or coronary artery procedures;
(8) number of beds set up and staffed and total inpatient days (excluding newborns) in each basic inpatient service category;
(9) inpatient statistics, including:
　(a) number of licensed hospital beds (excluding bassinets and long-term care beds);
　(b) number of admissions (excluding newborns);
　(c) number of discharges (including deaths);
　(d) number of deaths (excluding fetal deaths);
　(e) census on last day of reporting period (excluding newborns);
(10) information on other services, including number of rooms or units, number of inpatient and outpatient procedures, and number of outpatient visits in at least the following areas:
　(a) emergency room;
　(b) organized outpatient department;
　(c) x-ray, ultrasound, nuclear medicine, cobalt therapy, CT scans;
　(d) physical therapy;
　(e) respiratory therapy;
　(f) renal dialysis;
　(g) other ancillary services;
(11) information on changes in total number of beds during the reporting period;
(12) whether there is a separate long-term care unit, and if so, how many beds;
(13) patient origin data, including every town of origin and number of discharges;
(14) total Medicare and Medicaid admissions and inpatient days;

(15) size of medical and non-medical staff, including number of active and consulting physicians, medical residents and trainees, registered and licensed professional or vocational nurses, and all other personnel;

(16) name of person to contact in the event the department has questions concerning the information provided in the annual report. (History: Sec. 50-5-103, 2-4-201 MCA; *IMP*, Sec. 50-5-106 MCA; *NEW*, 1984 MAR p. 27, Eff. 1/13/84.)

16.32.139 ANNUAL FINANCIAL REPORTS BY HOSPITALS Every hospital shall submit an annual financial report to the department no later than January 31 of each year on forms provided by the department. The annual financial report must be signed by the hospital administrator and must include the following information:

(1) hospital revenues for both acute and long-term care units, including:
    (a) gross revenue from inpatient and outpatient service;
    (b) deductions for contractual adjustments, bad debts, charity, etc.;
    (c) other operating revenue;
    (d) nonoperating revenue (such as government appropriations, mill levies, contributions, grants, etc.);

(2) hospital expenses for both acute and long-term care units, including:
    (a) payroll expenses for all categories of personnel;
    (b) nonpayroll expenses, including employee benefits, professional fees, depreciation expense, interest expense, others;

(3) detail of deductions for both acute and long-term care units, including:
    (a) bad debts;
    (b) contractual adjustments (specifying Medicare, Medicaid, Blue Cross, or other);
    (c) charity/Hill-Burton;
    (d) other;

(4) Medicaid and Medicare program revenue for both acute and long-term care units;

(5) unrestricted fund assets, including dollar amounts of:
    (a) current cash and short-term investments;
    (b) current receivables and other current assets;
    (c) gross plant and equipment assets; deductions for accumulated depreciation;
    (d) long-term investments;
    (e) other;

(6) unrestricted fund liabilities, including dollar amounts of:
    (a) current liabilities;
    (b) long-term debts;
    (c) other liabilities;
    (d) unrestricted fund balance;

(7) restricted fund balances, with identification of specific purposes for which funds are reserved, including plant replacement and expansion, and endowment funds;

(8) (a) capital expenditures made during the reporting period, including expenditures, disposals and retirements for land, building and improvements, fixed and movable equipment, and construction in progress;
   (b) whether a permanent change in bed complement or in the number of hospital services offered will result from any capital acquisition projects begun during the reporting period (specify);
   (c) whether a certificate of need or Section 1122 approval was received for any projects during the reporting period, and if so, the total capital authorization included in such approvals. (History: Sec. 50-5-103, 2-4-201 MCA; *IMP*, Sec. 50-5-106 MCA: *NEW,* 1984 MAR p. 27, Eff. 1/13/84.)

16.32.140 ANNUAL REPORTS BY LONG-TERM CARE AND PERSONAL CARE FACILITIES Every long-term care and personal care facility shall submit an annual report to the department no later than January 31 of each year on forms provided by the department. The annual report must be signed by the facility administrator and must include the following information:

(1) the facility's reporting period, and whether the facility was in operation for a full 12 months at the end of the reporting period;
(2) a discussion of the organizational aspects of the project, including the following information:
   (a) the type of organization or entity responsible for the day-to-day operation of the facility (e.g., state, county, city, federal, hospital district, church related, nonprofit corporation, individual, partnership, business corporation);
   (b) whether the controlling organization leases the physical plant from another organization. If so, the name and type of organization that owns the plant;
   (c) (i) any changes in the ownership, board of directors or articles of incorporation of the facility during the past year;
       (ii) the name of the current chairman of the board of directors of the facility;
   (d) if the controlling organization has placed responsibility for the administration of the facility with another organization, the name and type of organization that manages the facility. A copy of the latest management agreement must be provided;
   (e) if the facility is operated as a part of a multi-facility system (e.g., medical center, chain of hospitals owned by a religious order, etc.) the name and address of the parent organization;
(3) utilization information, including:
   (a) licensed bed capacity (skilled and intermediate);
   (b) whether the facility is certified for Medicare or Medicaid;
   (c) number of beds currently set up and staffed;
   (d) total patient census on first day of reporting period; total admissions, discharges, patient deaths, and patient-days of service during the reporting period;

(e) patient census on last day of reporting period, broken down by sex and age categories;

(4) financial data, including:
 (a) total annual operating expenses (payroll and non-payroll);
 (b) closing date of financial statement;
 (c) sources of operating revenue, indicating percent received from Medicare, Medicaid, private pay, insurance, grants, contributions, and other;

(5) staff information, including number of full and part-time registered and licensed professional nurses;

(6) patient origin data, including patients' counties of residence, and number of admissions from state institutions and from out-of-state;

(7) name of person to contact should the department have any questions regarding the information in the report. (History: Sec. 50-5-103, 2-4-201 MCA; Sec. 11, Chapter 477, Laws of 1987; *IMP*, Sec. 50-5-106 MCA; *NEW*, 1984 MAR p. 27, Eff. 1/13/84; *AMD*, 1987 MAR p. 1074, Eff. 7/17/87.)

16.32.141 ANNUAL REPORTS BY HOME HEALTH AGENCIES Every home health agency shall submit an annual report to the department no later than January 31 of each year on forms provided by the department. The report must be signed by the administrator of the agency and must include the following information:

(1) whether the agency has Medicare certification, and if so, the term of such certification;

(2) the agency's reporting period, and whether the agency was in operation for a full 12 months at the end of the reporting period;

(3) a discussion of the organizational aspects of the project, including the following information;
 (a) the type of organization or entity responsible for the day-to-day operation of the agency (e.g., state, county, city, federal, hospital district, church related, nonprofit corporation, individual, partnership, business corporation);
 (b) whether the home health agency is owned by the same organization that controls it. If not, the name and type of organization that owns the agency;
 (c) (i) any changes in the ownership, board of directors or articles of incorporation of the agency during the past year;
  (ii) the name of the current chairman of the board of directors of the agency;
 (d) if the controlling organization has placed responsibility for the administration of the agency with another organization, the name and type of organization that manages the facility. A copy of the latest management agreement must be provided;

(e) if the agency is operated as a part of a multi-facility system (e.g., medical center, chain of hospitals owned by a religious order, etc.) the name and address of the parent organization;

(4) a listing of specific services provided by the agency, and the number of people served and number of visits made for each service;

(5) a description of the geographic area served by the agency;

(6) the number of persons served by the agency and the number of new cases acquired by the agency during the reporting period;

(7) financial data, including:
   (a) payroll and non-payroll expenses;
   (b) closing date of financial statement;
   (c) sources of operating revenue, indicating percentage received from Medicare, Medicaid, private pay, insurance, grants, contributions, other;

(8) staff information, including number of full, part-time and contracted registered and licensed professional nurses, home health aids, student nurses, and others;

(9) the name of the person to contact should the department have questions regarding the information in the report. (History: Sec. 50–5–103, 2–4–201 MCA; *IMP,* Sec. 50–5–106 MCA; *New,* 1984 MAR p. 27, Eff. 1/13/84.)

16.32.142 ANNUAL REPORTS BY ALCOHOL AND DRUG TREATMENT FACILITIES Every alcohol and/or drug treatment facility shall submit an annual report to the department no later than January 31 of each year on forms provided by the department. The report must be signed by the facility administrator and must include the following information:

(1) the facility's reporting period, and the number of days the facility was open during the period;

(2) type of licensure (hospital, long-term care facility, other);

(3) duration of inpatient treatment program;

(4) the type of organization or entity responsible for the day-to-day operation of the facility (e.g., state, county, city, federal, hospital district, church related, nonprofit corporation, individual, partnership, business corporation);

(5) utilization information, including number of inpatient beds, admissions and patient-days, and number of outpatient clients and service contacts;

(6) total inpatient and outpatient alcohol unit revenues;

(7) number of first admissions, listed by age, race, sex and education;

(8) percent of revenue received from Medicare, Medicaid, insurance, private pay, CHAMPUS, Indian health service, and other sources;

(9) number of clients who have received previous treatment;

(10) discharge data, including number of clients who completed treatment or were referred elsewhere;

(11) patient origin data, indicating number of patients from each county or out-of-state. (History: Sec. 50–5–103, 2–4–201 MCA; *IMP,* Sec. 50–5–106 MCA; *NEW,* 1984 MAR p. 27, Eff. 1/13/84.)

Appendix D

Recommended Retention Periods for Hospital Records

Use this table as a guide when your state or the federal government does not specify a retention period.

Record	Suggested Period of Retention	Remarks
Administrative Offices		
Accident (or incident reports)	6 years	
Annual reports	permanent	
Appraisal reports	permanent	
Audit reports	permanent	
Birth records to local government	permanent	
Census (daily)	5 years	
Communicable disease reports	3 years	
Constitution and bylaws	permanent	
Construction projects	permanent	
Correspondence	5 years	Retain only that of continuing interest. Review annually.
Death records to local government	permanent	
Doctor's personnel records	permanent	
Endowments, trusts, bequests	permanent	
Insurance policies, expired	6 years	
Licenses, permits, contracts	permanent	
Minutes of meetings of board of directors, executive committees, and medical staff	permanent	
Permits (alcohol & narcotics)	life of permit plus 6 years	

Record	Suggested Period of Retention	Remarks
Policies and procedure manuals	life of manual plus 6 years	
Property records		
Deeds, titles	permanent	
Leases	term of lease plus 6 years	
Reports (departmental)		Many daily and nonannual reports can be destroyed after year end statistics are compiled.
Statistics on admissions, services, discharges	permanent	

Admissions and Discharges		
Listings	6 years	
Register	permanent	

Business Office		
Alien—statement of income paid	so long as contents may be material in the administration of an Internal Revenue law (26 CFR 1.6001–1)	
Bank statements	6 years	
Budgets	5 years	
Cash receipts	6 years	
Cashier's tapes from bookkeeping machine	5 years	
Charge (slips) to patients	5 years	
Checks (cancelled)		
Payroll	7 years	
Voucher	10 years	
Check registers	6 years	
Correspondence		
Credit and collections	7 years	
General	6 years	
Insurance	4 years	
Deposits (bank)	2 years	
Equipment (depreciation records)	permanent	
Income (daily summary)	5 years	
Income tax returns	permanent	

Record	Suggested Period of Retention	Remarks
Invoices		
Fixed assets	permanent/life of asset plus 6 years	
Accounts receivable	6 years	
Accounts payable 6 years		
Journals (general)	permanent	
Ledgers (general)	permanent	
Ledger cards (patients')	7 years	
Payroll		
Bonds	10 years	
Insurance	8 years	
Individual earnings	term of employment plus 6 years	
Journals	25 years	
Rate schedules	6 years	
Social security reports	4 years	
Time cards	5 years	
Withholding tax exemption (W-4) forms	4 years	
Withholding tax statements (W-2 forms)	4 years after taxes paid	
Posting audits	7 years	
Unemployment tax records	4 years	
Vouchers		
Capital expenditures	permanent/life of item plus 6 years	
Cash	10 years	
Welfare agency records	7 years	

Clinic

Record	Suggested Period of Retention	Remarks
Appointment books	3 years	
Encounter statistics	1 year	daily and monthly reports
Medical records	10 years from date of last visit	
Patient's name index	permanent	
Social service confidential case histories	5 years	
Welfare agency records	7 years	

Record	Suggested Period of Retention	Remarks
Dietary		
Food costs	5 years	
Meal counts	5 years	
Menus	2 years	
Engineering		
Blueprints of buildings	permanent	
Calibration records	6 years	
Equipment records by location	life of equipment plus 6 years	
Equipment records in inspection and maintenance	5 years, including meter charts	
Equipment operating instructions	life of equipment plus 6 years	
Inspection of grounds and buildings	1 year	
Maintenance log	6 years	
Purchase orders	10 years	
Temperature charts	2 years	
Watchman clock dials	2 years	
Work orders	2 years	
Laboratory, Therapy and X-Ray		
Appointment books	3 years	
Blood banks		
Adverse reactions to transfusions	5 years	
Blood donor histories, examination, consent, reactions, and results of required tests performed on plasmapheresis and cytapheresis donors	5 years	
ABO and Rh types	5 years	
Blood tests results, interpretations, and release (issue) data for compatibility testing	5 years	
Final disposition of blood and components	5 years	
Refrigeration and blood inspection records	5 years	
Transfusion request records	5 years	
Electrocardiogram tracings	10 years; unusual cases, permanent until litigation is settled.	

Record	Suggested Period of Retention	Remarks
Electroencephalogram tracings	Uncut tracings to be retained in medical-legal disputes. 5 years for normal cutouts (reduced about 5/6). 10 years for abnormal cutouts.	
Fetal monitoring	permanent/10 years	
Index to patient's records	10 years; unusual cases, permanent	
Psychiatric reports to states health departments	permanent	
Radioisotopes (receipt, transfer use, storage, delivery, disposal, and reports of overexposure)	permanent	10 CFR 30.51
Registers (chronological of tests)	5 years or until hospital statistics are compiled	
Requests for tests	2 weeks	
Research papers published	permanent	
Test results (clinical laboratory)	3 months except for cases of unusual interest	
Therapy treatment records (inpatient and outpatient)	5 years where not duplicated in medical records	

Medical Records

Record	Suggested Period of Retention	Remarks
Annual reports to government agencies	permanent	
Birth registration copy	permanent	
Death registration copy	permanent	
Delivery room log	permanent	
Disease index	10 years to permanent	
Emergency room reports	10 years	
Fetal heart rate monitoring	10 years	
Operation index	10 years to permanent	
Indexes to patients' medical records	permanent	
Patient index	permanent	
Patients' medical records	10 years after most recent care usage	
Physician index	10 years	
Surgery log	permanent	
Tumor registry files	permanent	

Healthcare Records

Record	Suggested Period of Retention	Remarks
Miscellaneous Departments		
Housekeeping room record	5 years	
Returned goods memoranda	1 year if records are duplicated in business office	
Nursing		
Application (nonemployees)	2 years	
Attendance and time records	2 years	Copy in business office.
Minutes of meetings	permanent	
Personnel records	6 years after termination	
Policies and procedures	6 years after revision	
Private duty name file	6 years after last use	
Staffing records	6 years	
Training (course outlines and examinations)	permanent	
Personnel		
Absence reports	5 years	
Application (nonemployees)	4 years	
Employee health records	5 years after termination of employment	
Employee history	5 years in full; after 5 years, reduce to payroll card rate	
Garnishment records	7 years	
Job classifications	permanent	
Overtime reports	5 years	
Payroll and time records	5 years	
Pension records	permanent	
Vacation lists	2 years	
Volunteer service (certification of hospital workers)	2 years after termination	
Pharmacy		
Controlled substances (inventory and orders)	2 years	

Record	Suggested Period of Retention	Remarks
Controlled substances (dispensed and administered)	2 years. In a separate file, keep daily records showing kind and quantity of narcotics dispensed or administered, names and addresses of persons upon whose authority and purpose for which dispensed or administered (21 CFR 304.04).	
Methadone	3 years. Maintain clinical record for each patient showing dates, quantity, and batch or code mark (21 CFR 310.505).	
Other prescriptions	2 years	

Public Relations

Record	Suggested Period of Retention	Remarks
Clippings (historical)	permanent	
Contributor records	permanent	
Photographs (institutional)	permanent	
Publications (house organs)	permanent	

Purchasing and Receiving

Record	Suggested Period of Retention	Remarks
Packing slips	3 months	
Purchase orders	2 years Copy on record on voucher in business office.	
Purchase requisitions	3 years	
Receiving report	5 years Copy on record on voucher in business office.	
Returned goods credit	2 years Copy on record on voucher in business office.	

Appendix E

American Medical Association's Confidentiality Statement

Confidentiality

The information disclosed to a physician during the course of the relationship between physician and patient is confidential to the greatest possible degree. The patient should feel free to make a full disclosure of information to the physician in order that the physician may most effectively provide needed services. The patient should be able to make this disclosure with the knowledge that the physician will respect the confidential nature of the communication. The physician should not reveal confidential communications or information without the express consent of the patient, unless required to do so by law.

The obligation to safeguard patient confidences is subject to certain exceptions which are ethically and legally justified because of overriding social considerations. Where a patient threatens to inflict serious bodily harm to another person and there is a reasonable probability that the patient may carry out the threat, the physician should take reasonable precautions for the protection of the intended victim, including notification of law enforcement authorities. Also, communicable diseases, gun shot and knife wounds, should be reported as required by applicable statutes or ordinances.

Section 5.05, *Current Opinions of the Council on Ethical and Judicial Affairs of the American Medical Association*, 1989. Reprinted with permission.

Glossary

Abstract. A condensation of a record.

Accredited Record Technician (ART). A person who is certified as an expert, although not on as high a level as a Registered Record Administrator, by the American Medical Record Association.

Acquisition. The takeover of another business by a purchaser.

Admission. An acknowledgment that an allegation of the opposing party in a lawsuit is true.

Authentication. An attestation that something, such as a record, is genuine.

Consent. Voluntary agreement. Consent may be express (oral or written) or implied (demonstrated by silence or actions).

Defendant. The party against whom a plaintiff brings a lawsuit seeking some relief from a harm that the defendant allegedly caused the plaintiff.

Deposition. A written record of oral testimony, in the form of questions and answers, made before a notary or other public officer, to discover evidence for a lawsuit or to be read into evidence at trial.

Discovery. Pretrial proceedings in which the opposing parties get factual information concerning the matter in controversy. The tools of discovery are depositions, interrogatories, requests for admissions, inspections of documents, physical and mental examinations, and inspections.

Duplicate. One of two or more documents that are the same. Many state and federal laws provide that certain copies, such as microfilm copies, are duplicate originals.

Felony. A serious offense usually punishable by death or imprisonment in the state penitentiary for one year or more.

Informed consent. Agreement based upon complete understanding of the nature of the undertaking, including the risks thereof.

Interrogatories. Written questions used in discovery proceedings and asked by one side in a lawsuit to another party. The person queried must answer in writing, under oath.

Media. The materials upon which information is stored, such as microfilm.

Medical record. A record that identifies the patient and specifies the care the patient received.

Merger. The union of two or more businesses into one new business.

Microfilm. A photographic medium upon which documents can be greatly reduced in size.

Minor. A person who has not yet reached the age of majority so as to be considered an adult by law.

Misdemeanor. Any crime that is not a felony. A minor offense usually punishable by a lesser penalty than imprisonment in the state penitentiary for one year.

Negligence. A failure to use due care.

Original document. An authentic writing as opposed to a copy.

Plaintiff. The party who brings a lawsuit complaining of some harm done by the defendant.

Punitive damages. Sometimes called exemplary damages. Damages in excess of the amount that would compensate the plaintiff for injury suffered awarded to punish the defendant for misconduct.

Record. As a noun, the preservation of data or information on some media so that it may be read at some future time.

Records management. The supervision of records so that they are properly created, processed, stored, retrieved, and disposed of.

Records retention program. The plan that specifies how long a facility keeps its records.

Regular course of business. Doing business activities in accordance with your usual habit or custom.

Regulation. A rule issued by a governmental agency other than the legislature. Unless a regulation conflicts with the constitution or a statute, it has the force of law.

Registered Record Administrator (RRA). A person who is registered as an expert by the American Medical Record Association.

Statute of limitations. A period of time, fixed by federal or state law, during which a plaintiff may bring a lawsuit and after which the claim is barred.

Subpoena. A subpoena commands a person to appear at a trial or other hearing and give testimony.

Subpoena duces tecum. A subpoena duces tecum commands the person to bring certain records or documents in the person's custody or possession to a place the subpoena specifies.

Index

Access to medical records *see*
    Medical records
Accreditation Manual for Hospitals, 4
Acquisitions *see* Closings, disposition
    of records
Alabama
    Administrative records
        Contents, 74
        Media, 123
    Child abuse reporting, 153
    Communicable disease reporting, 179
    Court Order, 203
    Inspections for licensure, 193
    Medical records
        Access, 219
        Administrator, 74
        Confidentiality, 179, 234
        Contents, 4–5
        Disposal upon closing, 280
        Inspection, 193, 234
        Media, 123
        Ownership, 62
        Removal, 203
        Retention, 74–75
        Storage, 139–40
    Physician-patient privilege, 234, 256
    Reports, 75, 153
    Subpoena *see* Alabama, court order
Alaska
    Business records, media, 123
    Child abuse reporting, 153
    Controlled substances, 172
    Court order, 204
    Drugs, records of, 76
    Medicaid records, 76
    Medical records
        Access, 220
        Administrator, 75
        Confidentiality, 234–35

        Contents, 6–7
        Destruction, 272
        Disposal on closing, 280
        Media, 123
        Research, release for, 215, 234
        Retention, 75–76
        Storage, 140
    Physician-patient privilege, 153, 256
    Research, 215
    Subpoena *see* Alaska, court order
Alcohol abuse reporting, 171–77
Altering records, 147–49
American Hospital Association
    guidelines, 85
American Medical Association's
    Ethical Principles, 268
Arizona
    AIDS reporting, 179
    Blood, records of, 78
    Business records, media, 123
    Child abuse reporting, 154
    Communicable disease reporting, 179–80
    Controlled substances, 172
    Disaster plan, 77
    Food and dietetic records, 77
    Hospital records
        Destruction, 272
        Disposal on closing, 280
        Media, 123
        Pharmacy, 172
        Requirements, 76–79
        Storage, 140
    Investigations, 194
    Laboratory records, 78–79
    Medical information
        Access, 220, 235–36
        Confidentiality, 235–36
        Definition, 7

        Retention, 76–79
    Medical records service, 77
    Personnel records, 77
    Physician-patient privilege, 154, 194, 256
    Quality assurance records, 78
    Records retention, 76–79
    Respiratory care reports, 78
    Social services information, 78
    Subpoena, 194, 204
    Surgical records, 77
Arkansas
    AIDS Testing Program,
        confidentiality of patient
        identification, 236
    Alcohol abuse records, 172
    Business records,
        reproduction, 123–24
    Child abuse reporting, 155
    Communicable disease and infant
        sudden death reporting, 180
    Emergency room records, contents, 10
    Investigations, 194–95
    Medical records
        Access, 220
        Confidentiality, 194–95, 215–16, 236
        Contents, 7–10
        Department, 79
        Destruction, 272
        Disclosure, 194–95, 215–16
        Investigations, 194–95
        Media, 123–24
        Ownership, 62
        Research, 215–16
        Retention, 79
        Storage, 140
    Newborn records, contents, 9

312 Index

Nurse's notes, contents, 9
Obstetrical records, contents, 9
Outpatient records, contents, 9
Physician misconduct, reporting, 194–95
Physician-patient privilege, 155, 256
Reports, 180
Research, 215–16
Retention, 79
Subpoena, 204–5, 236
Venereal disease reporting, 180
Assessing patient care, 193–201

California
Alcohol and drug abuse reporting, 172
Child abuse reporting, 155
Communicable disease reporting, 180
Crime reporting, 172
Inpatient records, contents, 10
Laboratory records, 82–83
Licensing violations, release of information about, 195
Medical records
Access, 220–21, 236–37
Confidentiality, 140–41, 216, 220–21, 236–37
Contents, 10–11
Destruction, 141, 273
Disposal on closing, 280
Media, 124
Ownership, 62
Release of information, 155, 195, 205–6, 216, 220–21
Reproduction, 124
Research, 216, 220–21, 236
Retention, 79–83, 140
Service, 79
Storage, 140–41
Medi-Cal records
Code I restriction documentation, 81
Contents, 80
Prescription documentation, 81
Records, 80–82
Nurse's notes, contents, 11
Personnel records
Contents, 83
Retention, 83
Pesticide poisoning reports, 180
Pharmacy records, 82
Physician-patient privilege, 257
Reports, 180
Research, 216, 220–21, 236
Retention, 79–83
Subpoena, 205–6
Charge-out system, 141
Child abuse reporting, 151–70 see also specific state listings
Civil Rights Act, 71
Climate control, 138–39

Closings and disposition of records, 279–84
Colorado
AIDS reporting, 180
Business records, media, 124
Child abuse reporting, 156–57
Confidentiality, 157, 180, 237
Drug abuse records, 173
Hospital records
Media, 124
Requirements, 83–84
Retention, 83–84
Storage, 142
Medical records
Access, 221
Confidentiality, 142, 180, 237
Contents, 11–13
Definition, 11
Department, 84
Destruction, 273
Ownership, 62
Retention, 83–84
Storage, 142
Newborn records, contents, 13
Nursing records, contents, 12
Obstetric records, contents, 12–13
Personnel records, 84
Physician-patient privilege, 257
Retention, 83–84
Surgical records, contents, 12
Communicable disease reporting, 179–91 see also specific state listings
Comprehensive alcohol and abuse and alcoholism prevention, treatment, and rehabilitation act, 171–72, 232–33
Computer security, 121–22
Conditions of participation: Medical Records Services Health Care Financing Administration, 285–86
Connecticut
Business records, media, 124
Child abuse reporting, 157
Communicable disease reporting, 181, 237
Industrial health facility records
Content, 85
Retention, 85
Licensed maternity hospitals
Contents, 84–85
Retention, 84–85
Medical records
Access, 221–22
Confidentiality, 237
Contents, 13–14
Department, 84
Destruction, 273
Media, 124
Retention, 84–85
Storage, 142

Nursing and rest homes medical records
Contents, 14, 84
Retention, 84
Storage, 142
Obstetric records, contents, 13–14
Physician-patient privilege, 257
Retention, 84–85
Subpoena, 206
Confidentiality
Drug abuse records, 171, 233–54
Generally, 233
Oath of, 138
Patient access and, 219–30
Correcting records, 147–49
Custodian, 137–39
Credentialing, 193–201
Crimes
Altering records, 147–49
Obtaining medical records or information, 62

Delaware
Access to records, 222
Child abuse reporting, 157–8
Confidentiality, 237–38
Communicable disease reporting, 181, 237–38
Physician-patient privilege, 158, 257
Retention, 85
Department of Labor, record-keeping requirements, 70–71
Destroying records, 271–78
Destruction schedule, 69, 271
Disclosure of Information, 151, 219–30
Discrimination, 71–72
Complaints, 71
Records of nondiscrimination, 72
Disposal, 271–78 see also Destruction
Disposition of records, 279–84
District of Columbia
Confidentiality, 238
Disclosure of information, 195
Primary health record
Definition, 14
Media, 124
Physician-patient privilege, 257–58
Drug Office Abuse and Treatment Act of 1972, 171, 233
Drugs
Abuse reporting, 171–77
Abuse research, 171
Antibiotic drugs, Records of, 72
New drugs, records of, 72
Duplicate originals see Media, duplicate originals

Employee Retirement Security Act of 1974, 71
Employees
Benefit plans, records of, 71

Index   313

Exposed to toxic substances, 73
Federal, 70–73
Injuries, 71
Equal Employment Opportunity
  Commission, 71–72
Ethics *see* Medical ethics

Fair Labor Standards Act, 70–71
Federal Employees' Compensation
  Act, 71
Federal laws
  Confidentiality, 233–34
  Destruction of records, 272
  Media and, 122–23
  Ownership of records, 62
  Physician-patient privilege, 255
  Privacy Act, 148
  Record-keeping requirements, 70–74
    Department of Labor, 70–71
    Equal Employment Opportunity
      Commission, 71–72
    Food and Drug Administration, 72
    Health and Human Services
      Department, 73–74
    Health Care Financing
      Administration, 72
    Internal Revenue Service, 72
    Occupational Safety and Health
      Administration, 73
Federal Rules of Evidence, 122
Federal Tort Claims Act, 70
Fifth Amendment, 151
Florida
  Adverse incident reporting, 195
  AIDS reporting, 181
  Alcohol testing, 173
  Child abuse reporting, 158
  Disciplinary proceedings, 195
  Medical records
    Access, 222
    Altering, 148
    Confidentiality, 173, 238
    Contents, 15
    Destruction, 85
    Media, 124–25
    Microfilm, 85, 124–25
    Retention, 85
    Storage, 142
  Physician-patient privilege, 158, 258
  Risk management program, 195
  Sexually transmitted disease
    reporting, 181
  Subpoena, 195, 206
  Freedom of Information Act, 219

Georgia
  AIDS reporting, 181, 238
  Altering records, 148
  Business records, media, 125
  Child abuse reporting, 158–59
  Confidentiality, 181, 238

Drug dependent persons' records
  173, 238
Health maintenance organizations,
  86, 238
Health records
  Access, 222
  Confidentiality, 181, 238
  Contents, 15
  Media, 125
  Ownership, 62
  Retention, 85–86
Medical review committee records,
  confidentiality of, 238
Personnel records, 86
Physician-patient privilege, 258
Subpoena, 206
Government
  Authority to enforce sanctions, 67
  Authority to require record-keeping,
    67
  Laws *see* Federal laws, specific
    state listings

Hawaii
  Child abuse reporting, 159
  Media, 125
  Medical records
    Access, 222
    Basic information, 15–16, 87
    Confidentiality, 238, 273
    Destruction, 273
    Disposal on closing, 280
    Media, 125
    Retention, 86–87, 238, 273, 280
  Physician-patient privilege, 159, 258
  Subpoena, 206
Healthcare records *see* Medical records
Hippocratic Oath, 268

Idaho
  AIDS reporting, 181
  Child abuse reporting, 159
  Confidentiality, 196, 239
  Disciplinary actions, reports of, 196,
    239
  Drug abuse reporting, 173
  Employment records, 87
  Medical records
    Confidentiality, 196, 239
    Destruction, 239, 273
    Ownership, 62
    Media, 125
    Retention, 87
  Physician-patient privilege, 159, 258
  Subpoena, 207
  Venereal disease reporting, 181
Illinois
  Business records, retention of, 88
  Child abuse reporting, 159
  Communicable disease reporting, 182
  Infant records, contents, 16–17

Inspections, 196
Medical records
  Access, 223
  Confidentiality, 239
  Department, 87
  Media, 125–26
  Minimum requirements, 16–17
  Retention, 87–88
  Storage, 142
Obstetric records, contents, 16
Personnel records, 88
Physician-patient privilege, 259
Reports, 88
Indiana
  AIDS reporting, 182, 239
  Birth Problems Registry, 182
  Cancer reporting, 182, 240
  Chemical tests on blood, urine, or
    other bodily substances, 173
  Child abuse reporting, 160
  Communicable disease reporting,
    182, 239–40
  Confidentiality, 196, 239–40
  Destroying or falsifying records, 148
  Emergency and outpatient records,
    contents, 18
  Health records
    Access, 223, 239
    Confidentiality, 126, 216, 239–40
    Contents, 17–18
    Definition, 17
    Destruction, 239, 273
    Disposal on closing, 281
    Media, 126
    Ownership, 63, 239
    Research, 216
    Responsibility for, 88
    Retention, 88–90
    Storage, 143, 239
  Hospital records, 88–90
    Media, 126
  Inpatient hospital records, contents,
    17–18
  Peer review committees, 196, 239
  Physician-patient privilege, 173, 259
  Research, 216
  Subpoena, 207–9
  Traumatic injury reporting, 182, 240
Infectious disease reporting *see*
  communicable disease reporting,
  specific state listings
Inspections, 193–201
Investigations, 193–201
Iowa
  AIDS reporting, 182, 241
  Child abuse reporting, 160
  Communicable disease reporting, 182
  Drug abuse records, 174
  Emergency records, contents, 19
  Hospital records, 90–91

314   Index

Medical records
  Confidentiality, 160, 240–41
  Contents, 18–19
  Destruction, 126
  Media, 126
  Research, 240
  Retention, 90–91
  Storage, 90
Physician-patient privilege, 259

Joint Commission on Accreditation of Healthcare Organizations (JCAHO), 4

Kansas
  AIDS reporting, 182
  Communicable disease reporting, 182–83
  Drug Abuse Reporting, 174
  Investigations, 196
  Medical records
    Access, 196, 216, 241
    Confidentiality, 216, 241
    Contents, 19–20
    Destruction, 274
    Disposal on closing, 281
    Drug abuse, 216
    Media, 126
    Ownership, 63
    Research, 216
    Retention, 91
    Service, 91, 143
    Storage, 143
  Physician-patient privilege, 260
Kentucky
  Administrative reports, 91
  Child abuse reporting, 160
  Communicable disease reporting, 183
  Medical records
    Access, 223, 241
    Confidentiality, 241
    Contents, 20
    Disposal on closing, 281
    Media, 126
    Ownership, 63
    Retention, 92
    Service, 92
    Storage, 143
    Tampering, 148
  Personnel records, 91–92
  Physician-patient privilege, 160, 260
  Subpoena, 209
  Surgical records, contents, 20

Litigation, minimizing litigation losses, 68
Louisiana
  AIDS reporting, 183
  Cancer reporting, 183
  Child abuse reporting, 160–61
  Communicable disease reporting, 183

Hospital records
  Access, 223
  Contents, 21
  Definition, 21
  Disclosure, 196
  Media, 127
  Microfilm, 92, 127
  Ownership, 63
  Patient access to, 63
  Retention, 92
Investigations, 196
Physician-patient privilege, 161, 196, 260
Subpoena, 209
Venereal disease reporting, 183

Maine
  Adult Protective Services Act, 242
  AIDS reporting, 183, 223–24, 241–42
  Child abuse reporting, 161–62
  Media, 127
  Medical records
    Access, 223–24
    Confidentiality, 241–42
    Contents, 21
    Department, 92
    Media, 127
    Retention, 92–93
  Physician-patient privilege, 162, 260
  Subpoena, 209
Malpractice
  Altering records and, 147
  Avoiding litigation losses, 68, 121
  Claims, 4
  Statutes of limitations, 69–70
Maryland
  AIDS reporting, 184, 243
  Business records, retention of, 93
  Child abuse reporting, 162
  Communicable disease reporting, 183–84, 242–43
  Confidentiality, 184, 242–43
  Drug and alcohol abuse records, 174
  Media, 127
  Reproduction, definition of, 127
  Medical records
    Access, 224, 243
    Altering, 148–49
    Confidentiality, 143, 242–43
    Content, 21–22
    Correcting, 148–49
    Definition, 21
    Destruction, 274
    Disclosure, 196, 210
    Media, 127
    Research, 216, 243
    Retention, 93
    Storage, 143
  Medical review committee, 196
  Physician-patient privilege, 260–61

Research, 216, 243
Subpoena, 210
Venereal disease reporting, 183–84
Massachusetts
  AIDS testing, confidentiality of, 243–44
  Child abuse reporting, 162
  Clinical records, contents, 23
  Communicable disease reporting, 184, 243–44
  Confidentiality, 197, 243–44
  Hospital records
    Disclosure, 197, 210, 224
    Requirements, 93
  License revocation, reporting of, 197
  Medical records
    Access, 224, 243–44
    Confidentiality, 243–44
    Contents, 22–23
    Destruction, 274
    Disclosure, 197, 210
    Disposal on closing, 281
    Media, 127
    Retention, 93
  Operative reports, contents, 23
  Physician-patient privilege, 261
  Subpoena, 210
Media
  Destruction, and, 271
  Duplicate originals, 122
  Federal law and, 122–23
  Original, 121–22
  Output, 121
  Retention requirements and, 121–22
  State laws and see specific states
  Technology and, 121–22
Medical ethics, 268
Medical information see Medical records
Medical malpractice see Malpractice
Medical records see specific state listings
  Access, 193–201, 219–30
  Altering, 147–49
  Confidentiality, 171–72, 193–201, 233–54
  Contents, 3–59
  Correcting, 147–49
  Destruction, 271–78
  Disposal on closing, 279–84
  Drug abuse, 171–77
  Inspections, 193–201
  Media, 121–35
  Ownership, 61–65
    Federal, 62
    State see specific state listings
  Patient's rights to information therein, 61
  Removal, 61
  Research, 215–18
  Retention, 67–117

Security, 137–39 *see also* Security
Storage, 137–39
Subpoena, 203–14
Transfer to another facility, 61
Medical research *see* Research
Medicare, records, 73
Mergers *see* Disposition
Michigan
  Business records, media, 127–28
  Child abuse reporting, 162–63
  Medical records
    Contents, 24
    Destruction, 93
    Media, 127–28
    Retention, 93–94
    Storage, 143
  Physician-patient privilege, 261
Minnesota
  AIDS reporting, 184
  Child abuse reporting, 163
  Communicable disease reporting, 184
  Disciplinary boards, 197
  Hospital records, 94
    media, 128
  Maternity records, contents, 25
  Medical records
    Access, 197, 224
    Confidentiality, 216, 244
    Contents, 24–25
    Destruction, 274–75
    Research, 216
    Retention, 94
    Storage, 143
  Narcotics records, 94
  Newborn records, contents, 25
  Physician-patient privilege, 261
  Reports, 94
  Research, 216
Mississippi
  AIDS reporting, 184
  Business records
    Definition, 25
    Media, 128
    Retention, 95
    Retirement, 95
  Child abuse reporting, 163
  Communicable disease reporting, 184
  Hospital records
    Access, 224
    Confidentiality, 244
    Definition, 25
    Destruction, 275
    Disposal on closing, 281
    Media, 128, 275
    Ownership, 63, 244
    Patient access to, 63, 224
    Retention, 94–96
    Storage, 143
  Physician-patient privilege, 261
  Subpoena, 210
Missouri

Child abuse reporting, 163
Communicable disease reporting, 185
Inspections, 197, 225
Media, 128
Medical records
  Access, 225
  Confidentiality, 244
  Contents, 25–27
  Destruction, 97, 276
  Disposal on closing, 281
  Inspections, 197, 225
  Management, 96
  Media, 128
  Ownership, 63
  Removal, 63
  Retention, 96–97
  Services, 96
  Statutes of limitations, and, 96
  Storage, 63, 144
Nursing homes records
  Contents, 26–27
  Medication, 96
  Retention, 96–97
Physician-patient privilege, 163, 261
Montana
  AIDS reporting, 185
  Child abuse reporting, 164
  Communicable disease reporting, 185
  Delivery records, contents, 28
  Infirmary records, contents, 29
  Medical records
    Confidentiality, 244
    Contents, 27–30
    Core records, 29
    Destruction, 276
    Hospices, of, 29
    Media, 128
    Ownership of, 63
    Release of, 63
    Retention, 97
    Storage, 144
  Newborn records, contents, 28
  Obstetric records, contents, 28
  Outpatient records, contents, 29
  Personal care facility records, contents, 29
  Physician-patient privilege, 164, 262
  Reports, 97

National Cancer Institute Clinical Cancer Education Program, 73
National Cancer Institute grants, 73
National Heart, Lung, and Blood Institute grants, 73
National Institute of Health, 73
National Library of Medicine, 73
Nebraska
  AIDS reporting, 185
  Cancer Registry, confidentiality of, 244
  Communicable disease reporting, 185

Inspections, 197
Medical records
  Confidentiality, 197, 244
  Contents, 30
  Destruction, 276
  Disposal on closing, 281
  Media, 128
  Retention, 97–98
Physician-patient privilege, 262
Nevada
  Cancer reporting, 185, 245
  Child abuse reporting, 164
  Communicable disease reporting, 185
  Controlled substances, 174
  Drug and alcohol abuse, 174, 245
  Healthcare records
    Access, 225
    Confidentiality, 174, 244–45
    Definition, 30
    Inspections, 197
    Media, 129
    Retention, 98
  Inspections, 197
  Physician-patient privilege, 164, 174, 262
  Reports, 98, 245
New Hampshire
  AIDS reporting, 185–86, 245
  Business Records
    Media, 129
    Retention, 99
  Child abuse reporting, 164
  Clinical laboratory accession logs
    Contents, 33
    Retention, 99
  Communicable disease reporting, 185–86
  Confidentiality, 174, 197, 245
  Drug records, 174
  Home healthcare records
    Access, 225
    Business records, 99
    Contents, 33–34
    Retention, 98–99
  Inspections, 197
  Medical records
    Access, 225
    Confidentiality, 174, 245
    Contents, 30–34
    Destruction, 276
    Disposal on closing, 282
    Media, 129
    Retention, 98–99
    Storage, 144
    Subpoena, 210
  Outpatient clinic medical records, contents, 33
  Physician-patient privilege, 164, 263
  Residential treatment and rehabilitation facility records, contents, 33

Index

Sheltered care facility medical records
  Contents, 32
  Retention, 98
  Subpoena, 210
New Jersey
  Child abuse reporting, 164
  Communicable disease reporting, 186
  Hospital records, 99
  Inspections, 198, 245
  Medical records
    Access, 225–26
    Confidentiality, 144, 198, 245
    Contents, 34–36
    Definition, 34
    Department, 99
    Disposal on closing, 282
    Inspections, 198, 245
    Media, 129
    Ownership, 64
    Removal, 64
    Retention, 99–100
    Storage, 144
  Personnel records, 100
  Physician-patient privilege, 263
  Reports, 100
New Mexico
  Communicable disease reporting, 186
  Child abuse reporting, 165
  Drug and alcohol abuse information, 175, 245–46
  Malpractice claims, access to medical records for, 198
  Medical records
    Access, 198, 226, 245–46
    Confidentiality, 216, 226, 245–46
    Contents, 37–38
    Correcting, 149
    Destruction, 276
    Media, 129–30
    Ownership, 64
    Patients' rights to access, 64
    Research, 216
    Retention, 100, 276
  Physician-patient privilege, 263
  Subpoena, 175, 210–11, 246
New York
  Accounts, 104
  Child abuse reporting, 165
  Communicable disease reporting, 186
  Controlled substances, 175
  Drug treatment program patient records, confidentiality of, 175
  Emergency service records, 103
  Hospital records, 100–104
  Maternity records, contents, 39
  Medical records
    Access, 149, 226
    Confidentiality, 144, 165, 175, 226, 246
    Contents, 38–39
    Correcting, 149
    Media, 130
    Retention, 100–104
    Storage, 144
    Subpoena, 211
  Newborn records
    Contents, 39
    Register of births, 103
  Personnel records, 100
  Pharmacy records, 102
  Physician-patient privilege, 263
  Quality assurance programs, 198
  Reports, 101–4
  Subpoena, 211
North Carolina
  Child abuse reporting, 165
  Communicable disease reporting, 186
  Medical records
    Access, 226
    Confidentiality, 144–45, 198, 246
    Contents, 39–40
    Department, 104–5
    Destruction, 276
    Disposal on change of ownership, 282
    Media, 130
    Ownership, 64
    Retention, 104–5
    Storage, 144–45
    Subpoena, 211
  Medical review committees, 198
  Nursing home records
    Access, 226
    Contents, 40
    Responsible employee, 104–5
    Retention, 104–5
    Storage, 145
  Physician-patient privilege, 246, 263–64
  Subpoena, 211
North Dakota
  Child abuse reporting, 165
  Clinical records of long-term care facilities, contents, 41–42
  Communicable disease reporting, 187
  Medical records
    Access, 227
    Confidentiality, 227, 246
    Contents, 40–42
    Department, 105
    Media, 130
    Retention, 105
  Physician-patient privilege, 187, 264
  Reports, 187
  Subpoena, 246
Nursing Student Loan Program, 73

Oath of Confidentiality, 137–38
Occupational Safety and Health Administration, 73, 219
Ohio
  AIDS reporting, 187
  Cancer reporting, 187
  Child abuse reporting, 165
  Communicable disease reporting, 187–88
  Drug treatment programs, 175
  Financial records, 105
  Inspections, 198
  Maternity home medical records
    Contents, 42
    Retention, 106
  Maternity hospital records
    Contents, 106
    Retention, 106
  Medical records
    Access, 198, 227
    Confidentiality, 246–47
    Definition, 42
    Media, 131
    Retention, 105–6
  Nursing homes
    Required records, 106
    Retention, 106
  Physician-patient privilege, 264
  Reports, 105–6, 247
  Rest homes, 106
  Sexually transmitted disease reporting, 187
  Subpoena, 211
Oklahoma
  Child abuse reporting, 165–66
  Communicable disease reporting, 188, 247
  Confidentiality, 175, 188, 199, 227, 247
  Drug and alcohol abuse, 175, 227
  Medical malpractice claims, reporting, 198–99
  Medical records
    Access, 227
    Altering, 149
    Confidentiality, 175, 188, 227, 247
    Media, 131
    No definition of, 42
    Retention, 106
  Physician-patient privilege, 264
  Venereal disease reporting, 188
Oregon
  Child abuse reporting, 166
  Communicable disease reporting, 188
  Drug and alcohol abuse, 175
  Healthcare facility records, 106–7
  Media, 131
  Medical records
    Access, 227
    Confidentiality, 247–48
    Contents, 42–44
    Disposal on closing or change of ownership, 282
    Media, 131
    Ownership, 64

Index

Removal, 64
Retention, 106–7
Review by the Health Commission, 199
Storage, 145
Obstetric records, contents, 43
Physician-patient privilege, 264
Psychiatrist/psychologist-patient privilege, 166, 264
Surgical records, contents, 43
Original *see* Media
Output *see* Media
Ownership of records *see* Medical records, ownership, and specific state listings

Patient behavior, charting, 4
Patients
  Employees' records, 71
  Medical records, right to information therein, 61
Pennsylvania
  AIDS reporting, 188
  Child abuse reporting, 166, 248
  Communicable disease reporting, 188
  Confidentiality, 199, 248
  Malpractice reporting, 199
  Media, 131
  Medical records
    Access, 227–28
    Confidentiality, 64, 212, 228, 248
    Contents, 44
    Destruction, 277
    Disposal on closing, 282
    Facilities, 107
    Media, 131
    Ownership, 64
    Removal, 64, 131
    Retention, 107
    Service, 107
    Storage, 131, 145
  Physician-patient privilege, 265
  Subpoena, 212
Personnel records *see also* specific state listings
Personnel security *see* Security
Physical security *see* Security
Physician-patient privilege, 255–68
  Federal, 255
  States, 256–68 *see also* specific state listings
Privacy
  Generally, 231, 233
  Medical ethics and, 268
  Patients' right to, 233–54
Privacy Act, 148, 233
Project grants for public medical facility construction, 73
Protection of records of the National Fire Protection Association, 145–46

Psychiatrist/psychologist-patient privilege *see* Physician-patient privilege

Records *see also* Medical records
  Access to, 219–30
  Altering, 147–49
  Contents, 3–59
  Correcting, 147–49
  Definition, 3–59
  Destruction, 69, 271–78
    Documentation, 69, 271–72
    Schedule, 68–69, 271–72
  Disposition of, 279–84
  Employment *see* specific state listings
  Generally, 3
  Media, 121–35
  Medical *see* Medical records
  Ownership, 61–65
  Personnel *see* specific state listings
  Removal, 61–65
  Retention *see also* specific states
    Period, 68–69
    Schedule, 68–69
    Statutes of limitations, and, 69–70
  Retirement *see* Destruction
  Security, 137–39 *see also* Security
  Storage, 137–46
  Tax *see* records
Regular course of business, 122, 272
Release of records, 137–39
Requisitions, 139
Research
  Drug abuse, 171–77, 233–34
  Grants for research projects, records of, 73
  Medical research, 215–18
Retention schedules, 68–69, 297–303
Retirement *see* Destruction
Rhode Island
  Child abuse reporting, 166–67
  Communicable disease reporting, 188
  Confidential healthcare information
    Definition, 44
    Disclosure, 176, 217, 248–49
  Confidentiality, 199, 248–49
  Drugs, 176
  Medical records
    Access, 199, 228, 246–49
    Confidentiality, 199, 217, 248–49
    Contents, 44–45
    Department, 108
    Media, 132
    Reproduction, 108, 132
    Research, 217
    Retention, 108
    Storage, 145
    Subpoena, 212–13
  Peer review committees, 199
  Physician-patient privilege, 167, 265

Reports, 108
Research, 217
Subpoena, 212–13
Right to privacy *see* Privacy

Schools, receiving grants, 73
Security, 137–39
  Personnel, 137–38
    Computer security, 137–38
    Identification, 138
    Oath of confidentiality, 138
    Screening, 137
    Security consciousness, 137–38
    Verification, 139
    Warnings, 137–38
  Physical, 138–39
    Access, limiting, 139
    Climate control, 138–39
    Custodian, 139
    Storage, 138–39
  System, 139
    Charge-out system, 139
    Copying, 139
    Destruction, 139
    Register, 139
    Release of records, 139
    Requisitions, 139
    Transfer, 139
Self-incrimination, 151
South Carolina
  Business records, copies of, 132
  Communicable disease reporting, 188–89
  Drug and alcohol abuse, 176, 217
  Intermediate care facilities—mental retardation, records of, 108
  Nursing home residents' health records
    Contents, 47–48
    Retention, 108
    Storage, 145
  Medical records
    Confidentiality, 176, 217, 249
    Contents, 45–48
    Destruction, 277
    Disclosure, 176
    Disposal on closing or change of ownership, 282
    Media, 132
    Ownership, 64
    Removal, 64
    Research, 217
    Responsibility for, 108
    Retention, 108, 277
    Storage, 145
  Newborn records, contents, 46–47
  Nursing home records
    Contents, 47–48
    Storage, 145
  Physician-patient privilege, 265

318 Index

South Dakota
  Child abuse reporting, 167
  Drug and alcohol abuse, 176, 250
  Media, 132–33
  Medical records
    Access, 228
    Confidentiality, 109, 176, 189, 250
    Contents, 48–49
    Department, 109
    Media, 132–33
    Storage, 145
  Physician-patient privilege, 167, 265
  Venereal disease reporting, 189
Statutes of limitations
  State statutes of limitations table, 69–70, 287–90
  Tax, 72
Storage, 137–46, 279 see also Records, Medical records, Security, and specific state listings
Subpoena see also specific state listings
  Definition, 203
  Duces tecum, 203
  For medical records, 203–14
  Receipt, 203
System security see Security

Tax records
  Employment tax, 72
  Income tax, 72
  Withholding tax statements, 72
Tennessee
  Business records
    Definition, 49
    Excluded from definition of hospital records, 49
    Media, 109, 133
    Retention, 109
  Child abuse reporting, 167
  Drugs, 176
  Emergency room medical records, contents, 50
  Hospital records
    Access, 199, 228
    Confidentiality, 176, 250
    Contents, 49–50
    Definition, 49
    Destruction, 277
    Disposal on closing, 283
    Media, 105, 133
    Ownership, 64–65
    Patient access to, 64–65
    Responsibility for, 109
    Retention, 109
    Subpoena, 213–14
  Inpatient medical records, contents, 49–50
  Medical review committees, 199, 250
  Physician-patient privilege, 265

Sexually transmitted disease reporting, 189, 250
Subpoena, 213–14
Violation of records management statutes, 109
Terminology of the international classification of diseases, 4
Texas
  Business records, media, 133
  Child abuse reporting, 167–68
  Communicable disease information, 189, 250
  Drug and alcohol abuse, 176
  Inspections, 199–200
  Medical records
    Access, 199–200, 228
    Confidentiality, 111, 176, 250
    Contents, 50–51
    Destruction, 277
    Disposal on closing, 283
    Media, 133
    Retention, 110–11
    Storage, 145–46
    Subpoena, 214
  Physician-patient privilege, 168, 176, 265–66
  Reports, 110–11
  Special care facilities medical records
    Contents, 51
    Retention, 110
    Subpoena, 214
Transfer of records 139 see also Security

Uniform Preservation of Private Business Records Acts, 3
Uniform Rules of Evidence, 3
Utah
  Child abuse reporting, 168
  Communicable disease reporting, 189
  Drug dependency reports, 176–77
  Emergency room records
    Contents, 52–53
  Hospital records, 111–12
  Inspections, 200
  Media, 133
  Medical records
    Access, 200, 217, 229
    Confidentiality, 217, 251
    Contents, 51–53
    Department, 111
    Destruction, 277
    Disposal on closing, 283
    Media, 133
    Ownership, 65
    Policies, 111
    Removal, 65
    Research, 217
    Retention, 111–12
    Storage, 146

  Newborn records, contents, 52
  Obstetric records, contents, 52
  Physician-patient privilege, 266
  Research, 217

Vermont
  Child abuse reporting, 168, 251
  Communicable disease reporting, 189–90, 251
  Inspections, 200
  Media, 133
  Medical records
    Access, 200, 217, 229
    Confidentiality, 217, 229, 251
    Contents, 53–54
    Media, 133
    Research, 217
    Retention, 112–13
  Nursing home records contents, 54
  Physician-patient privilege, 251, 266
  Reports, 112–13, 189–90, 251
  Research, 217
  Tuberculosis reporting, 190, 251
  Venereal disease reporting, 189–90, 251
Virginia
  Business records, media, 134
  Child abuse reporting, 168
  Communicable disease reporting, 190
  Inspections, 200
  Medical records
    Access, 200, 229, 251
    Confidentiality, 251
    Contents, 54–55
    Disposal on closing, 283
    Department, 113
    Media, 134
    Retention, 113
    Storage, 146
  Nursing home medical records
    Contents, 55
    Preservation, 113
  Physician-patient privilege, 267
  Subpoena, 214, 251

Washington
  Business records, media, 134
  Child abuse reporting, 168–69
  Hospital records
    Censuses, 114
    Inspections, 114
    Personnel records, 114
    Registers, 114
  Inspections, 200
  Medical records
    Access, 229
    Confidentiality, 229, 251–52
    Contents, 55–57
    Destruction, 278
    Disposal on closing or change of ownership, 284

Index

Media, 134
Retention, 114
Service, 113
Physician-patient privilege, 267
Sexually transmitted diseases, reporting, 190
Welfare and Pension Plans Disclosure Act, 71
West Virginia
  Administrative records, 115
  Business records
    Inspections, 201
    Media, 134
    Not included in definition of hospital records, 57
  Child abuse reporting, 169
  Communicable disease reporting, 190
  Hospital records
    Definition, 57
    Media, 134
    Preservation, 114
    Subpoena, 214
  Inspections, 201
  Medical records
    Access, 65, 229–30, 252–53
    Confidentiality, 252–53
    Contents, 57
    Definition, 57
    Media, 134
    Nursing homes, 114–15
    Ownership, 65
  Patient's right to access, 65, 229–30
  Reproduction, 114
  Retention, 114–16
  Personnel records, 115–16
  Physician-patient privilege, 267
  Subpoena, 214
  Venereal disease reporting, 190
Wisconsin
  AIDS testing, disclosure of, 190–91, 201, 217
  Child abuse reporting, 169
  Communicable disease reporting, 190–91
  Confidentiality, 190–91, 201, 217, 253–54
  Drug and alcohol abuse, 177, 217, 230
  Maternal medical records
    Contents, 58–59
  Media, 134–35
  Medical records
    Access, 230, 253–54
    Confidentiality, 177, 217, 253–54
    Contents, 58–59
    Correcting, 149
    Definition, 58
    Media, 134–35
    Removal, 146
    Research, 217
    Retention, 116
  Service, 116
  Storage, 146
  Newborn medical records, contents, 59
  Patient healthcare records
    Definition, 58
    Contents, 58–59
  Physician-patient privilege, 169, 267
  Reports, 116
  Research, 217
  Sexual abuse reporting, 169
Wyoming
  Child abuse reporting, 169–70
  Communicable disease reporting, 191
  Confidentiality, 191, 201
  Inspections, 201
  Media, 135
  Medical records
    Contents, 59
    Destruction, 278
    Inspections, 201
    Media, 135
    Removal, 214
    Research, 218
    Retention, 116–7
    Subpoena, 214
  Physician-patient privilege, 268
  Reports, 116–17, 191
  Research, 218
  Subpoena, 214
  Venereal disease reporting, 191

About the Author

Jonathan P. Tomes is the Dean of Students and an associate professor at IIT Chicago-Kent College of Law. Among the subjects he teaches is administrative law—the part of the law that deals with the rules and regulations that administrative agencies, such as Health and Human Services, the Federal Drug Administration, the Internal Revenue Service, and so forth, issue to control publicly regulated businesses such as healthcare providers.

Before going to law school, Dean Tomes served as an infantry platoon leader in Vietnam, where he won the Silver Star and the Combat Infantry Badge among other awards. Then he graduated first in his class at Oklahoma City University School of Law and won the Oklahoma Bar Association outstanding law student award. He is a member of the Oklahoma bar. Following graduation, he served in the Judge Advocate General's Corps, U.S. Army, until he retired as a lieutenant colonel in 1988. While in the military, he served as prosecutor, defense counsel, and military judge before becoming Chief of Special Claims, Tort Claims Division, U.S. Army Claims Service, where he was in charge of processing and adjudicating claims that occurred overseas against the military, primarily medical malpractice claims. While serving in this position, he became aware of the critical importance of proper record-keeping in avoiding malpractice losses. The military rewarded his twenty years' service by awarding him the Legion of Merit, the second-highest service award in the military, upon his retirement.

Among Dean Tomes's publications are *The Servicemember's Legal Guide*, legal articles in *Military Review* magazine, and law review articles in *The Practical Lawyer*, *The Air Force Law Review* (the U.S. Supreme Court cited his article in this law review), and *Richmond Law Review* (in press).